The Thundering Years

Rituals and Sacred Wisdom for Teens

Julie Tallard Johnson

BINDU BOOKS
ROCHESTER, VERMONT

Bindu Books
One Park Street
Rochester, Vermont 05767
www.InnerTraditions.com

Bindu Books is a division of Inner Traditions International

Library of Congress Cataloging-in-Publication Data

Johnson, Julie Tallard.
    The thundering years : rituals and sacred wisdom for teens / Julie Tallard Johnson.
        p. cm.
    Includes bibliographical references and index.
    ISBN 978-0-89281-880-8 (alk. paper)
    1. Teenagers—Religious life. 2. Spiritual life. I. Title.

BL625.47 .J64 2000
291.4'4'0835—dc21

                                                        00-057168

Printed and bound in the United States

10 9 8 7 6

Text design and layout by Priscilla Baker
This book was typeset in Cheltenham and Stone Sans with Post Antiqua as a display face

Contents

This book is dedicated to my daughter, Lydia,
and her Thundering Years, and to your thunder
— may it wake us all up from our sleep.

Acknowledgments

I am deeply grateful to all those who contributed their wisdom and creativity to this book: the many teenagers and Wisdomkeepers whose words fill up each page. Likewise, I am indebted to the spiritual teachers who have helped me along the way, and who have kept me on the path of the Spiritual Warrior.

Thank you Laurel Reinhardt, Shannon King, Tamara Truer, and Joan Oliver Goldsmith, for being containers of hope and inspiration; Colleen Brenzy and Davis Taylor for your sacred wisdom and guidance; Andrea Wunnicke and Eric Amlie for helping me through my Thundering Years with my humor and strength in tact; Mr. and Mrs. Kaiser for offering another home during those teen years; the Haygoods for offering me their country getaway; to my seventh grade English teacher whose name I have forgotten but whose kindness remains with me; to Shabazz (Alternative) High School for giving me another chance; and to my high school sweetheart, Bill Ishmael.

Thank you to Jon Graham for seeing the value in the book and getting it to a most talented editor, Jeanie Levitan; to Nancy Yeilding, Janet Jesso, Priscilla Baker, and Peri Champine for their creative touch to the book—each page holds within it their thunder.

And finally to Spirit who helped get this book into your hands.

Royalties from this book will be donated to **International Campaign for Tibet,** to help keep this indigenous spirit alive, and to **Honor the Earth,** to protect Native American communities and their sacred sites.

Listening to the Thunder

"The Thunder releases the water,
and the water is medicine
for everything. Water is the medicine
of Creation. The Thunder roars and
makes people frightened, but it brings
the rains that purify and nourish everything.
So bring us your Thunder,
so the RAINS will come."

—FLAMING RAINBOW WOMAN,
SPIRITUAL WARRIOR

SOME FIND A PASSAGE in a book. Or, a stranger says something that sticks with us; a story touches our soul and opens a new door; an oracle guides us on the right path; or we have a dream that won't let go. Through chance and synchronicities we find our way to what we need. And then, we usually discover we want more, more from our experiences and more from ourselves. Just more. Sometimes it is our longing for one thing that leads us to another.

The Thundering Years mark our journey into adulthood—a time of longing, of lost and found, of power, and of crossroads. Sacred wisdom refers to it as a "heroic journey," full of pitfalls and magic. Many of us know someone who did not make it through. Ultimately, the Thundering Years are a time of choices.

It is as if we begin gathering into an invisible medicine bag a collection of experiences, beliefs, fears, relationships, choices, dreams, and synchronicities that become the basis of who we will be in life. Whatever we fill our medicine bags with during our Thundering Years becomes part of our *life's* medicine. Everything in this book is offered to you as a possibility for your medicine bag— dream weaving, sacred and native wisdom, meditation practices, rituals, stories and myths, proverbs, elders, mentors, poetry, drumming, and nature medicine.

I journeyed through my Thundering Years long ago but still hold on to the medicine I gained during those years. Now, as an author and psychotherapist for teens and young adults, I put this book together in hopes of offering you more for your medicine bag. The wisdom contained in this book is "borrowed wisdom," borrowed from ancient traditions, and from such Wisdomkeepers of today as His Holiness the 14th Dalai Lama and Sobonfu Somé, a female African shaman.

Native American peoples use the words *medicine* and *power* interchange-ably. The power of something *is* its medicine. Sacred wisdom shows us that we all contain within ourselves an "original medicine," our own unique personal power. This is called by many names: our Buddha or Christ nature, the Atman,

"If one advances confidently in the direction of his dreams, and endeavors to live the life which he has imagined, he will meet with a success unexpected in common hours. . . ."

—HENRY DAVID THOREAU, AMERICAN ESSAYIST, NATURALIST, AND AUTHOR OF *WALDEN*

the Authentic Self, and the Self within the self. No one has the exact same medicine. We are all meant to bring our uniqueness into the world. Even while considering the ideas, sacred practices, and rituals of other traditions shown in this book, we are not meant to compare ourselves to others or try to be like someone else. The passage through our Thundering Years is about opening up to who we are as individuals, and beginning to fulfill our particular and valued purpose on earth. It's about listening to our THUNDER—our inner truth, dreams, and desires. It's about understanding our fears. Sacred wisdom can help us do this, as it has helped others for thousands and thousands of years, because it is *not* about giving answers. It is about opening ourselves to our own inner vision—so we have the self-awareness and self-acceptance to choose the road we want to travel.

Sacred wisdom will help you to know that you don't have to be afraid of who you are, or of who you think you are not. Remember, you can choose at any time who you want to be and how you want to live. It is my hope that the meditations, rituals, and teachings in this book will help you the way they have helped me in the past and still continue to help me today.

> "The journey between what you once were and who you are now becoming is where the dance of life really takes place."
>
> —BARBARA DE ANGELIS, AUTHOR OF *PASSION*

> "Lift up your eyes upon this day breaking for you.
> Give birth to the dream."
>
> —MAYA ANGELOU, AFRICAN AMERICAN POET, AUTHOR OF *I KNOW WHY THE CAGED BIRD SINGS*

MIRACLE

Listen.

Do you hear It?
I do.
I can *feel* it.
I expect a miracle is coming.
It has set loose this restlessness
inside of me.

Expect it.
Dream about it.
Give birth to it in your being.
Know! Something good
is coming down the line.
Finding its way to you.

—JEWEL,
SINGER, SONGWRITER, POET,
FROM *A NIGHT WITHOUT ARMOR*

Chapter One

The Way of the Spiritual Warrior

"The Warrior demonstrates a willingness to take a stand.
This is the capacity to let others know where
we stand, where we don't stand, what we stand for,
and how we stand for ourselves."

—ANGELES ARRIEN, ANTHROPOLOGIST/AUTHOR,
FROM *THE FOUR-FOLD WAY*

Ajo ajo	Journey, journey
Ajo mi re.	This is my journey.
Kini l'awa o?	What are we?
Ajo ajo.	Journey journey.

—SHANGO SONG, TRINIDAD

THE JOURNEY INTO ADULTHOOD is the *intended* time to claim the Warrior's way. All the intensity, beauty, difficulty, and questions of the Thundering Years are designed to challenge us to determine what path we are going to take in life. Most Native cultures believe this *is* the purpose of the THUNDERing Years—a time when we commit to the way of the Warrior.

A Warrior's way includes a journey to oneself and to one's purpose. It is a "Hero's" path because not everyone is willing to risk taking the journey; many people are *afraid.* They put their Thunder to sleep with drugs or alcohol, too much work, video games, or other distractions, or they hide their Thunder from criticism—only to find it emerge later in their adult life when they are in their 30s, 40s, or beyond. Usually it resurfaces as a crisis—a wake-up call to another chance to redirect one's life, to take the spiritual path. As Dante Alighieri put it in *The Divine Comedy, Inferno,* "In the middle of this road we call life I found myself in a dark wood with no clear path through." That is why the intensity of our Thundering Years is so powerful and meaningful. *This is the time of our life we are meant to begin this path.* We are meant to listen to our Thunder-energy, we are meant to be outrageous and, at times, difficult. This energy enriches us all. Ancient wisdom recognizes the need for this Thunder to be expressed in order for civilization to grow and change. When a community ignores this energy, or is too afraid of it, the entire community ends up in trouble. We can't keep such energy down, we can't repress it, without it resurfacing in some way.

Spiritual "Warriorship" is embodied in the ancient traditions of Tibet, China, India, Korea, Japan, Africa, Northern and Southern American Indians, and ancient Celtic communities. All these traditions have one thing in common when it comes to Spiritual Warriorship: they all are founded on the belief that there is a basic human wisdom within everyone that can be tapped into to solve our difficulties and to increase our happiness. This wisdom is the intense Thunder-energy that, when used wisely, propels us into our adult years. It is also the energy that can harm us if it is misdirected or suppressed.

A Spiritual Warrior is someone who acknowledges the great potential within

"My message to our young people—is to be aware of the important time you live in. You will be alive to see the greatest pain the world has ever experienced, or, the greatest splendor. I see you riding on a tremendous wave, landing where my eyes cannot go."

—KARYN BELL, IRISH-AMERICAN MENTOR

"A human being is part of the whole, called by us the 'Universe,' a part limited in time and space. He experiences himself, his thoughts and feelings as something separated from the rest—a kind of optical delusion of his consciousness. This delusion is a kind of prison for us, restricting us to our personal desires and to affection for a few persons nearest to us. Our task must be to free ourselves from this prison by widening our circle of compassion to embrace all living creatures and the whole of nature in its beauty. Nobody is able to achieve this completely, but the striving for such achievement is in itself a part of the liberation and foundation for inner security."

—ALBERT EINSTEIN, PHYSICIST

themselves and *believes* in this potential. Warriorship is about *true* fearlessness in one's search for happiness and meaning. Living the life of a Spiritual Warrior means to value being part of the whole and to understand that we are all connected. The Spiritual Warrior is able to live in this modern world while acknowledging our relationship to and dependence on the spiritual world. *Spirituality* is not some vague notion or religious doctrine. It is a simple but powerful part of our human nature. It is within us all. It can be, and is, expressed in many forms. Throughout time and cultures, this spiritual energy has been recognized as being especially intense and meaningful during our Thundering Years. Spiritual energy moves us to ask the questions, "What is the meaning of life? Where do we come from? and What is my purpose here on earth?"

"All of life is an experiment. The more experiments you make the better."

—RALPH WALDO EMERSON, AMERICAN ESSAYIST, POET, AND SPIRITUAL PHILOSOPHER

"I worry a lot about small stuff, unimportant stuff. But then I think about why we're here. I believe in a God and all that goes with that. I believe in fate. But Why? Why am I here? I would like to know this."

—LINDSAY, AGE 19

"I am told I am beautiful. But I don't feel beautiful. I am told I am brave, but the truth is, I am full of anxiety and fear. I am told to follow my dreams, but my parents imply that my decisions are

somehow wrong. I am told to stay near home, but I want to move far away and see new places. I am told to be patient, but I want to START MY LIFE NOW. I am told not to be afraid, but it feels like they don't like my choices. I just want to GO; I am ready."

—ALEXA, AGE 22

Alexa's parents are afraid that her dreams of wanting to be a choreographer are not sound, and that she should pursue a more "serious" career. They talked her out of taking a trip to South America with other students the summer she turned 18 because it seemed too risky. Alexa is full of anxiety. She is ready to start her journey into adulthood and wants her parents' support. Her anxiety is one expression of her suppressed Thunder-energy. Are your dreams supported?

It is such dreams and aspirations that are the foundation of our spiritual journey. Our longings and desires are what get us up and on with our lives. They are the trail we make through our lives and each of us must follow our own. A deep spiritual longing underlies all Thunder-energy. This is important to understand because as you have likely found out, the intensity of Thunder-energy is often misunderstood by others. But no one can feel too intensely. What is important is *how* you use this power—what you do with your Thunder. This energy, unique to your time of life, pushes you toward independence and is the thrust behind your hopes and fears. It can be the source of your creativity, or negativity.

You are standing at a crossroad, the forceful place where you are no longer a child but not yet a ripened adult. This crossroad is of great significance for you and others. This crossroad is also like being on top of a tremendous mountain—you can look back from where you have been, and you can also hold a vision of where you are headed. This place holds great potential.

> "Dreams count; the Spirits have compassion for us and have guided us."
>
> —CREE INDIAN PROVERB

Sitting on Top of the Great Mountain Exercise

Take a moment and imagine yourself on top of a great mountain. You are far above everything and can see for great distances in all directions. Use this great vision to see your life. . . .

Behind you is your life so far . . . all that has come to pass up to this moment. What do you see? What events brought you to this place in your life? What choices did you or others make that determined your life so far? How have you used this time? Can you see how one choice leads into another? What losses, trauma, or pain have you suffered? How have these affected you? What gifts, happiness, and opportunities have been given to you so far? Notice how all this has led you to YOUR LIFE NOW.

To your sides is your life now. Who are your friends? What do you give your time to? What pain are you experiencing? What gifts and opportunities are being offered to you now? What choices are you making that will determine what is to come? What are your dreams and fears? What problems and challenges face your community and the planet at this time?

In front of you is your future. What do you see? When you look in this direction it stretches out further, beyond all that you can see. But what awaits you in the near future, because of how you are living now? What do you see awaiting you and the planet in the distant future if you continue to go on as you are presently? Can you easily imagine that the future side of the mountain is vast and expansive, meaning there are many possibilities out there for you?

Now take a few moments to write down your thoughts, feelings, and responses to this exercise. Date it, so you can reflect on it later. After you have read this book, return to this exercise and experience it again. Now, what do you see as you sit on top of the great mountain?

"I saw myself on the central mountain of the world, the highest place, and I had a vision because I was seeing in the sacred manner of the world . . . the central mountain is everywhere."

—BLACK ELK,
OGLALA SIOUX
HOLY MAN,
FROM *BLACK ELK SPEAKS*

In most native cultures around the world, the spiritual journey is considered the central purpose of each and every life. Spiritual practice was, and is, part of everyday life. Native cultures use special ceremonies and rites to help Spiritual Warriors on their heroic journey into adulthood. In these traditions, young people are given the opportunity to express and confront their spiritual and creative selves. They are given ways to open up to their potential and to their dreams. Ceremonies and wisdom teachings are part of the communal respect

for the young Warriors and their Thunder-energy. They are offered rites-of-passage rituals, which help them open up to their many qualities and become recognized as adults. The spiritual thirst is understood as a longing for wholeness and a desire to belong to something great, no matter what form it takes.

"A warrior must only take care that his spirit is never broken."

—CHOZAN SHISSAI, JAPANESE SWORDSMAN

A Warrior's Coming-of-Age and Empowerment

When we are born, a place is made for us. And, when you connect with your Thunder in a humane way, you will be given the confidence you need to accomplish your dreams. In Australian Aboriginal culture everything is experienced as "dreamtime," because they believe Spirit cannot be separated from humanity. An Aboriginal elder shares that "the Thunder inside of the young is very real, and of great value to everyone." Aboriginals believe that the ancestors created the plants and peoples, the mountains and deserts, and the oceans. Thus, when you relate to your Thunder-energy in a respectful way, you respect what the ancestors have given you. And, then you are given the confidence to express yourself in the way the Creator invented for you.

Celtic warriors were viewed as "stewards of change." They were taught skills at a young age to carry as their medicine into their adult years—respect, self-confidence, recognition of fear, consciousness of their surroundings, and knowledge of their place in the great circle of life. In the Jewish coming-of-age ritual—the Bar and Bat Mitzvah—one becomes responsible for the *yetzer hara*, the good and bad desires known to exist within all of us. In this tradition, up to the age of 13 the child has innocence, a lack of responsibility. At 13, the intense journey into adulthood is acknowledged as beginning, which means one becomes responsible for both good and bad impulses and all the actions that result from these influences.

Buddhists throughout the world offer coming-of-age ceremonies. Burmese Buddhists send the boys into adulthood with a lavish ritual called *shin-byu*. Tibetan Buddhists have rites they call empowerments to initiate the person with certain spiritual energies and to infuse them with spiritual power. These empowerments are done many times throughout one's life, when one is ready to take on more sacred wisdom and powers. Those who choose to journey on the path of the Spiritual Warrior are "infused" or "empowered" with certain sacred powers through chants and words sung by one who is practicing in the holy ways and who has been empowered with this wisdom.

In the Navajo traditions such empowerments are called *haatal* (chantway), and the one being "sung to" is similarly infused with holy power by a holy person. Most Native American traditions have their own style of empowerment rituals, where one is "chanted" to and thereby receives certain holy energies. This can be compared to sacraments in Christian faiths, where one takes on the "body and blood" of Christ, thus being "filled" with his love and wisdom.

All these forms of empowerment are meant to guide and support us, and give us inner strength.

> *"I went to an empowerment offered by His Holiness the 14th Dalai Lama. He chanted to us, and over three hundred people sat quietly opening their hearts and minds to this energy. He infused us all with compassion. I felt empowered with love and more capable of being courageous and compassionate. So I would say that somehow the empowerment took hold inside of me."*
>
> —JACOB, AGE 19

We can also "empower" ourselves with sacred wisdom by calling on the energies and power of a Wisdomkeeper (see chapter 10). It is believed that all those who have taken the path of the Spiritual Warrior will share their energies and powers with us—we simply need to invite their energies into our hearts and minds.

To find Tibetan empowerment rites refer to the resources at the end of the meditation chapter in this book, look in the *Shambhala Sun* magazine, or contact your local meditation (Dharma) center. For more on Native American empowerment rituals check out your local tribes through the chamber of commerce in your area.

> "They waited until their children reached the intensity of adolescence, and then they used that very intensity's capacity for absorption, its hunger, its need to act out, its craving for dark things, dark knowledge, dark acts, all the qualities we fear most in our kids—the ancients used these very qualities as teaching tools."
>
> —MICHAEL VENTURA, COLUMNIST FOR THE *LOS ANGELES WEEKLY* AND ADVOCATE FOR TEENS

The Way of the Spiritual Warrior

In a classic journey of the Spiritual Warrior, as described in the Navajo tradition, a young Warrior prepares for adult life by harnessing the fierce power of the "Thunderers." The Thunderers are spirit guides that represent the many forms of intensity that are part of the young Warrior's life. But as many Navajo stories reflect, this Thunder-energy can be misused as well, causing harm to the Warrior and his or her entire tribe. When one of us overdoses, or harms ourself or others, everyone is harmed. The stories show that we need to find a balance by harnessing this intensity, this power we have and using it in creative and meaningful ways.

You who choose to travel the sacred path must be willing to journey into your dreams, your mind, your body and soul—to find your true power, your true medicine. You must be willing to journey to places inside and outside yourself to use sacred wisdom. *Sacred wisdom is everywhere.* To commit to this journey is to discover yourself and to find lasting fulfillment.

> "Warriorship is a continual journey. To be a warrior is to learn to be genuine in every moment of your life."
>
> —CHÖGYAM TRUNGPA, TIBETAN LAMA, FROM *SHAMBHALA: THE SACRED PATH OF THE WARRIOR*

> "Ehara taku toa i te toa takitahi
> Engari takimano, no aku tupuna;
> Te mana, te wehi, te tapu me te ihi,
> I heke mai ki ahau, no aku tupuna . . .
>
> My greatness comes not from me alone
> It derives from a multitude, from my ancestors;
> The authority, the awe, the divine, and the artistry
> I inherited these gifts, from my ancestors."
>
> —TE MAORI ART EXHIBIT, NEW ZEALAND

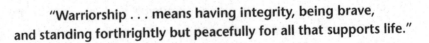

> "Warriorship . . . means having integrity, being brave, and standing forthrightly but peacefully for all that supports life."
>
> —STEVEN MCFADDEN, JOURNALIST AND ACTIVIST

The Circle of Life: Mitakuye Oyasin

"When we try to pick out anything by itself,
we find it hitched to everything else in the universe."

—JOHN MUIR, NATURALIST

In his young adult years, Jeffrey Miller went in search of himself and of a spiritual path. His parents were concerned when the spiritual longings of their Jewish son, who was raised in a town on Long Island, took him around the world to India. There he found a new sense of belonging. "Among a community of seekers living on Kopan Hill, my questions and search for purpose no longer seemed strange, weird, or out of place. Suddenly I discovered that it wasn't just me who wanted to find a deeper sense of meaning. My questions were the universal questions asked by generations of seekers—scientists seeking truth, mystics looking for a direct experience of the Divine, the pious seeking God. Buddhist, Jewish, Hindu, Christian, Muslim—it didn't matter—there was a whole world and an entire lineage of seekers, *of whom I was a part.* I belonged. At Kopan I discovered that a trail through the spiritual universe had already been blazed" (taken from his bestselling book, *Awakening the Buddha Within*). Jeffrey is now Lama Surya Das, a much-sought-after Buddhist teacher. In his book he confides how his parents came to accept and be happy for his choices. Just as he found that he belonged to something great, you also belong. Everyone who asks the big questions such as "Why?" or "Who am I?" belongs to all those who seek truth and purpose.

Mitakuye Oyasin is a Lakota slogan that translates into "all my relations." The Lakota are a Native American tribe that is also known as the Oglala Sioux, of which the great Oglala holy man Black Elk was a member. The words express the Lakota belief that everything and everyone is connected. We are all related to each other, as well as to the animals and plants who share this planet. This is a principle that we find in ancient traditions: **Each of us has a sacred and valued place in the circle of life.** This wisdom is important throughout our lives, and it can protect and guide you on your journey through the Thundering

"All things are tied together. When you cut a tree, whose roots connect with everything, you must ask its forgiveness or a star will fall out of the sky."

—LACANDON (MAYAN INDIAN) PROVERB

Years. When everything else is confusing and chaotic, or you are getting too much input from others, you can rely on this truth: *Remember you are part of something great.* Such wisdom can, and will, get you through the most difficult times. When you are in trouble, you can return to the voices of the ancient ones and the Wisdomkeepers who have gone before and made it through great difficulties of their own.

Tapping In to Sacred Wisdom

Sacred wisdom is a power we can tap in to at anytime. Such wisdom gives us the strength and insight to be brave—to take risks, and to help ourselves and others. This journey of the Warrior is about finding and knowing our place in this great circle. There is such strength and happiness when we find the way to know ourselves and to BE ourselves.

Here is a simple meditation that empowers you with this wisdom. It takes about ten minutes. All traditions that use such a practice, such as Native American, Tibetan, and Christian mysticism (to name a few), know that we gain substantial benefits by invoking the help of Wisdomkeepers. Such meditations are offered on the belief that when you invoke help, you will get it. What spiritual person, along with their wisdom and medicine, do you want to invite into your life right now? Consider this before you begin the meditation. They can be alive or dead. Does Gandhi appeal to you? Or perhaps Martin Luther King or Padmasambhava, the Buddha of Compassion, would be of help to you right now. Or it could be someone alive such as His Holiness the 14th Dalai Lama. There are many deities and Wisdomkeepers you can choose from, depending on what "medicine" you want to call forth: the courage of Black Elk, the love of Jesus Christ, the compassion of the Blessed Mary or Padmasambhava, the hope of White Buffalo Calf Woman, the power of Mother Earth, or the warrior energy of the Buddha. Once you have decided who you will be calling on, go ahead and begin the meditation.

"This we know: the earth does not belong to man, man belongs to the earth. All things are connected like the blood that unites us all. Man did not weave the web of life, he is merely a strand in it. Whatever he does to the web, he does to himself. All things are bound together."

—CHIEF SEATTLE,
OF THE
SUQUAMISH INDIANS

Find a room or place outdoors where you can be alone, undisturbed, for ten minutes. Sit down in a chair or on a mat or cushion on the floor or ground. Gently close your eyes. Let yourself settle into your body. Sit comfortably, yet alert. For a moment listen to your breathing. Feel the breath move through your body, making your stomach rise and fall. . . . Then begin to imagine in front of you the Wisdomkeeper of your choosing. . . . Invite this being to sit in front of you. Believe that your simple invitation is enough to have the spirit of this great teacher show up for you. Then, imagine this being sending you a ray of love and light from his or her heart into your heart. Let this light and love fill your entire body, filling every cell, every molecule, and every atom. Then silently ask this being to fill you with wisdom and courage. Allow this courage to become your courage and this wisdom to become your wisdom. This is why your chosen Wisdomkeeper walked the great path of the Spiritual Warrior, to help you now. Imagine yourself being infused with wisdom and courage. Then sit quietly, breathing softly, filled with the love, strength, and wisdom of this teacher. . . . Before opening your eyes, thank this teacher for being with you. Gradually open your eyes, and notice for a moment how you feel.

Also helpful is to find some written teachings by a Wisdomkeeper and read a few lines or paragraphs before beginning each day. When you read such a text, it sticks in your mind and influences your entire day in a good way.

These Wisdomkeepers are waiting for us to practice their wisdom, to borrow from their courage and strength, to learn from their mistakes. The Wisdomkeepers before us, and living today, know that each of us has the ability to accomplish great things in life. They know, through experience, the many obstacles and difficulties there can be on the way to a full adult life. They want you to know that there is no obstacle great enough to stop you from living a full and creative life.

"The human potential for intelligence and dignity is attuned to experiencing the brilliance of the bright blue sky, the freshness of green fields, and the beauty of the trees and mountains. We have an actual connection to reality that can wake us up and make us feel basically, fundamentally good."

—CHÖGYAM TRUNGPA, TIBETAN LAMA, FROM *SHAMBHALA: THE SACRED PATH OF THE WARRIOR*

Giving Up the Lie of Your Insignificance

> "Taking your journey requires you to
> leave behind the illusion of your insignificance."
>
> —CAROL S. PEARSON, AUTHOR OF *THE LESSON*

The sad truth is that many people today have lost touch with sacred wisdom and have given up on themselves and others. Sometimes to find wisdom we need to stop believing in a lie. Often, a lie is a belief that once may have had value but has outlived its usefulness *and truthfulness*. Examples of such outdated beliefs include "young women shouldn't go to college," "men don't have feelings," "women are too sensitive," "men should never be nurses or stay at home with the children," or "cigarettes aren't addictive." Lies are heavy baggage for the soul. It is as if you are putting heavy garbage in your medicine bags and lugging it everywhere you go. You get weighted down, and discouraged. Lies are a coverup for the truth. They *claim* to be the way things are, when in reality they are untrue. Men *do* have feelings and cigarettes *are* addictive. Like a mirage, lies appear to be one thing when in reality they are something altogether different. Cigarettes used to be advertised as benefiting one's health! Studies now show that "sensitivity" in a woman is part of her intuitive nature—not a flaw.

> "Since you are like no other being ever created since the beginning of time, you are incomparable."
>
> —BRENDA UELAND, AUTHOR OF *IF YOU WANT TO WRITE*

Lies restrict us. Lies "convince" us to believe something that ultimately can harm us. Living a lie, such as "I can never disagree with my parents," can hold us back. Has anyone ever lied to you, for example, by telling you "this won't hurt," or "it doesn't matter," when in fact it *did* hurt you, or it *did* matter? When we live by such lies, we have to generate a lot of energy to keep them from being discovered as a lie. That's why there are often secrets protecting lies from getting out. The cigarette companies put a lot of advertising into trying to convince us that smoking has its benefits! Alcohol and beer advertisements try to do the same—convince you that you won't have as much fun (or friends!) if you don't include *their* drink at your parties. When we are addicted to something we typically lie to ourselves about the problem: "Oh, I can stop when I want," or "I just do it on weekends."

Warriors work at seeing through lies and help bring out the truth for everyone to see. A Warrior in Tibetan culture, a *pawo,* is considered a person who is courageous enough to be authentic and honest. Pawos challenge themselves to be genuine in this world that often fights against such honesty. It takes a belief in oneself, along with intense courage, to bring truth and genuineness into our daily lives. *Spiritual Warriors have an urge to expose the lies that are around them, which threatens those who are invested in the lie.* From the view at the top of the mountain, you can see through the lies.

There is one lie that we all need to break free of, to take the path of the Warrior, and to move into our adult years with all of our Thunder-energy intact. It's **The Big Lie.** This lie convinces us that we are basically bad, weak, powerless, or insignificant. It tells us that we don't have any sacred "medicine" within ourselves. Those who believe in this lie let obstacles such as poverty, illness, bad weather, bad schools, abusive parents, negative (false) labels, social background, drug and alcohol addiction, or a disability stop us from setting goals and making dreams come true.

> *"The teachers at school worry about me because I enjoy the villains in Star Wars. And that's because they're so INTERESTING. I can spend hours coming up with new and exciting villain characters. So this means I'm dangerous? Is Stephen King dangerous because he's so good at writing dark tales? My 'dream' doesn't fit in to what others appreciate—so I am labeled bad news."*
> —Craig, age 16

The Big Lie may tell us that we might as well give up making a better life for ourselves. It may lead us to believe that we don't have choices, that life is basically a series of painful circumstances. For example, this lie tells us that if we are born poor, poor we will remain. That if our parents mistreat us, we will go on to mistreat others because this is what we were taught. This lie will convince us to give up on our dreams! It deceives us into believing that if we have a disability we cannot set our goals as high as others. It tells us we cannot get ourselves out of a harmful relationship. *This lie suggests that we cannot make different choices from our parents.* Don't be cheated and belittled by this lie.

"The greatest thing a man [or woman] can do in this world is to make the most possible out of the stuff that has been given him. This is success, and there is no other."

—Orison Swett Marden, founder of *Success* magazine

"Whoever you are whatever you are start with that, whether salt of the earth or only white sugar."

Alice Walker, African American writer, author of *The Color Purple*

17

In truth, we have the power to change or re-create our lives at any time. We are not victims of our situation—we can choose to respond to life's circumstances in a variety of ways. As the Revolutionary leader Thomas Paine said, "You have the power to change the world." And this change begins within ourselves. "We are the change we need." Even when we are under the control of others, we can make decisions about how we want to deal with this control. We all have choices. You have choices. You can choose how to use your intensity. You have this incredible medicine inside of you that is bigger than all the obstacles placed in front of you. This Thunder-energy can be connected with sacred wisdom to make incredible things happen for you. Only the "lie of your insignificance" (whatever form this lie takes) can keep you from this power.

> "My therapist kept telling me to believe that 'anything is possible.' But this was so hard for me. So much had gone wrong for me. She said I should just let the idea be with me for a while—that good things can and will happen to me. Her believing this helped. Then, things began to change for me. Once I let the idea in that anything is possible, I started to notice the opportunities that came my way."
>
> —NINA, AGE 18

Too many adults live by the lie that we cannot rise above difficulty or trouble. (You probably know a few.) One young person shared how her mother warns her not to dream "too big" because nothing ever really turns out. The mother teases her daughter when she shares her big dreams of becoming a scientist or a writer. Too many young people are inhibited by their *parents' fears.*

> "I want to fly helicopters. It seems impossible to my mother, and maybe she's right. What's the point? My parents think I can 'do something better.' Like what? They want me to get a master's degree in SOMETHING. Why can't they just leave me alone? It gets to the point I just want everyone to leave me alone."
>
> —JON, AGE 18

Our dreams develop during our Thundering Years. Never be talked out of your own dream. You don't have to believe the lie that you are "stuck with" a certain situation, relationship, or life. You can use your intensity, and your life

"Come to the edge, he said.

They said: We are afraid.

Come to the edge, he said.

They came.

He pushed them . . . and they flew."

—GUILLAUME APOLLINAIRE, POET

energy, your medicine, to create your own life's path—a spiritual path guided by the ancient wisdom handed down to help us. A path that leads you to an adult life full of opportunity, creativity, and companionship. Whatever you do, don't listen to others' fears and doubts about your abilities to fulfill your dreams. Find those who support your dreams. Believe in yourself enough to follow your dreams and ideals, regardless of limitations and doubts. All dreams, small and large, are worth consideration and respect. Sometimes the simplest idea becomes the greatest invention. It doesn't have to be something big to be great. All dreams are great. Believing in your dreams gives them incredible power. When you believe in your dreams, your life begins to open up in ways you or others may have thought impossible. When one of us rises above our limited or negative circumstance we offer an example to all others that come in contact with us. This is a great achievement. This is part of being a Spiritual Warrior.

> **"What lies behind us and what lies before us**
> **are tiny matters, compared to what lies within us."**
>
> —RALPH WALDO EMERSON,
> AMERICAN ESSAYIST, POET, AND SPIRITUAL PHILOSOPHER

> **"Every blade of grass has its Angel that bends over it and whispers, 'grow, grow.'"**
>
> —THE TALMUD, JEWISH SPIRITUAL TEACHINGS AND LAWS

Walking the Path

Before going on, consider the following questions and exercises. These questions will help you to get in touch with your Thunder-energy, making it more real for you. You may want to write your responses down in a personal journal so that you can reflect on them later. There is a lot of power in considering our lives and our choices, so a Warrior's way includes reflection. The power in reflection comes from our ability to be in the driver's seat of our lives, rather than being pulled around by circumstances. Reflection gives us insight and the time to make good choices. Most people who lose control of their lives don't stop and reflect.

- What beliefs may your family or community be living by that may no longer be useful or true for you?
- What beliefs are you likely challenging with *your* Thunder-energy/dreams?

The Way of the Spiritual Warrior

> "Change and growth take place when a person has risked himself and dares to become involved with experimenting with his own life."
>
> —HERBERT OTTO, AUTHOR OF *EXPLORATIONS IN HUMAN POTENTIALITIES*

> "Some candles burn themselves and one another up,
>
> Others taste like a surprise of roses in a room and you just a stranger who wandered in."
>
> —RUMI, SUFI MYSTIC AND POET

- Are you being discouraged from thinking for yourself? In what way?
- Are you being told something that doesn't feel right? What?
- Do your parents/friends/siblings abuse drugs or alcohol, or gamble too often? How does this affect you?
- Is someone you know hurtful with their sarcasm?
- What secrets are you keeping that may be covering up a lie?
- Do you feel insignificant in any way?
- Do you feel anxious a great deal of the time? Do you worry a lot? What about?
- What would make you most happy right now?
- Do you feel limited by your life situation?
- What do your parents fear? How does this affect you?
- What do you know of your parents' dreams for themselves? For you?
- Have someone else's fears gotten in the way of something you wanted to try?
- Can you find others that will support your dreams and goals? Make a list of them. Have you made contact with them lately?

Now write your thoughts and responses in your journal or simply take the time to reflect on your responses to the questions. Notice what feelings and concerns come up while you consider these questions. Do you find that there are reasons for you to take the journey of the Warrior? If you uncovered a lot of lies, sadness, or obstacles while reading the questions, you may have personal reasons to consider the wisdom contained in this book.

> *"I just need some other possibilities besides the same old shit from teachers and my parents. It's not that it's all bad, it's just not for me. I'm wanting MORE, even though I admit I'm not sure what the 'more' is. I believe I'm supposed to follow this feeling to its conclusion; I just want to see what's out there."*
>
> —DREW, AGE 20

Ideally, our lives are a balance of using the wisdom we have inherited from the past and the wisdom of the present.

Making a Medicine Bag

Indigenous cultures and ancient wisdom can give us guidance to help us use our Thunder-energy to make our dreams more real. One ritual that has been a powerful aid is making a medicine bag. Many indigenous and native cultures believe that we all hold an "original" and unique "medicine." To express this unique medicine, Native Americans, Celtic Warriors, and members of indigenous African tribes, among others, carry pouches or bags that contain symbols of power; symbols that represent their medicine.

A medicine bag is something physical and "real" to hold on to as we undertake our life's journey. You can make a medicine bag for yourself or buy one already made to hold objects that symbolize what you want to bring into your life as you journey into the adult years. You can collect pictures, rocks, words, quotes, herbs, dreams, favorite items, poetry, and/or prayers to put into it.

You can wear your medicine bag around your neck, keeping it close to your heart (or heart center), or you can place it on a private altar or in some other sacred place that is yours alone. Look into it when you need reminding of who you are and what you're becoming. Add to it along the way. Take out things that no longer feel right to you. Hold on to it when you're afraid. The medicine bag and its contents become symbolic of that part of you that no one can steal or destroy.

How to Make a Medicine Bag

- Find a piece of material that has value to you. It can have meaning because of its appearance or history. The material can be leather, velvet, cotton, or silk; whatever appeals to you. Leather and velvet work well because the ends don't fray after they are cut.
- Cut out a circle (it doesn't have to be perfectly round) the full width of your hand, or a small dessert plate.
- Punch a circle of holes about a quarter inch away from the edges and a quarter inch apart from each other. You can use a paper or leather hole puncher (depending on thickness of material), or you can use an ice pick

> **"Every child is born a genius."**
>
> —ALBERT EINSTEIN, PHYSICIST

> **"Pray to understand what man has forgotten."**
>
> —PROVERB, LUMBEE TRIBE, NORTH CAROLINA

21

to punch the holes in the fabric. When using an ice pick, place a wooden cutting board beneath the fabric and punch down through the fabric. The holes you punch need to be large enough to string something through the material to close the bag.

- Take a piece of rope, leather, hemp, or string of beads, about the length of a shoelace (24 to 30 inches), and lace it through the holes.

- Fill the bag with the power objects of your choice—artwork, poetry, quotes, favorite objects, stones or rocks, dried flowers, photographs—anything that has special meaning for you.

- Pull the string through until the ends meet and you can tie them, gathering the leather or fabric together. You can wrap some of the rope or string of beads just below the top of the gathering to close the pouch, or simply tie the two ends together. You can use the excess string to tie the bag around your neck if you like.

It is not necessary to punch holes and string your bag to keep it closed. You can simply gather your material into a pouch shape in one hand and loop some string or beads around the neck of the bag to keep your "medicine" from falling out.

Books, Resources, and Wisdomkeepers Related to This Chapter

The Four-Fold Way: Walking the Paths of the Warrior, Teacher, Healer and Visionary, by Angeles Arrien, Ph.D. (HarperSanFrancisco, 1993). A great additon to *The Thundering Years*, focusing on specific paths and exercises. Takes from a variety of Eastern and Western traditions.

The Gift: Poems by HAFIZ, translated by Daniel Ladisky (Penguin, 1999). A wonderful book of poems that support the spiritual journey.

The Kingfisher Book of Religions: Festivals, Ceremonies, and Beliefs from around the World, by Trevor Barnes (Kingfisher, 1999). Offers simple descriptions and pictures of the major world religions.

The Nag Hammadi Library, edited by James M. Robinson (HarperSanFrancisco, 1990). A must-have for any Spiritual Warrior. A collection of the Dead Sea Scrolls, including The Gospel according to Thomas.

Navajo & Tibetan Sacred Wisdom: The Circle of the Spirit, by Peter Gold (Inner Traditions, 1994). A great resource for those who want to go further into the two great spiritual traditions of the Navajo and Tibetans.

Yoga Journal, a monthly magazine that goes beyond yoga and offers excellent articles on physical, mental, and spiritual well-being. To subscribe call 1-800-600-YOGA.

Zen Soup: Tasty Morsels of Wisdom from Great Minds East and West, by Laurence G. Boldt (Penguin, 1997). Thoughts and quotes from Wisdomkeepers that will inspire you.

Online Resources

The Dharma Dance Bistro
www.ecstaticspirit.com
This site strives to help us connect with Spirit and nature through rhythmic drumming, dancing, and ritual in order to attain both personal and communal healing. The colorful background and graphics lead us through wonderful thoughts on the healing power of the ecstatic spirit. A very useful link page is included.

The Foundation for Shamanic Studies
www.shamanism.org
This site offers many resources and links regarding shamanism and Spiritual Warriorship in various world cultures. This is also the site of Michael Harner, author of *The Way of the Shaman* (HarperSanFrancisco, 1980).

Path of the Feather
www.pathofthefeather.com
A guide to one's personal journey of transformation and healing through shamanic journey, medicine wheels, spirit animals, and wisdom from the ancient ones. Contains numerous links to other interesting pages related to this one.

Spiritual Network
www.spiritualnetwork.net/native
This site contains lots of information on various topics with links to sections called the Rainbow Tribe; Sacred Earth Sites; the Medicine Wheel; Animal Totems; and Wisdom, Prophecies, Shamans. Many links to other useful sites are also included on this network. It is a site worth checking out.

"When I was seventeen years of age I had the small pox. I was left alone in a lodge, helpless, weak, and my eyes nearly closed. A bear came in and walked up to where I was lying. He sat down with his back pressed against me, and began to scratch his breast with his fore paws. By and by he got up and walked out of the lodge. Was I dreaming or had it really happened? While I was thinking it over the bear returned and, while I trembled for fear, went through the same motions again, and then went off, leaving me unharmed. I thought surely the bear has had mercy on me. When my father came again we talked it over and agreed that the bear had pitied me. After that I worshipped the bear, and in the dance I wore anklets of bear's teeth."

—POOR WOLF (GROS VENTRE),
FROM *NEWS OF THE UNIVERSE:*
POEMS OF TWOFOLD CONSCIOUSNESS
BY ROBERT BLY

Chapter Two

The Wisdom of the Crows

and the Power of Story

"The destiny of the world is determined
less by the battles that are lost and won
than by the stories it loves and believes in."

—HAROLD GODDARD, AUTHOR OF
THE MEANING OF SHAKESPEARE

" . . . it seems to me that these ancient myths are filled
with hints about things we urgently need to know."

—LYNDSAY CLARKE, AUTHOR OF
TRADITIONAL CELTIC STORIES

"The one who tells the stories rules the world."

—HOPI INDIAN PROVERB

CAN YOU FEEL YOURSELF at times with one foot in the world of the child and one foot in the world of the adult? Is the tension sometimes just too much to take? Hundreds of stories, myths, and legends are written to escort us on this journey into adulthood. If you let them, stories can act like mentors and Wisdomkeepers reaching out to you through time, offering you a path to walk on.

"I can still remember one of my first stories. I heard it from a Lutheran minister. I was about 14 years old. I don't remember anything else from his sermon but the story. It was about some monk who was hanging from a cliff. 'He couldn't climb up because there was a tiger above him waiting to devour him, and below him was a long fall to death. His hands were growing tired, and soon he knew he would have to climb up, or let go. As he hung there, a magnificent butterfly landed on a nearby rock. He watched the butterfly and in his last moments he reached out to it, and fell. . . .' That was my life then: I was between two awful places with nowhere to go. I'm not sure I knew it meant this to me at the time, but the story seemed to give me strength to deal with the ambiguity and confusion in my own life somehow. It told me we can always reach for what's beautiful, even in our last moments. It helped me look for this beauty in my own life. And it's not that I held on to the story, it is more like it held on to me."

—ADRIAN, AGE 24

Adrian discovered some hope within himself when he heard this story. The story "hung on to him" and its message has helped him through more than one difficult time. In many respects he's become a butterfly collector. He collects hope and beauty around him as a way to get through painful times. What stories are holding on to you? What stories speak to you now? And even more important, what stories are you composing with your own life?

When the Going Gets Tough the Tough Tell a Story

One way ancient wisdom is passed on to us is through the sharing of myths, stories, legends, and prophecies. Stories give us a place where we can find our life's purpose. They talk to our hearts, open our minds, and motivate us to act. Story is a way to connect with the soul and with others. How often have you and your friends remembered the same story? Stories help us answer the cosmic question, "Who am I?"

Stories reflect many profound beliefs found within the traditions from which they originate. Many are written for young Warriors, to assist them through the Thundering Years. They are called **initiation myths,** or **coming-of-age stories,** where the main character is "called" to an adventure: the adventure being the journey into adulthood. Most stories hold simple truths that apply to everyone. Many of these myths and legends came to the storyteller as a vision, some are events remembered and passed down, while others came as a dream. This is why it is recommended that you record your dreams (see chapter 7), particularly the ones that feel important to you. Your dreams are likely part of your own personal story or myth.

Each of us is an unfolding story, and every experience in life contains a story. We can use stories, as well as poetry and songs, to guide us through all our journeys. Or, we may use story to resurrect a significant event, like our first love, or some important achievement. Stories and myths help us make sense of our lives and what happens to us. Sometimes writing our stories and dreams can even save our lives.

> *"I had this dream, well a nightmare actually. . . . A man was chasing me with two kitchen knives—one in each hand. I ran from him, terrified. But then something happened where my FEAR shifted to RAGE. I stopped suddenly and turned to face my attacker. I looked at him and rolled back my sleeves, revealing my arms, already raw with cuts. 'What are you going to do to me?' I screamed like I've never screamed in waking life. 'Are you going to CUT me?!' Then as he stared in awe, I took one of the knives from him (incidentally it was the first knife I ever used to cut myself), and proceeded to cut my arms more. I was burning with anger—no longer scared. It didn't hurt, and I wasn't running. The man looked at me in shock and disbelief—HE HAD NO*

> "The ancient myths were designed to harmonize the mind and body."
>
> —JOSEPH CAMPBELL, PHILOSOPHER AND MASTER STORYTELLER, FROM *THE POWER OF MYTH*

> "We feel nameless and empty when we forget our stories, leave our heroes unsung, and ignore the rites that mark our passage from one stage of life to another."
>
> —SAM KEEN AND ANNE VALLEY-FOX, FROM *YOUR MYTHIC JOURNEY: FINDING MEANING IN YOUR LIFE THROUGH WRITING AND STORY TELLING*

> "Each of us is a story, and each day part of that story unfolds. Each of us is the author to the story of our life, holding within us the power to change the plot at any time. What you dreamt last night is a story—tell it to someone. Who you visited with over lunch is a story—tell it to someone. Who you love is a story— tell it to someone. Who you fear is a story—tell it to someone. The secret you hold in your heart is a story—tell it to someone. Tell it to us. . . .
>
> When you find the story that you are— you find your life."
>
> —FLAMING RAINBOW
> WOMAN, SPIRITUAL
> WARRIOR

POWER OVER ME. . . . This dream helped me understand that maybe my self-injury was a DEFENSE—'They can't hurt me if I hurt myself more.'"

—LIA, AGE 16

As difficult as Lia's dream-story may be, a large percentage of young people are known to cut themselves, often leaving scars for a lifetime. Lia began to cut herself at the age of 14. She tried many ways to stop but nothing really worked until she began to write out her stories in poetry, articles, and prose. She also gave up her regular use of marijuana, which had been adding to her depression and anxiety. This dream was one story that helped her understand WHY she was cutting herself, which ultimately helped her find a reason to stop. Now Lia fights back her fears through her stories and poetry. (See page 221.)

A Storytelling Circle

Try this with a group of friends, as part of a ritual or group, or even suggest it as a class activity. For a couple weeks look for objects that symbolize something significant about yourself, or about something that is going on in your life. Bring to the gathering the *one* object that most strongly represents something significant about you or your life right now. Have the group sit in a circle on the floor. Bring this object to the circle and place it in the center. (Keep the object in a paper bag so no one will know who brought which object.) Have someone remove all the objects from the bags and place them on the floor. Then, taking turns, each person chooses an object (not their own) that appeals to them. This person then shares with the group what it is that drew them to that particular object. Then the owner of the object is invited to tell their story of the object—what it means to them. "I brought a CD that has a song on it that expresses my feelings right now" (Nelson, age 16). Other objects brought to one circle included: earrings, artwork, a ceramic bowl (family heirloom), a telephone, a heart-shaped rock, and a photograph of a recently deceased sister.

What would you bring to your circle?

> "I am anonymous
> I am not to be named
> I am but a Teller of Tales
> A Keeper of the Mysteries and the Lore
> The Wisdom and the Teachings of the Old Ones
> Minatou of the Ways of the People
> Come closer around the fire
> And I will speak my story."
>
> —MANITONQUAT (MEDICINE STORY),
> STORYTELLER, WAMPANOAG NATION

Writing or Telling Your Own Stories: Keeping an Idea Book

Any and all parts of your life can be a story. In the example on page 28, everyone had a "story" to tell about the significant object they brought with them to the circle. We all tell stories every day. When you describe an event or situation that you experienced or when you write someone a letter or a poem, you are engaging in the ancient tradition of storytelling. Consider putting together a collection of your and your friends' stories. Let your Thunder be heard (or read)! Everyone loves a personal story—just look at the popularity of movies, plays, and novels.

The following poem was written by Kirsten at the age of 17. When Kirsten was 15, her English teacher suggested students keep an "Idea Book," a small pocket notebook to write down ideas, thoughts, poems, and doodles at any time. Even if you're sitting in science class, she suggested, and have an idea, bring out your book and jot it down.

After Kirsten died suddenly in a car accident at age 17, her mother came across Kirsten's idea book (from which a book of Kirsten's poems was later published). The following poem appears in Kirsten's poetry book, *She Would Draw Flowers* (see chapter resources).

> "We must accept that this creative pulse within us is God's creative pulse itself."
>
> —JOSEPH CHILTON PEARCE, AUTHOR OF *THE CRACK IN THE COSMIC EGG: CHALLENGING CONSTRUCTS OF MIND AND REALITY*

PURPLE VIOLETS

"A story is like water

that you heat for
your bath.

It takes messages
between the fire

and your skin. It lets
them meet,

and it cleans you!"

—RUMI, SUFI MYSTIC
AND POET

"Whosoever survives
a test,

Whatever it may be,

Must tell the story.

That is his duty."

—ELIE WIESEL, WIN-
NER OF THE 1986
NOBEL PEACE PRIZE
AND AUTHOR OF *ALL
RIVERS RUN TO THE SEA*

My path has never been strewn
With broken glass
And cutting words.
No,
I have walked my life
With feet pale and tender,
On pillows of purple violets,
Embraced by yellow voices
That enfold me,
Leading me, with trusting eyes closed,
Away from the sharp, slippery rocks,
Away from the sucking pool
Which threatens to pull me under,
Shielding me with gentle blue-sky wings
From the screaming, tearing, empty wind
Which tries to blow me away.

I did not ask for this path,
For the loving smiles
And guiding hands,
But they are mine.
This is how I am.
This is my path.
It is mine to walk,
To change as I please,
To take care of
Forever.
I must cherish my violets,
Or they will die.
So I will
Forever.
—FROM *SHE WOULD DRAW FLOWERS:
A BOOK OF POEMS*, BY KIRSTEN SAVITIR BERGH

Kirsten left a legacy of paintings, drawings, and poetry, which she wrote during her high school years. She lived the creative life. She had a community of people to draw upon. She, indeed, was a Spiritual Warrior. Her creative spirit lives on in her poems and in those of us who read them.

You, too, can keep an idea book, something you can always refer to as a resource of your thoughts, concerns, and personal stories. Some people write their stories like a myth, where the main characters are animals or heroes. Some of us make up short stories about our lives because it is the way we want our lives to go. All this is story making and storytelling, a powerful tool for healing, forming your identity, or focusing your goals and dreams.

Starting Your Story

Here are some questions/ideas you can ask yourself, or share with your storytelling group, to get started on identifying and recording or creating stories of your own:

- Write about the last meaningful event that happened in your life. Fill up three pages without stopping to think. Begin the page with *"This is what I remember about what happened . . ."* and then just write whatever comes to your mind. Don't edit or stop to consider if it makes any sense. You can always add to it later, or take something out if you don't like it.

- Write about what HURTS. Write about what is bothering you. Let all the feelings, thoughts, and opinions come out onto the page. Again, just let it flow—don't censor anything.

- What animal do you identify with? Imagine being that animal. Write a poem or a story about being that animal.

Thundering Stories

Myths hold clues for us about how we can respond to the many challenges that we face in life. They are meant to open our hearts and minds to more ways of dealing with life's circumstances. Stories can help us bring out the qualities we want in ourselves—strength, courage, compassion—all aspects of the Spiritual Warrior. Stories are an art form, so each person who hears or reads a story will respond to it in his or her own unique way.

> "Through imagery, character, and plot, stories mirror our own struggles and free the mind to imagine options for creative change. Stories seem to go directly into long-term memory and so become part of the fabric of our being, a spiritual handbook of information to draw on."
>
> —SHARRON BROWN DORR, STORYTELLER FROM THE FOX VALLEY STORYTELLING GUILD IN ILLINOIS

Stories are also important in understanding the visions we get on our vision quests, and to help us understand the teachings of the Wisdomkeepers.

"Mythology tells us that *where you stumble, there your treasure is.* **There are so many examples. One that comes to mind is in** *The Arabian Nights.* **Someone is plowing a field, and his plow gets caught. He digs down to see what it is and discovers a ring of some kind. When he hoists the ring, he finds a cave with all of the jewels in it. And so it is in our own psyche; our psyche is the cave with all the jewels in it, and it's the fact that we're not letting their energies (stories) move us that brings us up short. The world is a match for us and we're a match for the world. And where it seems most challenging lies the greatest invitation to find a deeper and greater power within ourselves."**

—JOSEPH CAMPBELL, PHILOSOPHER AND
MASTER STORYTELLER, FROM *AN OPEN LIFE*

"A healing story
has the power to
guide and inspire
for a lifetime."

—SHARRON BROWN
DORR, STORYTELLER
FROM THE
FOX VALLEY
STORYTELLING
GUILD IN ILLINOIS

In this interview, Joseph Campbell goes on to say that many stories are about how we get "stuck" in our lives, with the story offering ideas on how to get *unstuck.* Some of us are stuck in our feelings of anger, boredom, judgmentalness, jealousy, or fear; or stuck in negative outside circumstances, such as poverty, alcoholic families, and abuse, as mentioned in chapter 1. During the Thundering Years, we also can get "stuck" in being a child, lacking what it takes to move through these years. We may get older in age, but we never quite grow up. This happens because we are not given the tools to get past where we are stuck or we are too scared to take the initiative ourselves. And it is scary at times to feel the adult emerge in us. Like a thunderstorm brewing off in the distance we feel the adult pushing itself outward. Following are a few examples of the stories and myths that are here to assist us.

The first story, *Wisdom of the Crows,* is taken from the Japanese Buddhist tradition, offering a tale in leadership and the ability to see beyond the surface of things. It describes the importance of the child's mind transforming into the mind of an adult.

Every part of a story can actually be understood as *part* of one's own self. For example, each crow in the story is an aspect of ourselves. We are the elder (wise one), questioning ourselves about our readiness for adulthood. We also hold within us the unskilled archer *and* the skilled archer. All three of the young crows represent different parts of who we are when we are asked to prove ourselves. We each have the potential to see beyond the surface of things—to be a leader if necessary.

The second story is a Lakota legend. It speaks amply to the power and importance of our Thunder and how we can use it. This legend is known as *White Buffalo Calf (or Cow) Woman* and comes from the Oglala Sioux people, a tribe of the Lakota of the Great Plains. This myth holds great significance because it is believed to hold a message for all peoples, of all traditions, and particularly for those in their Thundering Years. It is a legend of how the sacred pipe (sacred wisdom) was given to the Lakota, and now is being passed on to you.

"This legend teaches our people that to hold on to a sacred tradition, even when their very lives and community are being destroyed, means to hold on to what is sacred in us all. To hold on to this sacredness means we can, and some have, survived the worst of times. The Oglala Sioux consider the pipe most sacred. We could sit and smoke the sacred pipe in secret. This allowed us to keep our culture alive when those around us were trying to wipe us out. This is why we were given the sacred pipe."

—ED McGAA, EAGLE MAN, OF THE OGLALA SIOUX TRIBE

The Oglala Sioux, Lakota of the Great Plains of North America, are a "warrior" tribe, warriors of strength, peace, and courage. This legend is a call to each of us to take our rightful place among the human "tribe" as a Warrior.

"It is time now to heal the sacred hoop."

—ARVOL LOOKING HORSE, 19TH-GENERATION KEEPER OF THE SACRED WHITE BUFFALO CALF PIPE

The Wisdom of the Crows

As retold by Sherab Chodzin and Alexandra Kohn

There comes a time in the life of every kind of creature when they have to go out on their own and join the company of their elders. Crows are no exception.

It happened one day that the elder crows were testing three young ones to see if they had reached the age when they had the wit and maturity to fly with their elders. To the first of the young ones, the leader of the crows put the following question: "In this whole world, what do you think crows should fear the most?"

The young crow thought a moment and then answered, "The most fearsome thing is an arrow, for it can kill a crow with one strike."

When the elder crows heard this, they thought it was a very clever answer. They flapped their wings and cawed with approval. "You speak the truth," said the leader. "We welcome you into the flock."

Then the leader asked the second young crow, "What do you think we should most fear?"

"I think a skilled archer is more to be feared than an arrow," the young one said, "for only the archer can aim and shoot the arrow. Without the archer, the arrow is no more than a stick, like the twig I am perching on." The crows thought this was one of the most intelligent comments they had ever heard. The parents of the second young crow cawed with pride and beamed at their brilliant child. The leader said, "You speak with great intelligence. We are pleased to have you as a member of the flock." Then she asked the third young crow, "And what do you think is the thing most to be feared in the world?"

"Neither of the things mentioned already," responded the young bird. "The thing in the world most to be feared is an unskilled archer."

Here was a strange answer! The bewildered crows stood about silent and embarrassed. Many thought the third crow was simply not bright enough to understand the question. "Why do you say a thing like that?" the leader of the flock finally asked.

"The second of my companions is right. Without the archer, there is nothing to fear from an arrow. But a skilled archer's arrow will fly where it is aimed. So when you hear the twang of the bowstring, you only have to fly to one side or the other, and his arrow will miss you for sure. But with an unskilled archer, you never know where his arrow will go. If you try to get away, you may fly right into its path. You never can know whether to move or stay still."

When the birds heard this, they knew that the third young crow had real wisdom, which sees beyond the surface of things. They spoke of him with admiration and respect. Not long afterward, they asked him to become the leader of the flock.

When have you seen beyond the appearance of things, and reached a deeper meaning? What do you think is the thing most to be feared in the world?

The Legend of White Buffalo Calf Woman

Adopted and retold with the help of Eagle Man (Ed McGaa, Oglala Sioux Tribe)

It was a time when many tribes were living on little food and the threat of starvation was close. A council fire was built and many bands from neighboring tribes gathered together to try and solve their shared problem. The council chose two young Warriors to go out in search of food. They traveled far but found nothing. They were on foot since this was before the Lakota had horses. They climbed a large hill to look over the land and saw something, or someone, approaching them. As the figure approached they both saw that it was a beautiful woman.

She was dressed in a white buffalo skin and held something in her hands. She radiated a bright light around her and her feet appeared to be slightly off the ground as she walked. When she got close enough they recognized her as a holy woman, a *Wakan wiman*, in the Oglala Sioux language.

She spoke to them and said, "Do with me what you want."

One Warrior was in awe and respect that she was in the presence of such a sacred woman and would not even look upon her. Even in her thoughts she regarded the holy woman with great respect. The other young Warrior, however, began to desire the holy woman's body and clothes and wanted to posses her somehow. He reached out to grab her, and as he did this a great mist descended down upon them. When the mist lifted all that was left of him were white bones.

Then as White Buffalo Calf Woman walked off she spoke to the other young Warrior who remained kneeling before her. "Return to your people and tell them I have brought something for them; *tell them to prepare for me.*"

The young Warrior did as she was told and went back to her people and gave them the message. They immediately prepared for her visit by building a medicine lodge with an earth altar that faced the west.

After four days they saw the holy woman approaching, carrying a bundle in her hands.

She entered the medicine lodge and unwrapped the bundle, showing them what was inside. It was the sacred pipe and tobacco. She taught them the use of the sacred pipe. She predicted that the pipe would keep the Oglala Sioux Nation alive. Inside the sacred pipe was tobacco. She explained that the pipe was never to be used to hold anything but sacred tobacco. "The bowl of the pipe," she taught, "is made of red stone. It represents the flesh and blood of the Buffalo People and all other Peoples. The wooden stem of the pipe represents the trees and all things that are green and growing on this earth of ours. The smoke that is pulled through the pipe by your breath represents the sacred wind, the breath that carries prayers up to the Great Creator of us all." She told them many things to remember. She told how we must all follow the Red Road—the Good Road—the road of the Warrior, where we care for the earth and each other. The pipe is to help us hold on to what is of value in us all.

Then she spoke directly to the younger men and women of the tribe: "*You are the coming generation*, that's why you are the most important and precious ones. Someday soon you will hold this pipe, you will be the ones leading us. You will soon be smoking and praying with the pipe. Prepare to be the holders of the pipe." She turned and faced the elders, "It is your most important duty to prepare the young Warriors. Take this job seriously."

Before leaving she said, "I will return." Then, as she walked off into the horizon, she rolled her body over the earth four times. The first time she rolled she stood up as a black buffalo; the second time she turned into a brown buffalo; the third time into a red one, and finally the fourth time she turned into a white female buffalo calf.

This is *your* legend. Will you take hold of the pipe or pass away quickly into the mist and become a skeleton, like the one Warrior did in this story? The choice is yours—to refuse or accept sacred wisdom.

Which of the two Warriors do you feel like today? Are you grabbing for a quick fix, or can you be still and listen to the wisdom inside and around you? What wisdom do you hold within yourself to carry back to your "tribe" (family, friends, community)?

"When you pray with this Pipe, you pray for and with everything."

—"WHITE BUFFALO CALF WOMAN," AS TOLD BY BLACK ELK, FROM *BLACK ELK SPEAKS*

In the story of White Buffalo Calf Woman, the pipe became a symbol of power and hope and a link to the past and future. **The pipe is now being passed on to you.**

The final story is a short Sufi fable. Sufism is a mystical faith of Islam. Sufi practices and stories attempt to bring us closer to Spirit (in this case, Allah). They believe that each of us is in search of a personal relationship with a Greater Power (God/Goddess/Allah/Creator/Mother Earth). This story tries to teach us a simple truth about making choices. Perhaps it will be a timely truth for you now.

The Tiger and the Fox

Once there was a young woman who longed to know her place in the world and how to listen to God's wisdom. She went for a walk through the woods and saw a fox that had lost its legs, and she wondered how it lived. She waited and watched. At dusk she saw a great tiger with some wild game in its mouth. He had eaten much of it but took the rest of the meat to the fox. And the fox happily ate it.

The next day the young woman watched again, and saw the tiger once again bring some fresh game to the fox to eat. The young woman was moved by how God provided for the fox by means of the tiger. She thought, "That must be it! I am meant to go sit quietly in the woods and God will provide for me all that I need as well!" So, the next day she set out for a deep spot in the woods where she sat herself up against a tree and waited. She waited for God to bring her what she needed, and believed God would take care of her in the same way the fox was taken care of. Many days and nights passed, and the young woman was on the verge of starvation and death. As she laid her head down in defeat she heard a voice shouting at her: "Wake up, foolish girl, open your eyes to the truth! Follow the example of the tiger and stop imitating the disabled fox!"

Ideas for the Road

1. Keep a diary or journal. Write when the spirit moves you—don't be a slave to the task. There are no limits to what you can express in your writing or how you have to do it. (See "The Power of Journaling" in chapter 3.)

"When I have nowhere else to go, I write. It doesn't sound much like a 'guy thing' to most, but writing poetry and songs is what keeps me going. The only reason I look so together on the outside is because I write whatever I want in my songs."

—JOHN, "BEE," AGE 19

2. Create or join a "storytelling" group. This can be in the context of a support group (such as AA or therapy) or in a class or workshop on storytelling where everyone shares his or her story. There are also story circles and poetry jams, which offer examples of how to hold a storytelling group. Also, check out your local theaters for storytelling classes.

"I took a storytelling class at the Guthrie Theater where everyone had the chance to tell part of their own story. It felt great to hear and to tell our personal stories. Everyone's life is so unique."

—GAYLE, AGE 23

"The rituals of primitive ceremonies are all mythologically grounded and have to do with killing the infantile ego (our child selves) and bringing forth the adult, whether it is the girl or boy."

—JOSEPH CAMPBELL, PHILOSOPHER AND MASTER STORYTELLER, FROM *THE POWER OF MYTH*

3. Unleash a painful story or memory. Sometimes telling our painful stories can break the hold they have on us. Usually in our painful stories are some secrets that have power over us for as long as we keep them a secret.

"I told my story of how my brother abused me, and even though I have a ways to go to feel 'all together,' I do feel a whole lot better having told others this secret."

—LAURIE, AGE 23

> "Human connections are deeply nurtured in the field of shared story."
>
> —JEAN HOUSTON, SCIENTIST AND PHILOSOPHER, FROM *THE SEARCH FOR THE BELOVED*

4. Listen to your dreams. A lot of poetry and many popular stories originate from dreams. What dreams do you have that feel like a story to you? Consider writing these out in your journal for future storytelling material.

5. Think of the stories that have stayed with you. These can be stories that were told to you or ones you experienced. What stories in this book have stayed with you? What story would you add to this selection? Tell us and connect with others on the THUNDER's Web site: www.thunderingyears.com

Books, Resources, and Wisdomkeepers Related to This Chapter

Blackfoot Lodge Tales: The Story of a Prairie People, by George B. Grinnel (University of Nebraska Press, 1962).

Dictionary of Native American Mythology, by Sam D. Gill and Irene F. Sullivan (Oxford University Press, 1992). A great resource book on Native Americans.

The Four-Fold Way: Walking the Paths of the Warrior, Teacher, Healer and Visionary, by Angeles Arrien, Ph.D. (HarperSan Francisco, 1993). An excellent, easy-to-read resource for the Spiritual Warrior.

Rainbow Tribe: Ordinary People Journeying on the Red Road, by Ed McGaa, Eagle Man (HarperSanFrancisco, 1992). An easy-to-read book about non-Indians taking the "Red Road," the road of the Spiritual Warrior.

Return to Creation: A Survival Manual for Native and Natural Peoples, by Medicine Story (Manitonquat) (Bear Tribes Publishing, 1991). Medicine Story offers stories and anecdotes on living a more balanced life with nature.

She Would Draw Flowers: A Book of Poems, by Kirsten Savitir Bergh (Linda Bergh, 1997). A moving book of poems and artwork by a young woman who listened to her Thunder. Contact Linda Bergh at LindaBergh@aol.com.

Stories of the Spirit, Stories of the Heart: Parables of the Spiritual Path from Around the World, edited by Christina Feldman and Jack Kornfield (HarperSanFrancisco, 1991). A collection of stories and parables that inspire and teach lessons.

Way of the Peaceful Warrior: A Book That Changes Lives, by Dan Millman (H. J. Kramer, 1980). A story about an athlete who became a Spiritual Warrior. To contact Dan Millman and to find out more about his work, visit: www.danmillman.com

The Wisdom of the Crows and Other Buddhist Tales, retold by Sherab Chodzin and Alexandra Kohn (Tricycle Press, 1997). Excellent collection of tales, each of which teaches a lesson.

World Mythology, edited by Roy Willis (Henry Holt, 1993). A reference book with definitions, pictures, and illustrations.

The Circle: News from a Native American Perspective
1530 East Franklin Avenue
Minneapolis, MN 55404
(612) 879-1760
An excellent paper with news from around the country on Native Americans. A section called "New Voices" contains articles and poetry from young adults. They want young Native writers to submit material.

Michael Meade
Mosaic Multicultural Foundation
P.O. Box 364
Vashon, WA 98070
(206) 463-9387 Fax: (206) 463-9236
A resource of people and storytellers. Michael conducts workshops and storytelling performances all over the country.

Online Resources

Arvol Looking Horse
www.worldpeaceday.com
19th Generation Keeper of the Sacred White Buffalo Calf Pipe for the Lakota, Dakota, and Nakota Nation.

Encyclopedia Mythica
www.pantheon.org
A site with an extensive list of stories, mythology, folklore, and images from cultures around the world, including, Aboriginal, Celtic, Hindu, Egyptian, Japanese, Native American, and Yoruban.

Favorite Teenage Angst Books
www.grouchy.com/angst
A site of fiction books and book reviews that are worth a look or a read. A great place to meet other teen readers.

Poetry Slam, Inc.
www.poetryslam.com
This is a bright and colorful site introducing us to the art form of performance poetry. It includes a map of poetry slam listings in your region of the United States.

How
Did the rose
Ever open its heart

And give to this world
All its
Beauty?

It felt the encouragement of light
Against its
Being,

Otherwise,
We all remain

Too
Frightened.

—HAFIZ, SUFI MASTER,
FROM *THE GIFT: POEMS BY HAFIZ*

Chapter Three

Thunder Power

Bringing Forth Your Creative Spirit

"A creative approach to life begins with the
recognition that we have all that we need,
if we but know what to do with it."

—LAURENCE G. BOLDT,
AUTHOR AND CAREER CONSULTANT,
FROM *ZEN SOUP, TASTY MORSELS OF WISDOM
FROM GREAT MINDS EAST AND WEST*

"All life is an experiment."

—OLIVER WENDELL HOLMES,
U.S. SUPREME COURT JUSTICE FROM 1902–1932

E ARE ALL BORN with a creative spirit inside of us. It is what the Hindus refer to as the larger "Self within the self." We are all talented in unique ways. We each hold within us a creative potential—the RAINS waiting to be released. Our spiritual Self and creative Self are one and the same, and cannot be silenced by trauma, abuse, neglect, or drugs. This creative spirit cannot be abolished, but it can become so small it is just a rumbling sound that comes deep within us.

Abusing drugs or alcohol, hateful and violent acts, neglect of your needs, lack of love and attention from others, and any other form of abuse by others will cause your creative spirit to go into hiding. Consequently, you may feel you should just give up, that you weren't meant to be alive. But, the creative spirit can never be destroyed, *not ever*. You can choose to bring forth your creative power at any time.

Or, it just may be that you are unsure of yourself and the Thunder-energy you hold inside of you. You simply need some help in releasing it.

It's All in the Attitude

To live is to create. Creativity is not reserved only for certain people or professions; it is more a way we approach life. Creativity comes in as many forms as there are people. We can be creative in whatever we do. Creativity is an "attitude," an attitude that gives us power. As the Roman emperor Marcus Aurelius put it, "Very little is needed to make a happy life. It is all within yourself, in your way of thinking." Attitude is everything. A creative attitude includes:

- A belief in ourselves.
- Openness to our intuition.
- Being flexible with ourselves and others.
- An ability to stay focused.

A belief in ourselves means to give ourselves a break from criticism and to give this potential inside of us room to come out. If you have gotten this far in the book, no doubt you have a strong enough belief in yourself. At times it can

mean "acting as if" we believe in ourselves, because then the "acting" turns into reality. A Huron proverb advises, "Let your nature be known and proclaimed," and it will follow suit that you will be what you say you are.

Openness to our intuition means to trust the inner wisdom contained within each of us. When your "gut" speaks to you, listen. Take the time to slow down enough to listen for that inner wisdom. (There are lots of ways to do this described in this book, particularly in chapter 6.)

> "I knew I wanted to attend college in California, but I got scared. Then everyone else started feeding my doubts by talking negative about California and my 'moving so far away from home.' Now, two years into another school, I know this is not the place for me. I should have gone with my gut to start off with. Well, at least it's not too late. I am transferring to California next semester. There, they have the program that really interests me."
>
> —NATE, AGE 22

Being flexible with ourselves and others means not to take ourselves so seriously that we get all tied up in knots. The meditation chapter (see chapter 6) has a great deal on relaxing our minds, and not being so hard on ourselves or others. Life IS just an experiment. Every moment is new. When we are too up-tight, we break. To let our creative power out, we need to be flexible, to accept ourselves just as we are, and not put so much time into changing who we are. This is about relaxing enough to bring forth what *wants* to come forth. When we loosen up enough, good things begin to happen.

An ability to stay focused long enough to experience something being completed gives our creativity power. Any time we "succeed" at something—running a race, writing a poem, giving a performance, even playing a video game—it happens because we stay focused (interested) long enough to finish it. It is not about winning, or being perfect; it is simply about showing up for the "game" and playing it to the finish.

"Creativity is the natural order of life. Life is energy: pure creative energy."

—JULIA CAMERON, AUTHOR OF *THE ARTIST'S WAY: A SPIRITUAL PATH TO HIGHER CREATIVITY*

Which of the above traits do you need to develop in order to let out your creative power? Throughout this chapter and book are ways you can develop all these skills for yourself. As you will discover, it is a matter of *balance*.

> Speak to us of Reason and Passion.
>
> And he answered, saying:
>
> Your soul is oftentimes a battlefield, upon which your reason and your judgment wage war against your passion and your appetite.
>
> Your reason and your passion are the rudder and the sails of your seafaring soul.
>
> If either your sails or your rudder be broken, you can but toss and drift, or else be held at a standstill in mid-seas.
>
> For reason, ruling alone, is a force confining, and passion, unattended, is a flame that burns to its own destruction.
>
> Therefore let your soul exalt your reason to the height of passion, that it may sing.
>
> And let it direct your passion with reason, that your passion may live through its own daily resurrection, and like the phoenix rise above its own ashes.
>
> I would have you consider your judgment and your appetite even as you would two loved guests in your house.
>
> Surely you would not honor one guest above the other; for he who is more mindful of one loses the love and faith of both.
>
> —KAHLIL GIBRAN, ARTIST AND PHILOSOPHER, FROM *THE PROPHET*

Life Does Offer a Guarantee

Because it is always available to us, it can be simple to bring forth our Thunder Power. In addition, you will discover that *use* of your creative energy will make you feel more generous, more joyful, more confident, and more lively. You will tap into a deep reservoir of ideas and capabilities that will be yours for your lifetime. But *you* must begin the journey. For each of us who opens up to our creative Self, there is a guarantee—*there will be success.* This is because everything you are searching for is also searching for you. Many artists will tell you that their "work" found them. In the Chinese oracle, the I Ching, or *Book of Changes,* this is referred to as the "Creator meeting us halfway." In Christian mysticism we are each understood as "Co-Creators with God." Remember the Sufi fable in the previous chapter? We can't expect to just sit under a tree (or in front of the television) and wait for life to knock on the door. We have to get up and go after life, we have to do our part to make things happen. The help we need *will* meet us halfway. Then, with the power of our own creativity and the help of Spirit, we are guaranteed success.

Sadly, many reject their creative power, or are too distracted to feel this power inside of them. Part of our "personal responsibility for uplifting our lives," as the great Tibetan lama teaches, is to take responsibility for our creative power. As sacred wisdom claims, it is in our very nature to be creative, to express our passion . . . to ignore or suppress this creative force could cause us harm. *Unused* creative energy sooner or later turns into depression, cynicism, violence, addictions, or/and hopelessness.

Our creativity, which is part our True Nature, can be repressed in so many ways. Most likely, each of us has a story of how part of ourselves, our creativity, went into hiding.

> *"I was in fourth grade. I remember this day as the day my 'Indian' went into hiding. The teacher brought out our history books and placed them in front of each of us, saying, 'This week we are going to learn about Indians.' I was SO excited. She was talking about ME. My father is full Creek, and mother mostly Irish. I opened the pages to the chapter on 'American Indians,' and there were people dressed up like 'savages,' carrying around spears and tomahawks. Then I heard other kids talking about 'scalping' and 'killing children.' I was totally ashamed. This is ME. I stayed home sick that entire week and realize now that a big part of me hid from others and myself for a long time.*

"We have to accept personal responsibility for uplifting our lives."

—CHÖGYAM TRUNGPA, TIBETAN LAMA, AUTHOR OF *SHAMBHALA: THE SACRED PATH OF THE WARRIOR*

"What is man's will And how shall he use it? Let him put forth its power to uncover the Atman [the light within], Not hide the Atman."

—SWAMI PRABHAVANANDA, FROM *THE SONG OF GOD: BHAGAVAD-GITA*

47

"It wasn't until later, at the age of 21, that I began to realize that who I am is unique, and that I hold a very special place in this world. With the help of an elder, I began to let the 'Indian' in me out and instantly began feeling my strength. For me, everything comes down to being MYSELF and bringing this Indian self into the world. Instead of staying home sick, I am going to be Indian. If this makes others uncomfortable, too bad. I think that my Ancestors have big plans for me."

—Debra Lee Jackson, Creek Nation, mentor

Begin with Ourselves

"For what is inside of you is what is outside of you, and the one who fashions you on the outside is the one who shaped the inside of you. And what you see outside of you, you see inside of you: it is visible and it is your garment."

—*The Nag Hammadi Library*, Gnostic Scriptures

We each then need to begin with ourselves; to believe in our Self enough to give ourselves a chance. The creative and spiritual path always begins HERE. This means we need to put our trust in some things we cannot "see" with our eyes alone, such as the Spirit's help that will arrive for us as we take these steps, and the love and help of all those Wisdomkeepers who walked the creative road before us. They too, although invisible, can assist you on your journey. Nola James, an Australian Aboriginal elder woman, puts it this way, "A lot of people will say to you, 'I won't believe in anything unless I see it.' But that is wrong. You can see the dust rising and you can see leaves blowing. But can you see the wind? It's as simple as that."

In finding our own creative power, we discover it is really about opening up to what is *already* inside of us. It's not perfect. It might not even be what we expected! But it will be good. So, committing to the creative life is about committing to opening up to *ourselves*. It is not about pleasing others, or making the grade, or impressing our friends. It *is* all about befriending one's self, first, and taking better care of ourselves. The world then becomes a safer place. We find ways to be more kind and gentle with ourselves, instead of beating up on ourselves. That means we give ourselves a break once in a while! We stop harming ourselves with drugs and alcohol, and we stop fooling ourselves into believing that what we put into our bodies doesn't really matter.

Consider making a commitment to living the creative life, to tapping into your inner Self on a regular basis. This is a commitment of the Spiritual Warrior—to live the creative life; to let your Thunder roar and the RAINS come.

The Power of Journaling

A routine of writing and drawing in a journal is one way to open up to ourselves—to unleash creativity—and commit to the Warrior's journey. Journals are a doorway to our "True Natures," what Buddhists refer to as our "Buddha Nature," and what mystical Christians call the "Christ Within." It is the Atman, the Inner Light, our Higher Power, and our Spiritual Self. Journaling helps unleash what is stored inside our minds and hearts. Journals are also a way to keep a record of our lives and our experiences. Wisdomkeepers throughout time have journaled, and this is where we find most of their wisdom. Rumi, the Sufi poet, wrote hundreds of journals of his poetry and prose. Most sacred text was journaled first and then translated into books. Your journal will contain some sacred wisdom, even if it is only kept for yourself.

Write your thoughts, feelings, questions, poetry, impressions, ideas, and dreams in a journal. You could keep a journal in your computer. Sometimes you may want to draw or scribble. It's your journal to do with as you wish. Consider using a notebook that doesn't have any lines in it. (These can be found at art and office supply stores.) Use colored pencils, pens, paint, markers, or even crayons. These all help bring out the creative Self.

Commit to writing in your journal on a regular basis, even if it's just a few thoughts or pictures. Put your thoughts and feelings onto the page without stopping to correct anything or change a word. Once in a while, practice keeping your hand moving on the page until one entire page is full. This free-style writing allows your creativity to emerge because you are not trying to be perfect about it. Just let your words and images flow! A tree does not stop and think about its task of producing leaves. A tree simply expresses its true nature. Just like that, we can let ourselves create by writing in our journals whatever comes to us.

"Let your light shine before men, that they may see your good works."

—THE GOSPEL ACCORDING TO MATTHEW

Making Your Own Personalized Journal

Lia, age 16, personalizes her journals by collecting different pictures, words, and drawings that hold meaning for her. Sometimes she finds images and words that go with a certain theme, such as "Follow Your Dream," or "Just Do It." Some of her journals present a humorous perspective such as one journal cover that was all pictures and words about women's thighs.

What you need: a simple spiral notebook (with or without lines); a collection of pictures/images and words you like; scissors (although sometimes tearing paper gives a different creative effect); all-purpose glue; a sheet of laminate (found at art and office supply stores); and your creative juice. Cover the front of the notebook with the images and words, gluing them in place when you find the look you want. Then, when finished, laminate it with a "peel-off" sheet. Now there's your personalized journal.

"There is one thing stronger than all the armies in the world, and that is an idea whose time has come."

—VICTOR HUGO, FRENCH POET, NOVELIST, AND PLAYWRIGHT

Try This

Write out in your journal a WISH LIST. Include on this list experiences you would like to have, projects and activities you would like to do. This is a "Creativity" Wish List.

- What do you wish to create in your life right now, or in the near future?
- Is there a job you want? A place you want to travel to? A language you want to learn?

Nothing is too small or too big. You may have several wishes on your list, or only one. It is important that this be YOUR list (not your mother's, not your girlfriend's, not your grandparents'). Yours.

Through writing this list you have given yourself some quiet time to reflect on what is important to you at this time. Having something written out gives us something to look at—it starts to become more real when we put it in writing. Later you can refer to it; check in with yourself by looking over your list. You are likely to add to it and change it as time goes on.

Obstacles on The Path

As with all journeys, there can be many obstacles on our path—in every shape and form. In the Grimms' fable of *The Golden Key*, the young man had everything against him, but by pushing through each obstacle he was able to make his life turn around.

The Golden Key by the Brothers Grimm, retold by Julie Tallard Johnson

There was once a young man who never seemed to have any luck. His parents were too poor to care for him, so he was sent off to live with strangers. Many times the strangers treated him badly. He had no time for friends because he had to work all the time just to keep himself fed.

One shivering winter's day he went searching for some wood for the fire. He had no gloves and practically nothing on his feet to keep away the bitter cold. He had traveled far from the house and it was so cold that his hands began to turn blue. He began to fear for his life and decided he could either give up and lie down to die or try to build himself a fire right there in the woods.

As he scraped away at the ice and snow, clearing a space for the fire, he found something—a golden key. Although he knew he might soon die from the cold without a fire, he thought, "Where there's a key, there's a lock!" and so he dug and dug with his bare hands through the frozen ground, until he found something again—a box.

"If only the key fits," he said, "my luck is sure to change!"

He looked for the lock, but he couldn't find it. It was dark and difficult to see. He nearly gave up when a voice deep inside him said, "Look again!" And so he did, and there it was, a keyhole so tiny you could scarcely see it. Most people would surely have missed it.

He took a breath and put the key in the lock, and it fit perfectly. He began to turn the key, and he opened the box and looked inside. He was so warmed by what he saw that the snow and ice melted around him. And indeed, his life from then on did change for the better.

"In my weakness, do not forsake me.

and do not be afraid of my power."

—"THE THUNDER, PERFECT MIND," FROM *THE NAG HAMMADI LIBRARY*

51

All through our lives, it is about beginning again and again. The commitment to the path of the Spiritual Warrior is about never giving up on ourselves.

We have no greater enemy than fear. Many things can block our creativity, but fear tends to shut us down. In order to bring forth our creative Self, we must name and face our fears straight on. Dr. Laurel Ann Reinhardt, author of *Seasons of Magic: A Girl's Journey,* offers some wisdom on overcoming our fears. She works with people around the country helping them move through their fears.

Moving Through Your Fears

By Dr. Laurel Ann Reinhardt, psychologist and Dream Weaver

We all feel it at various times. It's always uncomfortable, but did you know that there are different kinds of fear? Some fear is helpful; when this kind of fear comes along it comes into our body and moves through it like a wave, staying just long enough to let us know that we are in some kind of "danger," and we need to take some action, or make some changes in our lives. It is actual "movement" of our bodies that helps the fear to move on. But so often these days, fear alerts us to dangers that we think we can't do anything about. This can be little things, like a teacher telling you your impulse to color the sky green and the grass blue is "wrong," and then giving you a D for it, which your parents are going to give you a hard time about; fear can also be caused by big things, like your dad hitting you for being excited about something you did well. In situations like these, we often end up not taking any action and not moving our bodies. The fear gets stuck, we get stuck, and we end up with less room to move around in. We end up losing some of our creativity, and a lot of what makes us special or unique.

What can you do?

Believe it or not, there is always some kind of action you can take. The most important thing is not to pretend that the D didn't really hurt your feelings, or that your father hitting you didn't matter—those things do hurt us, and they do matter, because they make us afraid to follow

our inspiration, our intuition, our feelings in the future. So, it's important to turn the hurt and fear into something else. **The easiest way to do this is to breathe into the place where you feel the fear,** which is often in the stomach, the heart, or the throat.

Fear in the stomach is related to feeling powerless, so while you breathe into your stomach, you might want to remember a time when you felt really powerful, as though you could accomplish anything!

Fear in the heart is related to feeling unloved, so while you breathe into your heart, you might want to recall a time when you felt truly loved, or loving toward someone else.

Fear in the throat is related to not being able to say something, so when you breathe into your throat you might think of what it is you need to say to yourself, your journal, or a friend. Secrets, especially ones we keep from ourselves, cause the most damage to our spirits.

> **"We are such stuff as dreams are made of."**
>
> —WILLIAM SHAKESPEARE, ENGLISH POET AND PLAYWRIGHT, FROM *THE TEMPEST*

Anything that takes away from our sense of worth, that somehow puts us down or limits us, robs us of something very important. It steals the truth about us—that we have within us a reservoir of potential. It is in our true nature to feel good about ourselves. It is in our true nature to accept our talents *and* our mistakes. It is in our true nature to express our creativity. As Chögyam Trungpa further expresses, "A great deal of chaos in the world occurs because people don't appreciate themselves." And when we get into a place where we don't appreciate ourselves, we might feel paralyzed or afraid or begin to act violently against ourselves or others.

Difficulties are not something necessarily to GET RID OF, or to "just get over." They are, in fact, an intricate part of the Warrior's journey. How is that? It is so, because all this "stuff" gives us something to work with.

> *"It is in fighting my addiction to bad relationships that made me into the person you see now. The possibility that I may stumble into another bad relationship AGAIN actually keeps me on my*

*toes. Keeps me conscientious. There is a part of me that is drawn
to abusive guys. So I have to stay on my toes."*

—TERESA, AGE 21

Teresa is a senior in college and is going on to learn a language overseas. She is now a confident and strong young woman who knows where she is headed. Even if your obstacle is very serious, such as Teresa's attraction to abusive relationships or a drug addiction, it is committing to recovery, attending support groups, and staying sober that IS your path. And from this commitment to recovery, the creative Self emerges.

"To live the creative life, we must lose our fear of being wrong."

—JOSEPH CHILTON PEARCE, AUTHOR OF *THE CRACK IN THE COSMIC EGG: CHALLENGING CONSTRUCTS OF MIND AND REALITY*

A Checklist

To help keep it simple, a group of teenagers came up with a short list of common obstacles to creativity. Read over the list and check the ones that you believe may be an obstacle for you:

- Alcohol use or abuse
- Drug use or abuse
- Neglectful or selfish parents (who are only focused on their own needs/lives)
- Abusive parents (physically, emotionally, sexually)
- Poor diet (too much sugar or junk food)
- Comparing yourself to others
- Fear of being criticized
- Fear of being manipulated
- Doubting your abilities, choices, or ideas
- Anxiety
- Inability to get started
- Feeling unimaginative (lacking desire)
- Low self-esteem (dislike yourself)
- Worrying about making a mistake

- Trying to be perfect (or to do it right)
- Lack of friends; lack of support
- "Friends" who encourage you to take harmful risks
- Codependent relationships (ones that take up all your time); controlling relationships
- Abusive relationships (someone is physically/sexually or emotionally abusing you)
- Too much television
- Too much time on the computer/internet/video games
- Feeling lazy
- Feeling bored; not knowing what to do with yourself
- Difficulty staying focused or finishing something
- What you want is different from what your parents want for you
- Reading or learning disabilities (such as dyslexia)
- Confusion about what you want, who you are
- No adults to help or guide you
- Friends that put you down
- A physical disability
- Already into one thing and don't know how to change

> "Be patient toward all that is unresolved in your heart and try to love the questions themselves . . ."
>
> —RAINER MARIA RILKE, GERMAN POET

Once we can name the obstacles, we can find what we need to do to get beyond them. We can discover how we can "work" with them like Teresa did in the above example. Half the battle is in naming the difficulty! It's like finding ourselves sick with some horrible illness. We are throwing up and experiencing horrendous headaches! We take aspirin but that doesn't seem to do the trick. Then finally through our efforts to find out what the problem is, we discover we are seriously allergic to strawberries! Then we know what we can do to stop getting so sick. Stop eating strawberries. You may find that many of the above obstacles apply to you, or you may find that only one applies to you at this time. Once you have named the problem, you can begin to take action to deal with it.

A Closer Look at Some of These Obstacles

Many of these obstacles can fall under a category together . . . we can call these the TRICKSTER obstacles. They are Tricksters because they are very clever at tricking us into believing we ARE being creative, when in fact WE ARE NOT. Excessive television watching, hours playing video games, staying indoors to be in cyberspace several evenings of the week, watching sports but not participating in them, reaching altered states on drugs and alcohol, and obsessive shopping are all examples of activities where we are not truly "creating" anything. Some of these activities are a result of boredom and low self-esteem. Unfortunately, these choices tend to generate more feelings of boredom and low self-esteem. For example, people who are attached to a lot of TV watching are "living" their lives through the dramas and stories of others. They are not actually experiencing their own lives so they often feel bored easily. Many Wisdomkeepers of today are concerned about the "voyeuristic" lifestyle we are manufacturing for ourselves. When we are "watching" other's lives—through sports, TV, and movies *too much of the time*, we are not actively living our own lives. We may feel *as if* we did something, feel *as if* we went somewhere, when actually we did not.

> "My boyfriend and I have broken up several times over the past 3 years. And it's always over the same thing. All he wants to do is 'tour' (go out driving and smoke pot). We're in our first year of college and all he cares about is getting high. He talks about how he's going to graduate and he makes big plans. But he would rather attend a RAVE than study. I know we are not going anywhere if we keep this up. Talk is cheap. I want to do more with my life."
>
> —APRIL, AGE 20

> "So many of us do things that take away from our goodness, from our creativity."
>
> —ERIN, AGE 17

A life out of balance with too much alcohol or drug use can also be one of these Trickster obstacles. Have you ever noticed how someone who smokes

"Creative minds always have been known to survive any kind of bad training."

—ANNA FREUD, AUSTRIAN PSYCHOANALYST AND DAUGHTER OF SIGMUND FREUD, THE FOUNDER OF PSYCHOANALYSIS

pot regularly talks and talks about his or her plans and dreams, but actually accomplishes very little? Drugs and alcohol, especially when abused, inhibit one's creativity. All our energy goes into getting high, and little or none of it is left over for creating. These Trickster obstacles also get you to forget or lose sight of the great passage you are undergoing in your life. When preoccupied by television or stoned on pot, it is hard to hear your Thunder and easy to forget that you are holding the fire of the future in your belly. You will forget that you are at a most important threshold of your life. You will likely drop the "Golden Key" and lose a chance for what is inside the box.

So beware of the Tricksters. . . .

A Few Words about Addictions

"When you find something appealing try it but don't go excessive. Test the water before you jump in. So many of us jump in and find ourselves drowning in something."

—AMY, AGE 17

Addictions **dis-able** our creativity. They dis-able us by making us "less-able." Even though, as shown above, addictive behaviors often give the *illusion* that we are accomplishing something, they often trick us.

Addictions dull us, harm our bodies, destroy relationships, block creativity, rob us of our self-esteem, and ultimately rob us of our life-source. Addictions thrive on *fantasy,* while they kill our creative spirit. Feeling creative is not just a fantasy. It is not hanging out in the "when I win the lottery . . ." realm. Your creative essence is something *real,* something tangible. Our creativity *results* in something meaningful and good. When we are hooked by an addiction, the rest of our lives is put on hold. People who are addicted are often afraid. They are afraid to live their lives free of such substances; they are afraid to just "be."

Do you believe *you* may have an addiction, or are you concerned that you may be getting addicted to something? In order to admit we are addicted to

"Never give up, no matter what is going on. Never give up. Develop the heart. Be compassionate. Work for peace in your heart and in the world.

Work for peace, and I say, Never give up. No matter what is happening. No matter what is going on around you. Never give up."

—HIS HOLINESS THE 14TH DALAI LAMA

"Many have fallen with the bottle in their hand."

—LAKOTA PROVERB

something, we need to be honest with ourselves. Really honest. This kind of honesty takes the courage of a Warrior and leads one to freedom. Television or food are okay in *moderation* but too much can be a sign of trouble. Too much food can lead to obesity, low self-esteem, and other problems. Too much alcohol can quickly lead to alcoholism, depression, boredom, and low self-esteem. Cigarettes can lead to shortness of breath, greater anxiety, and reduced stamina.

What You Might Do

Here's a simple way to get a better idea if you have an addiction and what you can do about it if you think you do.

Something may be an addiction for you when:

- the only way you feel you can connect with friends is to get high;
- others have brought it up as a concern they have about you;
- it takes away from other important things in your life;
- it takes up too much of your time, money, and energy (because you feel you have to have it);
- you find yourself bored or scared without it;
- doing it dis-ables you somehow—makes you less able to go to school, work, or be on a team;
- one or both of your parents have an addiction.

If you checked even one of these examples, you may have an addiction problem.

The most important action you can take if you even think you might have an addiction is seek some help. You'll find some resources listed at the end of this chapter. And consider seeking out a mentor as recommended in chapter 10. Because addictions are such a serious and widespread problem today, there is a lot of help available. Chances are, if you have parents that have an addiction, you too may become addicted to the same substance. (Lots of research has proven this to be so.) This means you have to be *extra* careful about your choices.

"It is within my power either to serve God or not to serve him. Serving him, I add to my own good and the good of the whole world. Not serving him, I forfeit my own good and deprive the world of that good, which was in my power to create."

—LEO TOLSTOY,
19TH-CENTURY
RUSSIAN NOVELIST

A Parallel Path

One helpful insight about addictions is, it's often an attempt to feel good about oneself. So, the *intent* is right on; it is the method that is the problem. An Australian elder once talked about the path of the addict as being parallel to that of the Spiritual Warrior: "Addicts are on a parallel path to the Spiritual Warrior—they are just confused and misguided about how to feel the Spirit alive within them. When someone quits abusing drugs or alcohol, especially after years of abuse, they find themselves greeted by Spirit. They 'fall down on their face' but when they get up, they are transformed. *If* they get up and start walking the Spirit's path, they will find that this is what they wanted all along. They will find that they have been walking alongside the right path all along." In a message from His Holiness the 14th Dalai Lama, he says, "As human beings, whether we are rich or poor, educated or uneducated, whatever our nationality, color, or social status may be, each of us is just like everyone else. We all want to be happy and we do not want to be miserable." No matter what form it takes, we are all striving for happiness.

> **"If grains of sand can become a reflection of the Divine, just think what can happen to the human being."**
>
> —His Holiness the 14th Dalai Lama

A Story of Addiction

Matthew began drinking at the age of 9, stealing from his parents' liquor supply. He found it very easy to get booze, finding both adults and other teenagers who could get him alcohol. Matthew went to school drunk, until he got suspended. His parents felt powerless. Finally, a friend of the family, who was a recovering alcoholic and artist, offered him another chance.

> **"It's no use to cling to rocks that are falling with you."**
>
> —Alan Watts, Spiritual Warrior and American Philosopher

> *"He said that I reminded him of himself, and that the only thing that helped him was being given something better to do than drink! So, I found out I could draw, and that I enjoyed writing poetry. I didn't return to school, but got my high school GED, with his help. My best friend and drinking buddy at the time got real weird when I started attending the art classes at the institute. I got in on a scholarship and this took away time that we had together. Besides, I wasn't drinking anymore and was attending some Alcoholics Anonymous groups. None of this went over very well with my friend. Finally, he said I was boring and that he was wasting his time with*

me. My mentor warned me about others being upset with me. He said I would have to give up my drinking buddies if I wanted to get on with my life."

—MATTHEW, AGE 18

Matthew learned the wisdom of letting go of harmful relationships.

Make More Mistakes

"A person's errors are his portals of discovery."

—JAMES JOYCE, 20TH-CENTURY IRISH AUTHOR

"If you only knew how wonderful you truly are, you would stop striving all the time and just be yourself."

—FLAMING RAINBOW WOMAN, SPIRITUAL WARRIOR

Another common obstacle is perfectionism. Are you trying to do everything "right" or "perfect"? Are you trying to be who you think others want you to be? Are you afraid or anxious about finishing up a project or commitment, or speaking out about something? Perfectionism steals the creative energy we carry within us and stomps all over it. It's the voice of "I'm never good enough"—or "what I *do* is never good enough." Trying to be perfect takes the fun out of most, if not all, our efforts. Perfectionism doesn't allow us freedom in what we do. Instead, our focus is on if it is "right or wrong," "good or bad." At some time in our lives most of us encounter this obstacle.

"Once when I was really stuck with trying to do something right (and I had the belief that there was only one right way), a mentor of mine told me: 'There's no right and wrong, Maureen, there's only right and left.' This helped me to get unstuck from trying to find the one and only 'right way.'"

—MAUREEN, AGE 21

Perfectionism slows us down, shuts us up, inhibits our creative spirit and isolates us from others. Be kind to yourself by being willing to do or say some-

"Last night, as I was sleeping,

I dreamt—marvelous error!—

that I had a beehive

here inside my heart.

And the golden bees

were making white combs

and sweet honey

from all my old failures."

—ANTONIO MACHADO, SPANISH POET, FROM *ANTONIO MACHADO: TIMES ALONE*

thing without worrying if others will approve of it. A book by Terry Cole-Whittaker has a title that says it all: *What You Think of Me Is None of My Business.*

This takes us back to the first and basic step on the path of creativity—being kind to ourselves. We cannot let our true nature out if we constantly inhibit ourselves with perfectionism. The funny thing is, when we lighten up on ourselves we do better! When Maureen let go of "having to do it just right," she found she felt and did much better. Let's say you want to join the theater club but you are afraid to try out because you believe you are not "good enough." You may feel too small, too slow, too fat, too thin, too *something,* or *not enough of something* else. *You are trying to be just right—to be perfect—instead of just trying.*

> *"I know that being different isn't bad. But sometimes it's hard to try something new. I feel like everybody is keeping a score card on me, including myself!"*
>
> —SHELBY, AGE 19

If Perfectionism Is an Obstacle for You . . .

Ask yourself: How many ways are there to do your hair? Most of us think there are only one or two ways to do things: a "right" way and a "wrong" way. We are told that there is a "good" way to look, dress, and behave, and a "bad" way. Many of us were taught to "color inside the lines." How many ways are there to do what it is you want to do?

Make a list, in your journal or in your head, of the many (many, many) ways you could do whatever it is you are wanting to do. Or, if it is a *past* event that you are ruminating over, write out the many ways it could have been done. Admit to yourself that the way you did it is only ONE of the many ways, and that this does not make it wrong (or right).

Perfection doesn't tolerate mistakes. But **excellence uses mistakes** and learns from mistakes. This is a sign of a true creative genius—one who creates from his or her mistakes. And, one who doesn't let the fear of making mistakes stop them.

"In creating, the only hard thing's to begin; A grass-blade's no easier to make than an oak."

—JAMES RUSSELL LOWELL, AMERICAN POET AND ESSAYIST, FROM *A FABLE FOR CRITICS*

Now make a list in your journal of past mistakes on one side of the page. Then, on the other side of the page, across from the mistake, write what you learned, or what good came out of it.

> "The message is that each of us has all that it takes to become fully enlightened. We have basic energy coursing through us. Sometimes it manifests as brilliance and sometimes it manifests as confusion. Because we are decent, basically good people, we ourselves can sort out what to accept and what to reject. We can discern what will make us complete, sane, grown-up people, and what will keep us children forever."
>
> —Pema Chödrön, Buddhist nun,
> from *The Wisdom of No Escape and the Path of Loving-Kindness*

Taking On a Beginner's Mind

> "In the beginner's mind there are many possibilities, but in the expert's there are few."
>
> —Shunryu Suzuki, Zen master

In traditional Zen Buddhist practice, teachers often talk about approaching your spiritual practice, and your daily life, with the "beginner's mind." A beginner's mind is a mind that doesn't worry. Instead, it is a mind that is more spontaneous and FLEXIBLE.

A beginner's mind is often referred to as unburdened or childlike—curious and playful in what it approaches and courageous enough to learn new things without the fear of looking foolish or wrong. To a young child, every moment is new. Everything is a game and learning from mistakes is a natural, acceptable way to grow. Practice having a beginner's mind by allowing yourself to be unique and to learn. Give yourself room to make mistakes. Those who feel successful in life talk triumphantly of the many mistakes they made and what they learned from them.

A beginner's mind is a playful mind. We all too often take ourselves too seriously. Being playful, even silly, is a very good thing for your self-esteem and creativity. Risk being silly. Many of us will consider harmful risks, but then shut ourselves down when it comes to being silly and playful. A lot can be accomplished when we stop taking ourselves too seriously and give ourselves room to just "be." With a playful attitude we will try different things out. There is a natural high in allowing ourselves to be silly because we allow our body, mind, and emotions to stretch to limits they may not have yet experienced. Remember what the author Oliver Wendell Holmes said, "All life is an experiment."

Having a beginner's mind also speaks to our way of thinking and to the assumptions we hold about life. Most of us hold on to deeply ingrained beliefs about ourselves and others that limit us. For example, we think, "I am never going to get this right," or "When I am around other people I always say stupid things," or "You can't really trust anyone," or "Things never really ever work out." All these thoughts prevent us from experiencing something for the first time because we go into situations loaded with negative expectations. (For more thoughts on this refer to "Training the Wild Mind" in chapter 6.)

Take a Road Trip

To cultivate the beginner's mind, take a trip to a new place, alone. This place can be a neighboring town or an undiscovered street in the city. If you can't drive, take a bus or train. Take your journal along. Feel the newness of the place. Introduce yourself to new people. Notice the smells, the sights, the architecture, and the people of this new, unknown place. What do you notice? What does being in a new place feel like? What new thoughts or feelings arise in you while you are in this new place? Write about it or draw a picture of it in your journal.

Every place we visit each day of our lives can be approached with this "road trip" mentality. Every experience, no matter how many times we have done it, holds something new in it. Now, take a "road trip" to a place you frequent

"If you try to adjust yourself in a certain way, you will lose yourself. So without any intentional, fancy way of adjusting yourself, to express yourself freely as you are is the most important thing to make yourself happy, and to make others happy."

—Shunryu Suzuki, Zen master, from *Zen Mind, Beginner's Mind*

"Seataka is the term in Yaqui meaning *personal medicine,* or, one's personal power. This power is considered a great gift we are given at birth. Literally, Seataka means 'flower body,' suggestive of a kind of power, although Yaqui people hold that the English word 'power' is inadequate. Yaqui believe that individuals are born with specialized gifts. Seataka, the most important of these gifts, is said to be fundamental to Yaqui thought and life. Seataka is the channel between human beings and the rest of nature."

—*DICTIONARY OF NATIVE AMERICAN MYTHOLOGY*

regularly. Can you see, smell, and experience it for the first time? Write about it or draw it in your journal or turn it into a story. As Mark Twain put it so eloquently, "The trouble with most of us is that we know too much that ain't so." Try leaving some of your assumptions, positive and negative, at home, and see the world from a fresh perspective.

Finding Your Creative Community

"Never spend time with people who don't respect you."

—MAORI PROVERB

"Tell me whom you love, and I'll tell you who you are."

—AFRICAN AMERICAN PROVERB

"People are free when they belong to a living, organic, believing community."

—D. H. LAWRENCE,
20TH-CENTURY ENGLISH NOVELIST AND POET

People who get beyond their obstacles to express their creative Self do not typically do it alone. When we risk being creative we need the endorsement of others who care about us. You too will need help—the help of a supportive community. *You can start with just one person who supports you.* Consider a relative, another student in a class, a neighbor, a student adviser, or maybe even a counselor.

Surround yourself with people who appreciate your desire to live the creative and spiritual life—who take you and this desire seriously. Those who appreciate you are able to *show you* respect. Those who respect you will support your creative ideas and adventures. Those who respect you will *show* they care about your well-being and invest their time, energy, and love in you and your projects.

Warrior Beware

You will encounter many people who are not using their creative potential. Some are afraid, and, weakened by their fears, choose instead to just "get by." Some will feel too limited and will not try to stretch their imaginations, giving up on the idea that they can live a creative life. *Be careful of these people.* Because of their own fears, addictions, or limitations they may try to convince you that the creative life is a waste of time. Don't believe them. The creative life is the only one worth living.

"Be brave enough to live creatively. The creative is the place where no one else has ever been. You have to leave the city of your comfort and go into the wilderness of your intuition. You can't get there by bus, only by hard work, risking, and by not quite knowing what you're doing. What you'll discover will be wonderful: yourself."

—ALAN ALDA, ACTOR

When someone is jealous or judgmental of our creativity, our way of life, they are most likely blocked from their own creativity. These people will often get a "kick" from challenging us or from stewing in their own negativity. Oftentimes they will talk on and on about what they *could* be doing or *will* be doing. Or they may talk about how "life sucks" and "what's the point?" These people are dangerous to our creativity. They believe so strongly in their fears and limitations that they want others to share in their fears. You've probably heard the saying, "Misery loves company." This tends to be true. Alcoholics hang out with other drinkers. They don't hang out with those who attend Alcoholics Anonymous! Those who gossip find others who like to gossip. *Surround yourself with those people who are like what you want to become.* Hang out with people who are living the creative life, and you will find it easier to live the creative life. Don't allow others' anger, negativity, and fears to keep you from your Creative Power.

When you are afraid or are having difficulty ending a relationship that is holding you back, consider the advice in this Aesop's Fable....

The Old Lion and the Fox

An old lion, too weak to hunt for his own prey, thought he could get his food by being clever. So, he laid himself in front of a cave and *pretended* to be sick. Every time an animal came to visit him, the lion would coax it into the cave and eat it! He had already captured many animals this way when a fox walked by and began to visit with the lion. "So, how's your health?" the fox asked the lion.

"Oh it is bad. But I'm sure to get well soon and I'll be up and running about the rocks," commented the lion. "But, come in and stay awhile. There is much we can visit over. I have seen much in my lifetime."

"I would come in and gladly listen to all your stories," replied the fox, "if I hadn't seen so many animal footprints that go *into* your cave but don't come out!" And with that the fox went on his way.

Going on alone, without certain people, may be what keeps you healthy and safe. If you choose instead to enter the lion's den, there may not be anything left of you but a few footprints. Know that when you walk *away* from that lion's den, you are walking *toward* your creative community.

Sacred Places That Invoke Creativity

In Australian Aboriginal culture, a few people will gather at a sacred site, such as a rock or a water hole. This sacred site has been infused with the power of the ancestors. A fire will usually be built and the sacred rock or water will be covered with the smoke from the fire. Or, the dust of the rock, or water from the hole will be thrown into the air. All this is done to *release* the ancestors' creative power, and to *release* the creative potential within the individual doing the ritual.

You can borrow from such a tradition, by finding your own sacred place to invoke the help of the ancestors' creative powers, and to open up to your own creative Self. Much like the Bible says, "Knock and the door shall be opened," the help of the ancestors is just a simple knock, or request, away.

Where might such a sacred place be for you? In all cultures, many seek sacred wisdom from places in nature. There are many books that will tell you where to find traditional "sacred sites," places where you can go and invoke the help of the ancestors. You may also find and create for yourself such a place, that you know holds such power. The next chapter (chapter 4, Nature as Your Oracle) gives many ways to create such a sacred relationship with the wilderness.

"I live on 40 acres of woods and fields. My parents actually built a ritual site for us to share in family ceremonies. But my favorite place is deep in the woods, where there is a gathering of old oak trees. I am told they have been there for at least 75 years. It seems to me a good place to seek ancient wisdom. My father told me that one way places become sacred is when they are visited over and over by those who bring in spiritual intentions, and this infuses the place with sacred energy. When you visit a sacred place, you will know what I mean."

JOSH, AGE 18

> **"Growth is the only evidence of life."**
>
> —CARDINAL NEWMAN, THEOLOGIAN

Places that impart sacred wisdom include meditation centers, churches or temples, libraries or bookstores, art galleries or museums, historical sites, sports halls of fame, monuments, or nature sanctuaries. Such places hold inspiration and encouragement to live the creative life. Your sacred place may also be where you spend time alone. Wherever it is, we all need a place where we can go to open up to ourselves. Ideally, you have a place in your home where you can at times retreat to write, meditate, or simply hang out alone—a place where your creativity can be nourished and grow.

Ideas for the Road

Living the creative life means to make your own, unique way in the world. But the journey of the creative life is filled with challenges. There are days when all will seem so wonderful and others where it all will feel hopeless. Sometimes it can be helpful to have a simple list of reminders to refer to on those more diffi-cult days. . . .

1. Seek good company.

2. Take a little time every day to be with yourself in a peaceful and restful way (write in your journal, meditate, or take a slow nature walk).

3. Pay attention; the invisible help of Spirit *is* available to you.

4. Be kind to yourself every day (don't compare yourself to others).

5. Be interested in your life. Be curious about everything or anything. Approach the same old thing with a new curiosity about it. Use your beginner's mind.

6. Allow yourself to make mistakes. (Lots of them!)

7. Be kind to your body; it is a living, breathing entity.

8. Find a poet you appreciate and read from his or her book regularly, or when you need to be inspired.

9. Spend time with those people who might help you get what you want on your Wish List.

Books, Resources, and Wisdomkeepers Related to This Chapter

The Artist's Way: A Spiritual Path to Higher Creativity, by Julia Cameron. (G. P. Putnam's Sons, 1992). A helpful 10-week workbook on ways to discover your creativity. See online resources below for Web site information.

Life's Companion: Journal Writing as a Spiritual Quest, by Christina Baldwin (Bantam Books, 1990). Lots of exercises, quotations, and techniques to nurture you, the writer and Spiritual Warrior.

The Millennium Whole Earth Catalog, edited by Howard Rheingold (HarperSanFrancisco, 1994). A great resource of contacts and ideas on living the creative life.

Room to Write: Daily Invitations to a Writer's Life, by Bonni Goldberg (Jeremy P. Tarcher/Putman, 1996). Great daily exercises to get you writing.

Wild Mind: Living the Writer's Life, by Natalie Goldberg (Bantam New Age Books, 1990). A book that helps release the creativity in you.

Wishcraft: How to Get What You Really Want, by Barbara Sher (Ballantine, 1979). Motivational book for all ages that helps you get free from letting others run your life, and to find your own creative spirit.

Writing Down the Bones, by Natalie Goldberg (Shambhala Publications, 1986). How to get the muse moving in you.

Cocaine Anonymous World
P.O. Box 2000
Los Angeles, CA 90049-8000
(310) 559-5833
www.ca.org
Help for anyone recovering from cocaine addiction, or for those who have a close relationship with someone addicted to cocaine. See online resources below for Web site information.

Narcotics Anonymous
World Service Office
P.O. Box 9999
Van Nuys, CA 91409
(818) 700-0700
www.na.org
A community of recovering addicts who help each other stay clean. See online resources below for Web site information.

Smart Moves
Boys and Girls Clubs of America
Dept. P
1230 W. Peachtree St., N.W.
Atlanta, GA 30309
(800) 854-2582
A program where young people teach their peers to resist drugs, alcohol, tobacco, and sexual pressures. See online resources below for Web site information.

Youth to Youth International
700 Bryden Road
Columbus, OH 43215
(614) 224-4506 Fax: (614) 224-8451
A youth leadership and community-based drug prevention program. Provides leadership training for middle school and high school students.

Online Resources

Boys and Girls Clubs of America
www.bgca.org
For younger teens who are in need of mentors and community programs. Site links you to local clubs. Lists volunteer opportunities for older teens.

Cocaine Anonymous World
www.ca.org
This is the site of the Twelve Step Recovery Program for all people who want to stop using cocaine and maintain sobriety. The site contains contact information to find a program in your area, a self-test for addiction, and program information for the newcomer to the program.

Golden Visions
www.playback.net/vision/thevision/index2.htm
The purpose of Playback.net Golden Visions is to help groups with their media needs, "giving good causes the power of media." Worth checking out if your group has a need to express themselves through the media.

Narcotics Anonymous

www.na.org

Narcotics Anonymous is a "community-based association of recovering drug addicts" open to addicts of any drug. It values addicts working with other addicts and the practical value of a "spiritual awakening" for recovery. The site contains regional and area links to receive help in your area.

National Association of Anorexia Nervosa and Associated Disorders

www.anad.org

The site of the oldest national nonprofit association helping eating disorder victims and their families. Includes chat room, poems, stories, as well as lists of treatment centers and other health tips.

Positive Teens

www.positiveteensmag.com

An online magazine for and by teens. Can also give you ideas for starting your own magazine. According to their mission statement, this site "accentuates the positive in talents, lives, skills and voices of the youth today."

The Secret Diary

www.spies.com/%7Ediane/journals

A personal Web site by someone who journals. Lots of suggested readings, ideas, and links. Great resource on journaling.

Thundering Years

www.thunderingyears.com

Submit your poetry, thoughts, and ideas for the "articles" page. Send e-mail to Thundering Years at thunderingyears.com or contact Julie at Jewelhrt8@aol.com.

Youth Media Producers

www.ListenUp.org

An excellent site and resource for teens who want to get their message and creativity into films. Check this out if you have a movie idea, or to see other teen films!

Writing the Journey

www.writingthejourney.com

This site is an online journal-writing workshop with tools and exercises to get in touch with our hearts through journaling, such as writing about anger and keeping a dream journal. This site has lots of great information.

Chapter Four

Nature as Your Oracle

"Fox lurking in the night,
I see your eyes.
Go tell the growing moon
that my mind is dark."

—POMO SONG, FROM *SHARED SPIRITS*

"We can't have a sense of Self, without a sense of place."

—JED SWIFT, MEDICINE WALK GUIDE

"In all things of nature there is something of the marvelous."

—ARISTOTLE, GREEK PHILOSOPHER

"Every natural object is a conductor of Divinity."

—JOHN MUIR, NATURALIST

FOR ALL INDIGENOUS CULTURES, nature is a source of spirituality, where they connect with their spirit world and with themselves. Through their relationships with their natural surroundings they come to hold a deep understanding of their purpose here on earth. Malidoma Patrice Somé, an African shaman, explains that "indigenous people are indigenous because there are no machines between them and their Gods." He also believes that there is an indigenous soul that dwells in each of us and that to connect with the natural world means to bring forth this indigenous soul.

For all of us, nature helps define our place in the great Cosmos and circle of life. Wisdomkeepers of today warn us that if we become too disconnected from the natural world we will all perish. It is nearly impossible to feel our place in the circle of life without a real connection with the wilderness. Many ancient traditions lead us closer to nature. Native American traditions can be understood as an "Earth Spirituality." The mystical Jewish text, the Kabbala, explains that it is through one's relationship with nature that one finds the Divine. Christianity has a strong bond with nature as well. Al Cornell, a Christian minister and internationally recognized wildlife photographer, believes that God is *actively* involved in the universe and all of nature. He says, "The Bible frequently refers us to nature so that we might see the works of God's hands and sense his presence. The poetic Psalms reference nature many times, using language that helps us feel the presence of God in ordinary, natural things. Jesus frequently draws our attention to things in nature to help us understand spiritual things. While teaching from the mountainside, Jesus pointed out the birds and the lilies. Butterflies, chickadees, and roses help us to perceive our awesome Creator."

"Today, like every other day, we wake up empty
and frightened. Don't open the door to the study
and begin reading. Take down a musical instrument.

Let the beauty we love be what we do.
There are a thousand ways to kneel and kiss the earth."

—RUMI, SUFI MYSTIC AND POET

"I have always told my mom when she feels upset about me not going to church that my church is the outdoors. That's where I find God."

—KEVIN, AGE 25

The outdoors is a place we can go for answers to our problems, calm ourselves when we are tense, learn more about ourselves and our planet, act out our rituals, and meditate on plant and animal life. Nature is also there to be consulted when we are trying to make a decision or get closer to our spiritual Self.

Nature is a personal, real link to Spirit and to the wisdom you contain within yourself.

"Ask who keeps the wind

Ask what is sacred."

—MARGARET ATWOOD, POET, AUTHOR OF *CIRCLE GAME*

Consulting Nature

"Perhaps the truth depends on a walk around a lake."

—WALLACE STEVENS, POET

"Nature is one of the languages God speaks."

—ROBERT BLY, POET AND AUTHOR OF *IRON JOHN*

Do you have an issue that you need more help with? Maybe even something that, at this time, feels too private to share? Consulting nature as you would a spiritual teacher or an elder can bring you great insight and guidance. Nature can be an oracle for you. An "oracle" is a truthsayer, a means to better understand God or Spirit. It is also a way for you to have a deeper understanding of yourself.

Consulting nature is a way to get guidance or an insight. Much like dreams, contact with the wilderness can be a provocative and meaningful experience. Encounters with *wild*life can help us step outside of ourselves and listen to the truthsayers in nature—the deer, coyote, ants, lizards, eagles, and other creatures with whom we share this planet. Consulting nature, even by sitting quietly

"The current is in the stream of energy which flows out of the soil into plants, thence into animals, thence back into the soil in a never ending circuit of life."

—ALDO LEOPOLD, ECOLOGIST AND AUTHOR OF *A SAND COUNTY ALMANAC*

under a tree, is recognizing our deep connection with Earth, and ultimately our dependence on Her. Native Americans relied on nature as directing every decision in their lives. Every day they would consult Mother Earth or Father Sky. Jesus gave his talks to the crowds *outside,* never inside man-made temples. So when we consult nature, we are relying on a powerful and widely used source.

In consulting nature, or any oracle for that matter, there are a few basic skills. First, you will need to trust yourself. When you walk out into the woods, for example, you need to *trust* the experience, trust that Spirit will communicate with you. Furthermore, you will need to trust what comes to you. Just as you trust a repetitive dream as holding some significance, trust that your connection with the spirit world is real and can be made through nature and your relationship with it. Have faith that you are part of this great circle of life, and that it wants to relate to you in a very personal and dynamic way.

Another skill you will need is an understanding and acceptance of synchronicity. All Wisdomkeepers rely on this principle as a way to listen to the spirit world. The literal meaning of *synchronicity* is "meaningful coincidence." The psychologist Carl G. Jung popularized this term, but earth religions have always relied on this form of communication with the spirit world. When an inchworm falls on your shoulder during your visit with nature, this is a synchronicity.

"On one of my nature walks with my daughter a stick bug was on our path. These are rare encounters. The meaning for me at the time was in my daughter's response to the bug. It was a stick with legs! So, to her, everything was alive! What a great reminder for me, how everything holds the energy of life within it."

—FLAMING RAINBOW WOMAN, SPIRITUAL WARRIOR

Synchronicity is happening all the time—we just need to train ourselves to pay more attention to what crosses our path every day. What this means *is that Spirit is always trying to get through to us!* Have you ever had a book fall off the shelf at the bookstore, and it turns out to be of great help to you? Have you ever met someone by "accident" and had it turn out to be a meaningful encounter?

> "Nature constantly sends us messages —omens that point the way, signs that help us follow our dreams."
>
> —CHUNGLIANG AL HUANG, MENTOR AND COAUTHOR OF *MENTORING: THE TAO OF GIVING AND RECEIVING WISDOM*

In the woods you go searching for insight about a relationship and a crow calls out to you. You are grieving the death of a friend and two flying squirrels fly from tree to tree above you. Your parents and you are at odds and in seeking nature's counsel you discover a family of river otters. These are all synchronistic encounters, which hold a special message for the seeker. When we consult nature, we are meant to perceive synchronistic encounters as the way Spirit communicates with us. Trust your synchronistic encounters with wildlife. Watch for what appears to you while you are on your walks or vision quest.

Finally, take an attitude of curiosity and *awe* with you into the wilderness. To be in awe means to hold an open mind, a beginner's mind of *appreciation and wonder* for all that is alive and wild. To be in awe means to recognize we are part of the circle of life—*not* outside of it and *not* the center of it. We, too, are "wild." When we go into the wilderness with a sense of awe, we recognize the strength and beauty of the eagle *and* the earthworm.

> "Only that day dawns to which we are fully awake"
>
> —HENRY DAVID THOREAU, AMERICAN ESSAYIST, NATURALIST, AND AUTHOR OF *WALDEN*

Taking a Medicine Walk

"The clearest way into the Universe is through a forest wilderness."

—JOHN MUIR, NATURALIST

"Remember, that all the peoples before us, even in your own family heritage, lived more *with* the earth. Medicine walks help heal the distance we have with our planet."

—JED SWIFT, MEDICINE WALK GUIDE

A medicine walk is done alone, although you can know that others are nearby experiencing their own walk. Find an area that is available to take at least an hour walk, although a two- to four-hour walk is recommended. The place can be a state or national park, someone's private land, or a nature sanctuary. You need to be in a place where you will not be disturbed by the noise and congestion of the city. Plan your walk with a friend or family member or as a planned group outing.

Preparing Your Question

Before you begin your walk, think about the question or concern you want help with. As you walk, you will present this to whatever you consider your source of help: God, your guardian angel, the spirit world, or Mother Earth. You can put the question "out there" to the Unknown, trusting that the natural world of animals and other wildlife will hear your concern. Hold this question or concern in your heart throughout your walk. Some examples of questions may be:

- How can I deal with this relationship?
- What do I need to do to feel less alone and afraid?
- What is stopping me from making a decision about my relationship?
- How can I feel better about myself?
- What wildlife would be good for me to understand and imitate?
- What needs my attention at this time?
- What would be a good way to use my intensity/Thunder?

Ask for insight and help with this issue as you enter your walk with trust, receptivity to synchronicity, and a beginner's mind. Let yourself be moved by the conversation you are about to have with the natural and spirit world and then let nature respond to your question.

Creating a Threshold

This is an important part of the medicine walk because it symbolizes our stepping out of the ordinary world into the world where we are communicating with nature and Spirit. The threshold is where we cross over from being in an ordinary state of mind to the medicine walk—where we begin to receive our insights and messages from the natural and spirit worlds.

This is particularly meaningful when we are at a threshold in life. At these times a medicine walk has even more significance and power. That is why a medicine walk is often a part of a traditional initiation ceremony (see chapter 5). You may want to have one of your medicine walks be about acknowledging the threshold you are at in your life. You may ask such questions as:

> "Go find the wild prairies, and you will find yourself."
>
> —WILLIAM E. ISHMAEL, WILDLIFE BIOLOGIST AND MENTOR

- What is my purpose?
- Where might I get my power?
- Where is my place in the world?

To create a threshold for your medicine walk you need something to step over or to walk though. In the Shinto worship of Japan a *torri* is created as a passage from the ordinary world into the sacred in order to go into a place of worship. You can place a special stick on the ground. Many have used feathers, rocks, and other cherished objects to step over. You can create a gateway to step through with a collection of branches and other objects placed together.

> *"On our land, we have an arbor to walk through when anyone wants to go on a medicine walk."*
>
> —JOSH, AGE 17

Once the threshold is built, step over or through it, holding your issue/question/prayer in mind. If you are in a group, each one steps through the threshold one at a time. When your walk is complete, you will return to this place to cross back into the ordinary world and return to a more ordinary state of mind.

The Walk

A medicine walk is done in silence and alone. Walk as quietly as you can, stopping to notice all that is going on around you, and *inside* of you. Pay particular attention to any animals, animal sounds, tracks, birds, feathers, and insects that appear on your walk. If you are not sure what they are, write a description or sketch them for later reference. The farther out in the country you can get the more likely you are to encounter wildlife. The rule of thumb is, any animal, bird, or insect that appears without wanting food from you, carries a message (or its medicine) for you. Notice also any plant life that catches your attention, or that "catches on to you," such as a burr or thorn.

One young man found himself surrounded by wild blackberry bushes. He was not sure how he got to the center of them without ripping his clothes. He sat down for a while and watched the different birds and bugs that came to eat

> "I caught a glimpse of a woodcock stealing across my path, and felt a strange thrill of savage delight, and was strangely tempted to seize and devour him raw; not that I was hungry then, except for that wildness which he represented."
>
> —HENRY DAVID THOREAU, AMERICAN ESSAYIST, NATURALIST, AND AUTHOR OF *WALDEN*

the ripe blackberries. Up until then, he had never wept over the death of his grandmother, whom he had loved very much. He wept and wept when the blackberries brought back the smell and taste of the wild blackberry jam she would preserve every summer. He also remembered how much she loved and believed in him. He trusted the "coincidence" of finding himself in the middle of a berry patch and knew his grandmother was with him.

> *"I was changed after this experience. So much so, some of my friends teased me and didn't seem to understand the power of this experience. Alone in the blackberry bushes I was finally able to cry over losing my grandmother."*
>
> —STEPHAN, AGE 18

"We are all the children of . . .

A brilliantly colored flower,

A flaming flower.

And there is no one,

There is no one

Who regrets what we are."

—RAMON MEDINA SILVA, POET, FROM *THE HEART OF THE GODDESS*

For the entire walk, remain in a quiet and reflective mood so that you can focus on receiving nature's message. Pay attention to what catches your eyes or ears. Is a crow calling out to you? Is a squirrel following you? Has a lizard crossed your path, or a butterfly landed on your shoulder? What tree seems to stretch out to you? What makes you feel safe? Afraid? What is your walk communicating to you? One young man had three hawks circle around him on his first walk, another time a young woman was serenaded by a cardinal. Many find special objects such as feathers, rocks, tracks, odd-shaped sticks, or animal bones.

Whatever comes up on your walk is part of your "medicine." This "medicine" carries with it a message for you. First, interpret the "message" by thinking what the object or animal means to you. Again, remember to trust the experience. *What you need to know will be revealed to you.* Jed Swift, who takes people of all ages on such walks (see resources on page 90), recommends having the mind-set of "Courting the Mystery"—allowing for the unexpected and unknown to appear. It is being open and light, not too serious, yet respectful of what appears. He also recommends that we have a soft gaze, a meditative gaze. Allow yourself to be like you are walking gently in a dream, noticing the symbols and meanings of the dream as you walk. You will notice what holds meaning for you.

The Return

Return to your threshold at the time agreed upon. Cross over, or through, the threshold, passing from your more meditative state to a more ordinary state. This signifies the end of this visit with the spirit world.

Silently meet up with your group or partner, if you have one. If you are with a group, your mentors or a leader may have a circle or fire built for your return around which you can all gather together. Or you may find a big rock or log to sit on alone. Whether by yourself or with a group, take some time in silence to write down your experiences. Write down any questions you may have for the leader or group or that you want to ponder. Once everyone is finished with their writing begin to listen to each medicine walk story. Share whatever you are comfortable with. Ask each other for input on interpreting the wildlife you encountered on your walk.

Interpreting the Meaning of Your Medicine Walk

The use of nature to help with decisions and to gain more insight is a well-established and still-practiced tradition. But what does it mean when an opossum crosses our path, or a striped butterfly lands on our shoulder? What message might the circling hawk be carrying for us? In Tibetan culture, animals are often considered *auspicious* signs. That means they are bringing us a blessing or a message that this time is favorable for us. Tibetans will often inquire what animals visited a child the day they were born. They consider that the appearance of a certain animal or bird means a rebirth of an evolved spiritual teacher. Crows are known to have shown up for the rebirths of several recent Dalai Lamas, for example. Many Native Americans are named after animals that signify an encounter with that animal.

When we open up to an animal, a tree, a bird, or other forms of wildlife, we are opening up to these aspects *within* ourself. We are calling out to them to come forth, so they can reveal to us the strengths and weaknesses that are within us. How are you like the circling hawk? What is the hawk searching for? How are you like a fox, or an ant, or a 100-year-old oak tree? This is one way to

> "One day there will suddenly appear
>
> An image of light;
>
> When you know that,
>
> You yourself are it."
>
> —SUN BU-ER, FEMALE TAOIST TEACHER AND POET

interpret your encounters—look for what they mean to you, and *what they may say about you.*

Initially, come up with some of your own interpretations. Trust what you make of the encounter. When you are on your walk, certain forms of nature "appeared" to you, and got a certain response from you. Having written this down, you can later take time to reflect on your experience. Make note of the emotions and thoughts you held while you had this encounter. Someone who found herself under a very very old tree realized that the tree would be there long after she was gone. This made her concern seem less urgent (but no less important). She further encountered some animal's home in the base of the tree, with tracks going in and out.

"It's hard to describe to someone if you haven't done it yet. But all of you know what I mean. I could feel the power of that tree. I realized it was probably over a hundred years old. And here I am only 18 years old. I knew the tree would be here long after I am dead and gone. Then I started imagining myself coming back as a fox that might sleep under its shade. It's hard to explain but being so small and young made me feel a part of something awesome. I wrote this poem:

Dear Tree
   Mother, Father, Sister, Brother,
Take me with you
   into tomorrow.
     With
Roots to my past,
   So deep it takes me beyond this time
till I visit again and again
   this time as a woman, next as a fox,
     and then woman again."

—LIZA, AGE 18

Liza experienced a feeling of connectedness to all of life, and that she did, indeed, belong here. This gave her the courage she needed to face her difficul-

"The aspect of Nature is devout. Like the figure of Jesus, she stands with bended head, and hands folded upon breast. The happiest person is the one who learns from Nature the lesson of worship."

—RALPH WALDO EMERSON, AMERICAN ESSAYIST, POET, AND SPIRITUAL PHILOSOPHER

80

ties. Afterward, in a circle with the others that went on a walk at the same time, she discovered that the tracks were likely those of a badger. As it turned out, the badger was likely trying to eat whatever was in the tree! For her and the others, badgers represented "fierceness" as their strength, and "others being afraid of them" as their weakness. This shared interpretation gave her even more insight and help with her issue. Later she read in the book *Animal-Speak* that "bold self-expression and reliance" are traits of the badger. This added another dimension to her encounter.

We can continue our interpretations after we return from our medicine walk. It can be helpful to get books on birds, insects, and animal behavior. There is an abundance of such books available at every library and bookstore. Following an encounter with wildlife, our understanding can grow if we do a little investigative research about that particular animal. The history and mythology of wildlife is also available and can be helpful in interpreting our encounters with something wild. The meaning will change as we change. Then there may come a time when we need to get more insight, so we take another medicine walk.

Gear you will need for a medicine walk:
- day pack
- watch
- water bottle (drink regularly on your walk to stay ahead of your thirst)
- tissue
- rainwear/warm clothes (if needed)
- hat/mittens (depending on weather)
- sunglasses
- sunscreen
- journal and pen

For further help on medicine walks refer to the resources given at the end of the chapter.

"We all come from the Mother

And to Her we shall return

Like a drop of rain

Flowing to the ocean."

—ZSUZANNA E. BUDAPEST, WICCAN AUTHOR OF *GRANDMOTHER OF TIME: A WOMAN'S BOOK OF CELEBRATIONS, SPELLS, AND SACRED OBJECTS FOR EVERY MONTH OF THE YEAR*

More Medicine from Nature

If you don't have time for a long medicine walk, consider other ways to listen to nature's wisdom:

- Sit outside and observe one square yard of earth for an hour. What you observe can be understood as a mirror reflecting your inner work or an answer to a question.
- Find an animal hole, where an animal resides, and sit and watch until something happens.
- Find a *vacated* animal hole, put your face within inches of it, and stare into it. Stay there until something happens (inside of you). Do you feel scared, excited, nervous, curious? Do you "see things" in the hole?
- Go find a rock, tree, creek, or bush. Then "talk" with it. Ask it a question and wait for a response. Trust what comes.

The places you find—holes in trees, creeks to sit by—can be returned to again and again. In your returns you are naturally creating your own sacred place. You are building this place's wisdom by your presence, questions, and intents.

Vision Questing

> "Our demons are our own limitations, which shut us off from the realization of the ubiquity of the spirit . . . each of these demons is conquered in a Vision Quest."
>
> —JOSEPH CAMPBELL, PHILOSOPHER
> AND MASTER STORYTELLER

> "Where there is no vision, the people perish."
>
> —PROVERBS 29:18

In the Sioux tradition vision quests are called *hanblecheya*, which translates into "crying for a vision." A vision quest is similar to a medicine walk, only it involves more and tends to be more intense. It is, quite literally, a "quest" for answers by going into the night wilderness "unprotected." Unprotected means

"This generation is serving as the midwife for the rebirth of the Shechinah. . . . This Goddess who shines on us as we study sacred texts is found in redwood groves and apple orchards. She is coming to us in the wind and the water, in the ocean and the mountains."

—RABBI LEAH
NOVICK, RITUALIST

to have as little clothing as possible without endangering oneself, and without food and other distractions. Many powerful experiences happen when we go out into the woods with only our curiosity to protect us.

Visions are sought after when we are about to take an important journey—like the great journey into adulthood. A vision quest can also be taken when we have an earnest prayer or request. In ancient cultures, many prophecies were the result of a vision that came to someone who sincerely and respectfully "requested" it. Sometimes a vision comes to us because we are in urgent need of one. A vision quest is a request made to the spirit world. No matter what faith or traditions we value, a vision quest can give us insight and help.

Like the vision quests of North American tribes such as the Dakotas *(Black Elk Speaks/White Buffalo Calf Woman)*, all indigenous cultures have their own way of seeking a vision. Many seek a vision through hours or even days of drumming and dancing, while others seek one through running miles until exhausted. Through these means the seeker reaches an altered state and then receives a vision or dream of some kind. Most have some form of "fasting" involved, not eating before and/or while on the quest (which can last up to four days). The Celts sent people out to an island alone to receive answers and insight. Aborigines in Australia do "walkabouts." Buddhists and Muslims go on pilgrimages, walking long distances to a sacred spot. Being alone in the wilderness and meditation are also common in most cultures' practices of vision questing.

All kinds of vision quests attempt to break down the barriers between the mundane day-to-day world and the spirit world. When this veil is broken, we receive a vision, an insight, or a dream that is helpful to us. These visions also hold messages for those in our circle (family, friends, community).

During our Thundering Years visions can be a powerful way to gain wisdom about our life's purpose. Because vision quests are understood as a valuable tool for young adults, many people offer these today (refer to the resource section of this chapter and chapter 5). A vision quest is set up to help you remove obstacles to a vision, to remove the distractions of life, such as food, television,

"As I dig for wild orchids

in the autumn fields,

it is the deeply-bedded root

that I desire,

not the flower."

—IZUMI SHIKIBU, ANCIENT JAPANESE POET, FROM *THE INK DARK MOON*

beepers, telephones, even music. It is you and the wilderness, and you can't help but have a memorable experience.

The Basics for Your Vision Quest

Unlike some of the other rituals within this book, **you will need a "council of elders"** to hold a vision quest. This council can include a vision quest guide, parents, teachers, grandparents, godparents, mentors, therapists, or religious leaders. All the council elders are adults you have a great trust and respect for, and who are willing to help with your vision quest. The vision quest guide is someone who has facilitated many such quests and is likely to charge a fee, or expect a "gift," for his or her services (a list of such persons is given at the end of this chapter). The council of elders is intended to help you interpret your vision. They will have a warm fire built for you on your return from your quest, at which time they will greet you, offer you food, and listen to your experience.

A vision quest is always done in the wilderness. You will need to plan for a place—it is important that you (and the others on the quest, if it is a group) have enough wilderness around you. Some national parks or retreat centers are good for this. There are retreat centers in most states that offer vision quests for young people. A vision quest is done in solitude, where you are out in the wilderness for at least a full day and night alone. Often one of the elders will guide you to a place far enough away from the council fire and others so you can feel the solitude.

To encourage a vision, it is advised by many that you fast at least the day of the quest, and that you take no food with you into the wilderness. Take some water but no other means of distraction with you. (Refer to the medicine walk list of what you will need [see page 81] and exclude the watch.) Some take a journal, but most guides and elders consider journals an obstacle to a vision. You will remember what happens to you and can record it after your return. Take a sleeping bag, or a couple blankets to keep warm, but no other cover such as a tent. You are meant to be "exposed" to the wilderness. If you are too protected, you won't get the vision you are "crying" for.

"And it was a good time to be alive. The Great Spirit right here, resting in the heartbeat of the people's drums. Showing them how to dance, how to find their voice. Teaching them to hear their own breath in the whisper of a raven's wing."

—GARY FERGUSON,
AUTHOR OF
*SHOUTING
AT THE SKY*

The entire idea of a wilderness vision quest is to take you away from the familiar and into the natural world. It is a genuine encounter with the Spirit of the wilderness. None of us can manipulate an encounter with the weather and the untamed wilderness, and this brings out something in each of us that resonates with the wilderness. It also brings out our need to compromise, to relax some of our "rules" since we can't control nature. When we can't manipulate, we find a flexibility in ourselves we didn't know we had. Some things that seemed big and important become small, and some small ideas become big.

Before you go out, you **"call for a vision."** It can be open ended or specific. You can share it with the council members before you go out on your quest, or keep it to yourself. Then, just as in the medicine walk, you will cross the **threshold** from the ordinary world into your vision quest. This is the same place you will pass through on your return to the elders' council.

The Vision

"A vision comes as a gift born of humility, of wisdom, and of patience. If from your vision quest you have learned nothing but this, then you have already learned much."

—From *American Indian Myths and Legends*

The loneliness of a night under the sky can easily bring up many feelings. So notice all your feelings, thoughts, and dreams as part of your vision.

"I didn't have some spirit walk up and talk with me, and I didn't see anything. But the night under the stars alone was awesome. I really wondered if I could even do it. There were times I was scared. Before it got dark, I was bored. But then when it started getting dark, my imagination went wild. And I did hear all sorts of animals and things walking around out there. And—it's hard to explain if you've never done this—but I found a piece of myself out there. A piece that was missing for a long, long time. If you ask me what my 'vision' was, it's this missing piece of me."

—Jeremy, age 18

"Nature is our only reliable and authentic teacher."

—Luther Burbank, PLANT SCIENTIST

Visions typically come as feelings of courage or peace with yourself, or as an awareness, like the one Jeremy had, or you might have a dream that holds significance for you.

> *"I thought I would never get to sleep, actually. Finally I did, and I had this dream: I was babysitting a little girl and we were at this place where there were swimming pools all over the place, and bars where people were drinking a lot. Most everyone had a drink in their hand, or they were swimming. My parents were there in some bar. At some point I asked a friend to watch the girl for a little while. And she said she would, so I went to get something. When I came back, my friend wasn't watching the little girl, and she couldn't be found. I started to scream for her and asked others to search the pools. But no one seemed to care. Then I found her in a pool and pulled her out. She was okay, but she had lost consciousness. I wrapped her up in a lot of warm towels and hugged her and kissed her and told her how much I loved her. She looked right into my eyes. When I awoke I knew that the little girl was me. I was saving myself from drowning by being involved with the vision quest and by hooking up with others who cared about me. I felt both sad and strong. I knew there were some people I couldn't hang around with anymore if I wanted to live."*
>
> —MEGAN, AGE 18

Nature Meditations

> **"I feel above me the day-blind stars waiting with their light. For a time I rest in the grace of the world, and am free."**
>
> —WENDELL BERRY, NATURALIST AND POET

We all need to "rest in the grace of the world." With all the intensity within you, like the "day-blind stars waiting with their light," meditation and sitting quietly in nature can bring great relief and freedom. Just to simply enjoy the quiet of the river, or the strength of a large tree as you sit against it. You can gain strength by being in such places. You can calm any mental confusion by having as little as ten minutes in the woods, away from the noise of the city. Just ten minutes of lying in a field, walking barefoot on the grass, or sitting against a tree can replenish you. Let the earth and fresh air comfort you.

Energizing Meditation

"Earth's crammed with heaven,
And every common bush afire with God."

—ELIZABETH BARRETT BROWNING, ENGLISH POET

Breathing in the fresh air, listening to the sounds of nature, feeling your feet on the earth, can renew the hope that lies dormant under all the heaviness we sometimes carry within us. We need the ability to experience a rebirth of energy and hope when we are feeling low or depressed. Too often we get stuck inside on the Internet, talking on the phone, or watching television—trying to find a way out of our gloom. But the best medicine can often be found *outside,* in a "common bush." Earth is "crammed with heaven," holding in it the ability to crack through our depression or sluggishness. Most rituals are held outdoors to elicit this "heaven" that the earth holds for us. As we light our ritual fires, feel the ground under our feet, and see the stars stretched above us, our spirits are lifted and our attitude improved. Sometimes just holding a rock in our hands or feeling the rain on our face can be of immense help in a time of darkness. When you are feeling down, let yourself be energized by a simple walk outside. Let the skin of your feet or hands touch the natural strength you can feel in the plants and soil. Take a walk in a nearby park, touch a tree, touch a common bush. Let the earth help you feel your natural strength and beauty.

"I have found that the best cure for the blues is a good walk outside."

—WILLIAM E. ISHMAEL, WILDLIFE BIOLOGIST AND MENTOR

Take ten minutes to sit comfortably outdoors. Sit on the ground and take a few moments to bring your awareness to your breath. Begin to imagine the earth breathing through you. . . . As you allow the breath to move in and out naturally, feel it connected to the sweet slow rhythm of the earth's breath. . . . As you breathe in, breathe in the strength and beauty around you, and as

you breathe out, release . . . release your heaviness into the earth. Sit and
breathe with the earth, feeling its strength and how it supports your body.

Appreciation Meditation

Whether or not we can get out into nature, we can bring nature's qualities into our *daily* life. Perhaps you know the story of the girl who walked three miles, on a busy street, to kill herself by jumping off a bridge. She looked into the faces of dozens of strangers as she walked slowly to the bridge. People either looked away or stared back at her. For three miles no one said hello or inquired about the stress and pain on her face. As she approached the bridge, where only a month earlier a friend of hers had jumped to his death, she saw the face of a man smiling at her. He was just an ordinary man, carrying a briefcase in one hand and walking fast somewhere. But he slowed down enough to give her *a big smile of recognition.* She had to smile back, even though he was a stranger. In her journal later that day she wrote, "An angel disguised as a man smiled at me today, and I decided if God was going to bother to send me an angel I could hang on."

"Before eating, always take a little time to thank the food."

—ARAPAHO PROVERB

Each day look at those who pass you by, catch the location of the sun as it rises in the sky, put your hands into a running stream, touch the falling snow, smell the cold air, eat an apple very slowly, listen to a bird sing, or feed a squirrel. . . . There are a thousand ways to kneel and kiss the earth right in our own front yards. We need only slow down a bit and appreciate what is around us. Our human neighbors are also part of the circle of life, we are all part of nature. Showing someone you recognize them as a "member of the human family," is a form of meditation in action. It is slowing down enough to do what would come more naturally to us if we weren't so distracted and caught up in things! Today take the time to "kneel and kiss the earth" in your own way. Be that angel in disguise and smile at a stranger. Eat that one apple slowly . . . tasting every bite.

"Brambles should be cut away,
removing even the sprouts.
Within essence there naturally blooms
A beautiful lotus blossom.

If you don't know essence and don't know life,
You will split the creative and receptive into two paths.
But the day you join them together to form the elixir,
You fall drunken into the jug yet have no need of support."

—TAN GUANGZHEN, CHINESE PHILOSOPHER

Books, Resources, and Wisdomkeepers Related to This Chapter

Animal-Speak: The Spiritual and Magical Powers of Creatures Great and Small, by Ted Andrews (Llewellyn Publications, 1996). A great resource for helping interpret your medicine walks. Includes a dictionary of animal, bird, and reptile symbolism.

Animal Wisdom: The Definitive Guide to the Myth, Folklore and Medicine Power of Animals, by Jessica Dawn Palmer (Thorsons, 2001). A comprehensive guide to the legends, rituals, and magical powers of animals. Includes worthwhile descriptions of the Thunderbeings. An excellent companion to this chapter.

A Crow Doesn't Need a Shadow: A Guide to Writing Poetry from Nature, by Lorraine Ferra (Peregrine Books, 1994). Helps connect the creative spirit with the great outdoors.

Lame Deer: Seeker of Visions, by John (Fire) Lame Deer and Richard Erdoes (Washington Square Press, 1976). Lame Deer shares the story of his reckless youth, and his quest of a vision.

Lost Borders: Coming of Age in the Wilderness (Two Shoes Productions, 1998), 84-minute video. This moving documentary explores an ancient rite of passage that is being revived in North America. For ordering and further information visit the Web site: www.bullfrogfilms.com.

A Sand County Almanac, by Aldo Leopold (Ballantine Books, 1949). A nature lover's classic. An example of a published journal.

365 Days of Nature and Discovery: Things to Do and Learn for the Whole Family, by Jane Reynolds, Phil Gates, and Gaden Robinson (Bellew Publishing, 1994). Useful and fun guide to help create your own nature walks and to gain a better understanding of the natural world.

Contact your local **Department of Natural Resources**. They offer year-round free outdoor workshops and trainings. They also have booklets of local wildlife and pamphlets of animals tracks to help you identify what may have appeared on your medicine walk. They also have a list of parks and sanctuaries where you can hold your medicine walks.

Jed Swift
Medicine Walk Guide
4859 10th Street
Boulder, CO 80304
e-mail: Jedswift@earthlink.com
Leads people of all ages through medicine walks and offers workshops on improving our relationship with nature.

Tom Brown's Tracker School
Tracking, Nature, and Wilderness Survival
P.O. Box 173
Ashbury, NJ 08802
(908) 479-4681
Fax: (908) 479-6867
e-mail: TrackInc@aol.com
www.trackerschool.com
Resource of classes (links on the site), books, and events. Excellent resource for the adventurous soul. Includes shamanic healing and nature

rituals. Make sure you check out their excellent links page.

Bob Burton
Visionquest, Inc.
P.O. Box 12906
Tucson, AZ 85732-2906
(520) 881-3950
www.Vq.com
Visionquest is a private corporation that contracts with public agencies to provide programs for teens. The vision quests vary depending on a given group's needs. Sweat lodges are also offered. Check out their Web site for class information.

Wonder Camp
Jamie Charles, Camp Director
15423 N. 54th Street
Scottsdale, AZ 85254
(602) 765-9551
Fax: (602) 765-0691
e-mail: liltiger@amug.org
Offers many rituals and rites of passage for teens. Web site offers readings and more information on the camp, and links to other helpful sites.

Online Resources

American Camping Association

www.acacamps.org

This site provides useful information about finding an American Camping Association camp near you, successful camping tips, volunteer and job opportunities, and what can be expected during one's first experience at camp.

ANASAZI Foundation

www.anasazi.org

Outdoor healthcare and wilderness encounter classes for those in need of a place to recover from addictions or other difficulties.

Cedar Creek Nature Studies

www.CedarCreekNatureStudies.com

Learn about the school located in Hot Springs National Park, Arkansas. They offer classes in tracking, observing nature, and more.

Connecting with Nature

www.ecopsych.com

An extensive site on many ways to connect with nature. Includes educational opportunities.

Native Cultures

www.spiritual-endeavors.org

An index of information and resources on Native cultures, including vision quests, and resources on Mother Earth spirituality.

Skillsalive

www.skillsalive.com

A site that teaches many primitive skills such as drum making, creating shelters, and finding edible plants. Will host classes in your area.

Temagami Experience

www.northwaters.com

This is the site of the Northwaters Wilderness Program at the Temagami Forest Reserve in Ontario, Canada. They specialize in wilderness canoeing adventures and "creating opportunities for learning from the land and one another in a spirit that honors awareness, personal growth, cooperation, balance, and trust." There are programs created especially for youth.

Wilderness Rites

www.wildernessrites.com

Wilderness Rites is an organization based in Oregon and California that specializes in wilderness quests, youth rites of passage, medicine walks, and "self-generated ceremony and intentional transformational experiences" to connect to the natural world and ourselves.

The Song of Return

I had a date in the bush
With all the Gods,
So I went.
I had a date in the bush
With all the trees,
So I went.
I had a date in the mountain
with the kontomble.
I went because I had to go,
I had to go away to learn
How to know.
I had to go away to learn
How to grow.
I had to go away to learn
How to stay here.
So I went and knocked at doors
Locked in front of me.
I craved to enter.
Oh, little did I know
The doors did not lead outside.
It was all in me.
I was the room and door.
It was all in me.
I just had to remember.
And I learned that I lived
Always and everywhere.
I learned that I knew everything,
Only I had forgotten.
I learned that I grew
Only I had overlooked things.
Now I am back, remembering.
I want to be what I know I am,
And take the road we always
Forget to take.
Because I heard the smell
Of the things forgotten
And my belly was touched.

—DAGARA TRIBE, WEST AFRICA, FROM *OF WATER AND THE SPIRIT:
RITUAL, MAGIC, AND INITIATION IN THE LIFE OF AN AFRICAN SHAMAN*

Chapter Five

The Ceremonial Circle

Rituals and Rites of Passage

"We may never hear
The Thunder come out
of the lion's mouth.
We may never see his claws—
The claws that once served
The peace of the village.
How much longer can we survive?
Ye Ye Ye."

—INITIATION SONG, DAGARA TRIBE, WEST AFRICA

RITUALS ARE A WAY TO ACKNOWLEDGE what we value in our lives. They are a way to bring the spirit world into our daily lives. Most likely, you already engage in some rituals. For example, many Christians take Communion as a spiritual ritual of accepting the body and blood of Christ. The wafer and wine are not actually the body and blood of Christ, rather, they represent, *symbolize,* his body and blood. This is a *blessing* ritual. You have been blessed by the life of Christ when you take Communion. Buddhism, Native American traditions, Hinduism, Judaism, and Wiccan practices are all rich with ritual. A common daily ritual for Buddhists, Hindus, and Native Americans is the care of an altar. Decorating a Christmas or Solstice tree is a ritual practiced by many of us. Jewish families engage in many rituals year round to acknowledge holy days. Many African Americans now celebrate Kwanzaa, a seven-day festival, founded in 1966 to help African Americans learn about the heritage of both their American and African traditions, build strong families, and promote unity. Blowing out candles on a birthday cake, brides throwing their bouquets at weddings, singing hymns at funerals, carving pumpkins for Halloween, saying family prayers before going to sleep at night, lighting the Menorah during Hanukkah, placing important objects on an altar, and dressing up are all ways we practice ritual in our lives.

"Even if it's one [tribe] a year carrying out its ceremonies, the earth can still be saved."

—BOB BROWN,
ONEIDA NATION
HIGH SCHOOL
TEACHER

Rituals are also a way of interacting with the *invisible* in our lives. In a sense, we touch the invisible through the practice of ritual by acting out a belief, story, or prayer. When we sincerely take Communion, pray, sing hymns, set up an altar, or practice community rituals (such as midnight mass on Christmas Eve) we are having a personal conversation with our *spiritual* source. For most of us, our spiritual source is invisible. Some, however, worship nature and the change in seasons, which are visible. But even those whose spiritual source is nature will speak of such invisible things as animal spirits. The invisible is known by many names: God, Goddess, Spirit(s), Ancestors, The Great Unknown, Guardian Angels, Buddha, Christ, Mother Nature, the Creator, Hope, Faith, and so on. *Ritual is a way to acknowledge and communicate with this invisible source of power.* It helps us to feel less alone in times of difficulty. Ritual is meaningful because it keeps us connected to something greater than ourselves. In fact,

94

that is the purpose of most indigenous ceremonies — to keep the individual and community actively involved with the spirit world.

A Message from Sobonfu Somé

Raised in a traditional Dagara village in Africa, Sobonfu Somé has personal experience in the tribal initiation of women and has benefited from years of mentoring by the elders of her tribe. Sobonfu, who lives in the United States part time and part time in her village, has become familiar with the ways of the West while holding on to the ancient teachings passed on to her. Her name, "Sobonfu," means "Keeper of the Rituals." Sobonfu invites us all to live an active life with Spirit and with each other. She knows the pain and the joy of trying to keep our connection with Spirit alive while living in this fast-paced world.

The indigenous voice of Sobonfu speaks to the indigenous voice alive inside all of us. Through ritual we can all come in contact with our ancestral wisdom.

"In the Dagara culture, it is understood that children need a vehicle to carry them into adulthood, a process that will awaken in them their connection to a deeper sense of purpose and community. Children are prepared from birth to know and fulfill their place in the community. All adults of the village nurture and foster their children's understanding of and connection to the spirit world. Adults and elders model the acceptance of the child's place in the community and the responsibility of living their purpose. The power and authority of adulthood is tempered by the individual's personal connection with Spirit.

"Initiation is the vehicle by which we build this intimate connection with Spirit. It is the process that connects us to ourselves and supports a greater connection between us and the community in which we live. Initiation is a ritual with the intensity necessary to match the emotional and spiritual energy that erupts during our Thundering Years. An initiation respects this powerful time in our lives.

"I have observed that the Western world is a very confusing place for young people. Often it seems as if there is little to connect you to yourselves, or to the greater collective (community, family, spirit

> "Where ritual is absent, the young ones are restless or violent."
>
> —MALIDOMA PATRICE SOMÉ, AFRICAN SHAMAN

"The survival of all Species depends on our grasping the significance of what was learned during the Beginning Times. And what we learned was this: The Ceremony is Life itself; it is the way we do things; it is the way we maintain Balance and Harmony with all our Relations; it is the way we Honor our Ancestors and protect the Earth for the Yet Unborn Generation."

—
GKISEDTANAMOOGK, CITIZEN OF THE WAMPANOAG NATION, FROM *ANOQCOU: CEREMONY IS LIFE ITSELF*

world). The nuclear family, as it exists in the West, seems limited in its ability to provide you with adequate support, thus fostering a sense of separation and isolation, both internally and externally. Young people are bombarded with mixed messages about what it means to be an adult. The messages about purpose, responsibility, and contribution to the greater whole are often overshadowed by messages of power and authority. There does not appear to be a clearly defined vehicle built into the structure of the society that connects you to yourself and Spirit. Without an attempt to harness the intense emotional and spiritual energy generated during our young adult years, it is easy for us to get lost and disconnected. As a result, I see many young people struggling. Gangs, violence, drug abuse, sexual acting out, and other self-destructive behaviors appear to me to be misdirected attempts at creating intense experiences to contain the tumultuous energy of the Thundering Years.

"In an attempt to provide you with authentic containers for this spiritual energy, many are rediscovering indigenous ways. The call to awaken our ancestral wisdom is strong. Personal and community rituals are ways of reuniting us when we are in a state of alienation and turmoil with Spirit.

"You deserve a life full of rituals and information to assist in your transformation into adulthood and the probing for your purpose."

—SOBONFU SOMÉ

Rituals that hold spiritual and cultural significance for us need to be brought back into our lives, and you can help. Practicing such purposeful rituals as Kwanzaa or coming-of-age rites can help to end the hostility, violence, and alienation many of us are experiencing in our lives. Through them we can help ourselves and others "maintain the balance and harmony" we are so lacking today.

"Drugs make us forget our dreams. Make us forget who we are and what we can do. Ritual helps me get in touch with the 'who' of who I am and can be."

—ERIN, AGE 17

Ritual is where we can induce natural highs and make a connection with the spirit world. Altered states are achieved through dancing, singing, meditating, chanting, shouting, prayer, playing musical instruments, and "acting out" stories and myths. An altered state is also achieved through the intense connection we have with others and with Spirit during ritual. This altered state is often felt as a deep sense of "belonging" to something important.

> *"Every ritual I participated in has brought me a feeling of 'oneness' with all beings, and a good feeling that usually lasted for a long while. Designing personal rituals helped me acknowledge important passages and times in my and my loved ones' lives. Rituals have also brought more community and friendship into my life. Every year I celebrate the changing of the seasons, the solstices and equinoxes, as well as events that are special to me, like graduations. When I share in a meaningful ritual with others, I feel closely connected to them, to myself, and to the spirit world. Malidoma and Sobonfu Somé, and other teachers of ritual, proclaim something I always found to be true—that every ritual I participate in has a lasting impact on me and the events in my life."*
>
> ANDREA, AGE 24

This chapter will offer you ways to bring ceremony into your life. First, we will start with the basics of ceremony, to help you design your own. Then, several specific rituals will be described as illustrations of what you can do. The anger ceremony is very popular among teenagers. Rites of passage, naming ceremonies, and initiations are rituals that acknowledge the important transition we are making during our Thundering Years. Seasonal rituals help connect us and our changing lives with the changing of the seasons and are meant to be fun as well as meaningful.

Creating new rituals or adding to traditional ones such as Passover or graduation is something you can also choose to do for yourself and your community.

> *"After attending my first ritual, I decided to change my graduation party. I borrowed the idea of giving gifts to those I wanted to recognize for helping me reach my goal of graduation. I made or bought small gifts and passed them out at my party, thanking each person for their help. My grandmother cried, and I could see*

that everyone was touched by my gifts. I encourage everyone to think about what they need to do to enrich holidays and traditions we already participate in. I was a little afraid others would be uncomfortable, but it was really great!"

—STEPHANIE, AGE 19

Ceremonial and Ritual Basics

"Ritual is a return to the ancient with a plea of help directed to the world of the spirit."

—MALIDOMA PATRICE SOMÉ, AFRICAN SHAMAN

Each of the rituals described in this chapter follows the same basic guidelines. You can use these guidelines as a framework from which you can add your own creative touches. While many of the rituals described are based on time-honored ancient traditions, you can also approach your rituals as an opportunity to express whatever it is you and your group want to explore—in your own way.

"Ritual keeps our culture alive."

—AMY, ONEIDA NATION, AGE 16

Preparation for Your Ritual

In preparation for a ritual, take the time in advance to consider what your ritual is about. What is the *purpose* of the ritual? Is it to acknowledge a transition in your life? Is it to manifest a goal? Do you want to express an emotion, such as anger, grief, or gratitude? Are you celebrating an important passage, such as a birthday, or acknowledging another season's arrival? Is it a holiday that you want to enrich with your own ritual? Many young people design rituals to initiate them into adulthood or a new way of life. Are you planning a coming-of-age ritual?

"It meant a lot to me to get my one year medallion in my AA group but I wanted more. I talked to my mom about having a

celebration. She agreed and told me to think about what I wanted. Mostly, I wanted to have fun, but I also wanted to be seen as a new person. With my mom's help we came up with a ritual and party! I made a cake in the shape of a six-pack. We ate it to symbolize my power over alcohol. We also burned things that were part of the old me. It meant a lot to me to share this with my mom and friends. I plan on having ritual be part of my life."

—KARYN, AGE 22

As you prepare for your ritual leave room for spontaneity. African shaman Malidoma Somé, in his book *Ritual*, says that leaving room for spontaneity is leaving room for the "spirit world" to become involved with your ritual. It also allows for more fun. Getting too rigid in your planning will stifle you and the other participants.

Preparation is also intended to make the ritual safe for you and all those involved. Being *uncomfortable* or nervous is usually good, since this means you are doing something new and different. However, it is important that you and others feel safe. *A safe ritual won't force anyone to do anything they do not want to; there is no harm, abuse, or manipulation of any kind.* Everyone attending the ritual will need to know its purpose, and what their role is. This helps in creating a safe experience for everyone.

> **"The one thing in the world of value, is the active soul."**
>
> —RALPH WALDO EMERSON, AMERICAN ESSAYIST, POET, AND SPIRITUAL PHILOSOPHER

Remember, the power and fun of your ritual is dependent on knowing the purpose of your ritual.

Ritual is rich with symbolism. When you send someone a birthday card or give someone a gift, these are *symbolic* of your affection for this person. The card or gift are objects that symbolize your feelings. An engagement ring, a hat with your team's name on it, gang emblems, costumes for sporting events, lighting a candle, wearing certain jewelry, putting up a poster, taking Communion, and flowers being thrown up on stage after a performance are just a few examples of the use of symbolic objects and behaviors to express ourselves and to connect with others.

Planning the Ritual

Once you have decided the purpose of the ritual, you can then begin to create it. In most cases, those involved in the ritual should be involved in the planning of it. Anyone who is not part of the planning needs to be given an outline of the ritual at least a few days before they arrive. In planning for the ritual you will want to decide *where* to have it, *what* you will need, *who* will attend, *what* will take place, and the *food* you will want to eat after the ritual is over.

Here are the typical makings of a ritual, first listed here and then briefly described:

1. Setting up an altar
2. Making a space for the ritual
3. Invoking the Invisible (Spirit, Nature, Ancestors, God, Goddess, Creator, etc.)
4. Heart of the ritual
5. Closing the ritual
6. Eating and sharing

Things you might need or want to have on hand:
- noisemakers/musical instruments/drums
- comfortable clothes or costumes
- safe containers for candles
- firewood (if a fire is part of the ritual)
- drinking water
- cloth or small table for an altar (or can be on ground)

Setting Up an Altar

"I sit in front of my altar when I need time to myself and to think things through."

—ERIN, AGE 17

Altars are set up to help us remember and focus on what is meaningful for us. During a ritual, an altar can symbolize the purpose of the ritual. It helps us focus, for example, on what we are thankful for in our Fall Equinox/Thanksgiving ritual, and what we hope for in our Summer Solstice ritual. Altars are designed to call our attention to what is important to us. We place on them symbols of empowerment, strength, and guidance. We also place food and other objects on them as offerings to the spirits and ancestors. The objects have meaning for us and are "symbolic" of what we may be praying or hoping for. Many people have photos of mentors, sponsors, and helpful people on their altar, along with other objects of spiritual and emotional significance. Altars are meant to inspire us. They often remind us of our connection and responsibility to nature or to our spiritual source.

> *"I sit by my altar and have a conversation with my dad, who died three years ago. He died of cancer. No one really knows I have an altar. But ever since I made one I feel less alone about my dad. If he were alive he'd say, 'Nice altar, Kevin.' I know he'd like it because he was open minded about things. My friends though, they might think it's strange."*
>
> —KEVIN, AGE 23

An altar can be used as a "message board" to our spiritual source. We can place on this message board objects that express our prayers and desires. Altars, such as the ones at many Tibetan rituals, are covered with sweets, drinks, and butter sculptures that are offerings to their deities, along with lamps and pictures of holy persons. Most churches and synagogues have altars with candles, incense, and certain sacred objects. In the Kwanzaa ceremony a Kinara (candleholder) is placed on the center of a table and is the focal point of the entire seven-day ritual.

Decide in your planning time what you want placed on your altar.

Making a Space for the Ritual

The space for a ritual includes the physical as well as the symbolic so you will need to make both a physical *and* a symbolic place to hold your ritual. Ideally, the location of your ritual is chosen well in advance. Many rituals are held in

> **"If you feel the real joy and the real spirit within you, they come out naturally. If you really go deep inside, everything is there. You feel and, if you want it to come out, it will come out."**
>
> —MAYUMI ODA, ARTIST AND ACTIVIST

the woods, often at campsites in state parks, which need to be reserved weeks or months in advance. A ritual can also be held in a large and private yard or in the comfort of someone's home.

After you have unloaded whatever you need for the ritual and set up your altar, all the participants gather together in a circle to start "shedding the everyday." This is a way to let go of the worries and concerns you may have brought with you to the ritual. It is how you create symbolic space. It's a time to let go of what you *don't* want in your ritual (worries about school, for example). A common way to shed the everyday in Native American rituals is smudging: a smudge stick or bundle of sage is lit and the smoke is wafted around the participants and the ritual space. The burning of incense and "smoking" an area is used in many cultures as a way to purify the area. Many religions, including Christianity and Buddhism, also burn incense as a way to "feed" the spirits. The smoke from the incense symbolizes food for the spirits and it is believed that honoring the spirits in such a way helps bring safety to the space where ceremonies or rituals are performed.

"Rituals must be performed with good and pure hearts."

—HOPI PROVERB

Smudging the area gives you a way to symbolically prepare for the ritual and feed the spirits you want to invite into the ritual. It symbolizes cleaning off any negative energy that may be hanging on to you. This then "prepares" *you* for the ritual. You can buy smudge sticks (usually made of sage, cedar, or sweet grass), at most food coops, natural foods stores, or stores that sell herbs. You light the stick and "smudge" each other with the smoke, by letting the smoke drift around your body. Make sure you have water to put out the smudge stick when you are finished. Another way to cleanse is to splash each participant with a little water or burn your favorite incense. It is the *intent* of cleaning the space that is important here; you can use whatever expresses this for you.

When you are finished smudging everyone and have put out the smudge stick, you can do a short grounding or breathing meditation. Read a meditation aloud (see chapter 6, Meditations for the Mindful Warrior). This is to help "center" you. To center means to bring you more into the moment so you can have a full experience of the ritual. It helps bring your attention into the ritual. If your thoughts and attention are elsewhere you will not be able to participate or receive the most from the ritual. The Sacred Tree Meditation (see page 160) is often used here or a simple five minutes of the Mindfulness Meditation (see page 146).

If you have candles on the altar, you may light them as a statement that the ritual is beginning. When the ritual is over, you blow them out as a statement that the ritual has ended. (Please have the candles safely placed on the altar in a glass or metal holder, so you don't have to worry about them during your ritual.)

Invoking the Invisible

According to many ancient traditions, invoking or "inviting" spiritual guidance into the ritual is the pivotal point of the ritual. Gkisedtanamoogk, a citizen of the Wampanoag Nation in southeastern Massachusetts and eastern Rhode Island, states in his book *ANOQCOU: Ceremony Is Life Itself* that "all the Ceremonies that I can think of have something to do with Thanking the Presence of the Creator." Ceremonies are then a way to acknowledge your gratitude and relationship with the Creator, Spirit, or nature. All great teachers of ritual warn us that our very thoughts and attitude affect what energies are invoked in a ritual. Therefore, it is important to call on the spirit world with awe and respect, and to come into the ceremony with an open and respectful attitude. You can invoke God, the Higher Power, the Creator, a hero or heroine, Buddha, Christ, the natural world (spirits of the trees, wolves, wind), or any of the mythological gods and goddesses. African shaman Malidoma Patrice Somé stresses the importance of who and what you invoke. Sobonfu Somé also stresses the importance of the spirits we invite into our ritual space. "Invoking Spirit," she says, "communicates to the spirit world: you are part of me and I am part of you. They *want* to carry on a conversation with us. Western people are too often discouraged and frightened from this conversation. I say, *talk* to your spirit world and let them into your ritual and into your life."

Invoking Spirit is inviting the invisible to be part of your ritual. Who or what invisible source would you like invited into your ritual? Many seasonal rituals invoke the guardians and spirits of the natural world, such as the warmth of the sun at Winter Solstice or Mother Earth, who gives us our food, during the Fall Equinox ritual. Many "invite" loved ones who have died.

"I invite into each ritual the ancestors that have gone before me so they can teach me and remind me of my purpose here. Ritual has saved my life and I am grateful that the ancestors have passed this on to me."

—SALAKWA, ONEIDA NATION, AGE 23

"You need to know what the Creator's intention is for you. Many people are confused and do not know where they come from or what purpose they have in their lives. They need ritual with the elders in their community. They need to connect with spirit and discover the richness of their life."

—ONEIDA NATION HEALER

Heart of the Ritual

This is the central part of your ritual, where you carry out its purpose and intention. This part of the ritual can involve many activities: prayer, shouting, acting out, gifting, creating something, meditation, drumming and dance, acknowledging a transition, burning items in a fire, wearing or the making of masks, and opening up to your emotions. Examples of several rituals are offered later in this chapter, along with resources and recommended readings. From these examples you are encouraged to design your own ritual.

Closing the Ritual

More often than not, you will have a sense when the ritual is finished. This too will have been part of your planning the ritual. In closing the ritual, it is important that you *thank the spirits you invoked*. For some, giving thanks is the *most* important part of ritual.

"At the beginning and end of every ritual and prayer, we thank the Creator. This is most important. Give thanks to all natural things. Thanks to what you need and are given in your life. But mostly thanks to the Creator. We burn our sacred tobacco. This is our personal ceremony of thanking the Creator."

—SALAKWA, ONEIDA NATION, AGE 23

You will have your own way to give thanks, perhaps something borrowed from your own heritage. But a simple statement of thanks is enough.

Many elders recommend that we "release" the spirits back to their place of mystery when we are finishing the ritual. This is accomplished by being grateful and saying farewell to any spirits you invited into the ritual.

You may have some closing statements to say to one another as well. Then, you close the ritual and blow out the candles (if any are lit). In many rituals a closing song is sung. Here is a version of a favorite, borrowed from an Irish blessing:

May the circle be open but unbroken
May the Love of the Creator/Goddess be forever in your heart
Merry we meet
And merry we part
And merry we meet again.

Eating and Sharing

The ritual is considered over now, but you are still enjoying the gathering of friends. This is the time to talk about the ritual or just enjoy some food and the company of each other. The food that is chosen can be related to the theme of the ritual. For example, above, Karyn baked a cake in the shape of a six-pack. All the other food at the gathering was brought by friends and family in celebration of her sobriety and new life.

Generally, rituals are considered confidential. This means the specialness and sacredness of the events in the ritual are contained within the group. This gives you and others the freedom to be silly, spontaneous, truthful, open, and emotional without the fear that others will be told about it. Much like the agreed upon confidentiality in AA or Al Anon groups, your privacy deserves to be respected in ritual. You may want to agree upon confidentiality during the planning of your ritual.

"The Thunderers— our people—our Beings—tell us when it is Time to feed our Ancestors and all those who have passed on."

—GKISEDTANAMOOGK, CITIZEN OF THE WAMPANOAG NATION, FROM *ANOQCOU: CEREMONY IS LIFE ITSELF*

Emotions in Ritual

Emotions are an important and natural part of ritual. You will find yourself experiencing many feelings throughout a given ritual. Try not to inhibit them; instead, express them. Open up to them. The grounding exercise and the various meditations suggested will help you invite the emotions and altered states that are part of every ritual. When an emotion does arise—such as rushes of excitement or the tightening of the throat with sadness—let it become part of the ritual. Instead of suppressing the feeling, let it out. Instead of closing around the feeling by tensing your body, relax and open up to what comes. When we allow for such emotional and physical states, we experience the natural highs in ritual.

Ritual isn't a passive high like drug- and alcohol-induced states. Ritual brings on altered states through our *active* participation. Unlike drugs and alcohol, the altered states in ritual affect our well-being in a lasting and positive way. Instead of a hangover or a "day after" depression from alcohol or drugs, we are uplifted. We feel better about ourselves. In ritual, as in art and sports, you are the drug.

"Taking a risk is at the core of a rite of passage. It needs to be a challenge that will reveal to yourself who you are."

—ELLEN HUFSCHMIDT, RITUAL CONSULTANT

Rites of Passage for the Thundering Years

"A time when young men go into manhood is a most sacred time that must be prepared for. Such ritual [rites of passage] is a way of life for me now."

—SALAKWA, ONEIDA NATION, AGE 23

Rites of passage are times in your life that hold great significance and change, such as moving from childhood to adulthood, young women getting their first period, graduation from one level of school to another, and becoming a member of a special group in society. Rites of passage can also be spiritual passages, such as dedicating your life to a spiritual order or practice. Now, during the Thundering Years, you are experiencing such a passage. Sadly, our Western culture has few rituals that initiate you into and through this passage, with the exception of Bar and Bat Mitzvahs in the Jewish tradition. This is disheartening, because you *deserve* to celebrate and experience this passage in a powerful and meaningful way. Such a rite should acknowledge that you are now a boy moving into manhood, or a girl moving into womanhood.

Boy into Manhood

> *"Manhood is represented in many cultures by a coming-of-age ceremony. In the melting pot of the United States, we have very little of a common religion left, and because of this we have lost the power of a universal coming-of-age ceremony. Our fathers recognized this step into manhood as one of their needs that went unfulfilled as they were young men. In teaching us the ways of manhood, they defined for themselves what they should be and justified their thinking as men."*
>
> —DAVID EDELI, AGE 17, FROM *BOY INTO MAN:*
> *A FATHER'S GUIDE TO INITIATION OF TEENAGE SONS*

How scary, frustrating, and painful it is not to know your place in the world or to be recognized (in a good way) for your entrance into manhood. Salakwa spoke to me of the importance of ceremony in helping him get his life together and bringing meaning into his previously drug-addicted existence.

> *"I learned a lot from 'Bob' [a teacher and shaman in his tribe] about ceremonies, culture, and language. This got me looking forward to my life instead of dreading what may be next. I was taught and experienced a lot of ceremonies about who we are as a people. My life would be empty without ceremony."*
>
> —SALAKWA, ONEIDA NATION, AGE 23

Salakwa went on to tell me how the Oneida offer young boys initiation rituals into manhood. The boys take time to prepare for a four-day fast, then go into the woods for four days and four nights alone. This is meant to happen during the age of puberty (12 to 14) but can happen later if one wasn't offered the ritual at this age. The boy being initiated is sent out by his community. He is sent out

"A bit of advice given to a young Native American at the time of his initiation:

'As you go the way of life, you will see a great chasm.

Jump.

It is not as wide as you think.'"

—JOSEPH CAMPBELL, PHILOSOPHER AND MASTER STORYTELLER

107

into the woods as a boy for the last time, *returning to his community a man*. On his return the men in the tribe greet him and celebrate his successful passage.

The following prayer expresses the sentiment of adults who participate in contimporary coming-of-age rituals for boys.

"For you, our beloved sons, we wish many things. We want you to love yourselves and to know how unique and precious you are. We want you to know your own gentleness and live compassionately with all life on this beautiful planet. We want you to acknowledge your own energy: creative, strong, forceful, and life-affirming. We want you to know the spirit within you, to nurture and to trust it. We want you to celebrate who you are and look forward joyfully to who you will become."

—BERNARD WEINER, AUTHOR OF *BOY INTO MAN: A FATHERS' GUIDE TO INITIATION OF TEENAGE SONS*

Boys need to realize that there are many, many ways to become a man and to live in the adult world. Too much emphasis is put on athletic achievement and "winning," when there are so many other talents and skills that demonstrate a young man's worth. A highly recommended book is *Boy into Man: A Fathers' Guide to Initiation of Teenage Sons*, in which the initiates take on the acting out of many male adult roles. This is meant to help them understand that the road of manhood is one of diversity and differences.

Girl into Womanhood

"We want to welcome our daughters into womanhood. Teach our young women and ourselves to tend to the fires of our creativity, intuition, and wildness, all of which ground us in our feminine power. The tradition of handing down this knowledge through the generations has been broken in our modern culture. Using time honored ways of ritual, art, and story, we can open our hearts to the gifts of wisdom that pass from our grandmothers to our daughters and back again. As we mend this connection through ritual we begin to reweave and mend the fabric of our communities."

—ELLEN HUFSCHMIDT, RITUAL CONSULTANT

For the first 30,000 years of human existence the earth itself was widely celebrated and worshiped as *female*. This is one reason we often hear the earth today referred to as "She" and "Mother Earth." The great mysteries of menstruation, pregnancy, and childbirth were recognized in early communities as sacred experiences to be honored by the entire tribe or community. In Mexico, Tlazolteotl was a popular Moon Goddess who again and again gives birth to herself just like the old moon gives birth to the new. A girl's coming-of-age ritual recognizes this revered ability to give birth, which can take many forms—the birth of a child, a poem, a creative or helpful act—or, like the Moon Goddess, as *the ability you have to give birth to yourself, and your adult life.*

In many indigenous cultures, a young woman beginning her menstrual cycle is recognized as passing through a natural rite of passage and in need of a coming-of-age ritual. Like young men, young women are also known to be initiated by going into the woods on a vision quest, returning recognized as women in their respected communities.

> *"I felt embarrassed at first when my mother suggested I have a rite of passage around my getting my period. This is not something that is easily talked about with older women! My mother explained that she was taught to be ashamed and embarrassed too and that she wanted to give me a new way, a better way, to experience my coming-of-age. The rite would acknowledge what my body already knew—that I was a woman now, with adult responsibilities and concerns. My mother and I planned this together and even though I felt a little embarrassed at first, the ritual came to mean a lot to me. I know it helped my mother to heal from the embarrassment she was taught about her period and her body as a woman."*
>
> —KATIE, AGE 15

"Black mother goddess, salt dragon of chaos, Seboulisa, Mawu.

Attend me, hold me in your muscular flowering arms, protect me

from throwing any part of myself away."

—AUDRE LORDE, AFRICAN AMERICAN POET AND ACTIVIST

Several Native American girls spoke excitedly of the cleansing and naming ritual that they would be part of with the adult women in their tribe. A naming ritual is where the young woman is given her spiritual name by a female leader in her community or tribe. She is symbolically "cleansed" of her childhood and is ready to step into womanhood. With this, the elders or women facilitators of the ritual give her a spirit name. See pages 117–22 for stories about the power of spiritual names.

The Call for Initiation/Coming-of-Age Rituals

According to ritual consultant Ellen Hufschmidt, the need for a rite of passage from childhood to adulthood is a biological one. If our adolescent self does not sufficiently *risk* itself to be seen and acknowledged by the larger community of adults, we will continue this yearning, this quest, into adulthood and carry with us a sense of incompleteness.

Do you

- find you are wanting to act out a lot;
- want to make a statement to others about who you are;
- often feel angry or/and depressed;
- experience panic attacks or a lot of social anxiety;
- feel as if you're not sure where you belong;
- abuse drugs;
- commit violent acts against yourself or others;
- feel misunderstood or invisible to adults;
- feel you've done something important but no one seems to notice;
- feel confused about your reason to be alive and maybe even hopeless about why you are alive;
- get recognition for something like an athletic or a musical achievement but still feel an emptiness inside;
- feel too much emphasis has been made on your negative behaviors or mistakes;
- lack purpose and direction in your life?

If any of these are true for you, an initiation or coming-of-age ritual may be what you need. Much of your confusion and anger is a result of not being recognized as being in an important transition. This confusion also reflects

"Buffalo Woman's energy is very strong in many of our hearts at this time. Buffalo Woman is willing to shine out through each of us who quiet ourselves and call."

—Brooke Medicine Eagle, Native American elder and author of *Buffalo Woman Comes Singing: The Spirit Song of a Rainbow Medicine Woman*

our culture's inability to offer you enough guidance on your way into adulthood. Sometimes the adults in your life may hold an agenda for you to "be something," but you haven't yet decided what you *really* want to be. Some of you may have been given mixed and confused messages of what adulthood is all about, while others of you may be clear about who you are and what you want. A coming-of-age ritual acknowledges that you are now on the road of making important decisions for *yourself*. It recognizes you as a unique and distinct individual. It recognizes you as a valuable part of the community.

Initiation rituals need to be facilitated by adults, however, because an adult is someone who has already made this passage. Thus they can help you over the threshold. Adults will "initiate" you into their "club," so to speak, recognizing you as a "member" once you are initiated. In most indigenous cultures, initiations or coming-of-age rituals are done with adults other than parents.

> *"Girls need women to bring us into our adult life. In our tradition a woman will give to a young woman a spiritual name and take her through a cleansing, as part of her initiation into adulthood."*
> —AMY, ONEIDA NATION, AGE 16

While you need adults to help guide you through this time, *you are joining the ranks of adulthood yourself* and are making many of your own choices. Therefore if you cannot locate any adult in your family, school, or community who can help you create the type of initiation ritual you want, refer to the resources at the end of this chapter.

Most initiation rituals include some symbolic "threshold" for the initiate to cross over—such as those described as part of medicine walks and vision quests in the previous chapter. A vision quest is often a powerful part of an initiation or coming-of-age ceremony. Ritual consultant Ellen Hufschmidt says that the risks and challenges—the thresholds—of rites of passage will be different for everyone. She recommends that if you are musically inclined that you create your own performance. If you are physically inclined then enter a race. The point is to have the threshold you cross be bigger than anything you've done

"Coming-of-age, traditionally, has meant taking responsibility for the food that we eat."

—JAMES A. SWAN, PH.D.
ECOPSYCHOLOGIST AND AUTHOR OF *THE POWER OF PLACE: SACRED GROUND IN NATURAL AND HUMAN ENVIRONMENTS*

111

before. Confront a fear, push past your inhibitions—all this can be part of your coming-of-age ceremony. Crossing these thresholds represents your transition from childhood to adulthood. Once you pass through this symbolic threshold, everyone in your community recognizes you as a young adult, and no longer a child.

An Initiation Ritual

An initiation ritual is a profound experience of renewal in which a new life, a new beginning, is entered into by the initiate. The word *initiation* comes from the Latin *initia*, which refers to the basic or true nature of any living thing. This means that as initiates we are opening up to our own True Nature in this ritual, and a new beginning for ourselves. You cannot have this experience and remain unchanged.

The first parts of the ritual—the planning of it, the setting up of the altar, lighting the initiation fire, and the crossing over the threshold—are between you, the initiate, and your chosen Wisdomkeepers *only*. Your chosen community members come to the welcoming into adulthood ceremony after you have completed your "trial" phase of the initiation.

Planning the Ritual

Unlike other rituals, a greater part of an initiation is in the planning and preparing for it with your mentors and elders or Wisdomkeepers. Depending how elaborate you (and the other initiates, if it's a group initiation) are getting, the planning phase can take several months. So take into consideration the time of year you want to hold the ritual so you have plenty of time to prepare.

It's during the planning phase that you identify what coming-of-age means for you, what your "trial" will be, and who you want involved in welcoming you into the community as an adult.

"In all the initiation/coming-of-age ceremonies we do there are ritual components symbolizing the shift from childhood to adulthood—sometimes a change in garments or a movement from one place in the ritual space to another. Also, we always include gifting of some kind for those initiated."

—SELENA FOX, PAGAN ELDER

Questions to help focus your initiation/coming-of age-ritual:

• What do I need to leave behind in my childhood?

• Who do I want to become?

• What do I want my test/trial to be? How does this challenge and symbolize my move into adulthood? How might this trial bring about a change within me that initiates me into my adulthood?

• Who do I want welcoming me back into the community as an adult? This can include anyone of your choosing—friends, immediate or extended family, teachers, religious leaders, neighbors.

• Who do I want to have the responsibility of giving me my Spiritual Name or new name on my return from my trial (if this is part of your ritual)?

All those welcoming you need to know when and where to show up, what to bring (stories about you, initiation gifts, and food to share), and what is expected of them. The Wisdomkeepers helping you plan and prepare for the ritual can send out invitations with all this information. Include an RSVP, so you know who will be coming to the ritual.

To help choose your mentors or Wisdomkeepers, take a look at the Wisdomkeeper chapter for some ideas. Most important is that these people represent the qualities of an adult that you aspire to. Also important is that they are trustworthy and believe in the power of such rituals. They should not want anything from you in exchange for their help—sex, money, or favors. You may hire someone like Ellen Hufschmidt or Malidoma Somé to be consultants to you and your mentors, and they would likely require a fee for their services, which you should work out with them before the actual ritual planning begins. However, elders in your community participate in your initiation ritual because it is a needed activity that they want to provide to you and others.

You can choose, if you like, to give your mentors a gift that expresses your appreciation for their role in your life and their part in the ritual. The gift can be offered during the gifting part of the ritual.

The initiation ritual described here is borrowed from many traditions, including Native American, African, and Celtic.

What you will need for this ritual:

- elder(s), mentor, and/or Wisdomkeepers to help plan and facilitate this ritual
- symbols of initiation for the altar
- gear for the "trial" phase of the ritual
- initiation fire, lots of wood
- objects symbolizing childhood to burn in the fire
- a threshold to cross over
- gifts from those welcoming you back from your trial
- favorite foods (provided by others) to eat after the welcoming
- initiation symbol (may be made ahead of time, such as a mask)

Setting Up the Altar

Bring objects that symbolize who you are becoming. Some objects can represent what you are leaving behind (these can be released into the fire prior to crossing over the threshold, if you want) or be protective guides for the journey ahead. Include candles of various colors, to represent the rainbow of possibilities life will offer you as an adult, and seeds of your choosing, to represent the potential within you. Ideally the altar will be outside, in the Eastern corner of the ritual site since the East is where the sun rises on a new day.

The elders and welcomers (friends, family, community) should place their unwrapped gifts on the altar.

Heart of the Ritual

After placing your symbols of initiation on the altar, the elders light the initiation fire and cleanse the space. They then place the threshold in its place (ideally the West end of the ritual site). For threshold ideas see chapter 4, page 76 (Creating a Threshold).

You are then smudged with the sage or incense by the elders. Next, you release into the fire anything symbolizing your letting go of your childhood. It can be something literal (someone once burned a picture of her abuser) or symbolic (someone one once released shells of sunflower seeds as symbolizing breaking through the shell of childhood).

Next you step over the threshold to enter your trial.

The Trial

If possible, the elders will have the fire burning until your return from your trial. Trials can be:

- sleeping under the stars alone
- running a race, a marathon, or a designated distance alone
- giving a performance of some kind
- doing your first hunt (see "Hunting Ritual" on page 136)
- writing an article for the local paper
- mountain climbing, rafting, or kayaking (all which you've prepared for)
- going on a 4- to 8-hour medicine walk (see page 75)
- going on a vision quest (see page 82)
- creating some artistic piece (painting, sculpture, poetry, a play)
- presenting a play or poetry jam (see page 220)

> "Ritual enables us to live a life that is much closer to what our souls aspire to."
>
> —MALIDOMA PATRICE SOMÉ, AFRICAN SHAMAN

Make sure that the trial pushes you beyond your comfort level. The trial is intended to initiate you into adulthood by creating some ordeal you have to get through. Not a harmful or unsafe ordeal, but one that does create some anxiety and discomfort. This experience will help prepare you for the hardships and challenges we all experience in our adult journey through life. As Dadisis Sanyika, an African American elder and musician, expresses, "The hardships imposed during initiation help to break down the resistance of your ego so that you will be receptive to new information and insights." The idea then is to have some insight and newness come to you during your trial that you can then bring back with you into your adult experience. It doesn't have to be earth shattering to be profound.

"My trial was putting together a collection of my poems into a chapbook and presenting them to an audience. The entire experience created a lot of anxiety and thought—but I did it! I finished a book and read it to others. I ended up with many insights about myself, and who I want to become. I feel more like myself now."

ZACH, AGE 17

"It took months and months to plan for my initiation ritual. And finally on the day of the ritual, everything broke open. When I went out into the woods for several hours before dawn to 'gather objects and thoughts that were me,' I felt afraid. What if nothing happened? How would I know what to do out there all by myself? Was there really going to be a community of people welcoming me back? All this stress built up in me and broke through while I was sitting out in the woods. I cried and cried, and I wasn't even sure why. All of us being initiated hadn't eaten for three days, and I felt tired and hungry. Something in me broke down. But when the light started coming up and it was time to return to the fire, I felt that I had cried something out of me. We had made masks for our return and were to wear them when we came back. But the mask didn't feel like me anymore. So, I put it on the back of my head facing out. When I came into the circle, and heard my name being called, I first walked in backward. Then, I turned and faced them and just started to shout and laugh with them.

"I hope everyone who wants can have such an experience."

—ANNA, AGE 17

> "The hero's journey always begins with the call. One way or another, a guide must come to say, 'look, you're in Sleepy Land. Wake. Come on a trip. There is a whole aspect of your consciousness, your being, that's not been touched. So you're at home here? Well, there's not enough of you there.' And so it starts."
>
> —JOSEPH CAMPBELL, PHILOSOPHER AND MASTER STORYTELLER

Welcoming Back and Closing the Ritual

On your return to the ritual site, you pass back over the threshold where those you've invited welcome you into the adult community. They sing, chant, make music, and shout your name. If you've been given a spiritual name or new name, your chosen elder will shout this out first. Everyone then shouts out your new name.

Then you are placed in the center of the circle of participants, safely near the fire or altar. You first share your trial experience and what it means to you. Then, everyone takes turns sharing stories about you, and their hopes and dreams for you. They can then give you the gift they brought for you. You may decide to offer your own gifts at this time, to show your appreciation to your mentors and the community as a whole. Your gift may be in the form of a song, a spoken poem, a dance, a skit, or playing an instrument. As always, allow for spontaneity. Remain open to how Spirit is going to show up in the ritual. When the gifting is through, end the ritual and begin the initiation feast!

Finding Your Natural or Spiritual Name

In most cases, a naming ceremony is part of an initiation or Summer Solstice ritual, or a vision quest. When you arrive back from your trial or vision quest, you can be given a Spiritual Name by a chosen elder. Or, as in the example below ("How I Came to Be Named"), a name can be given during a sweat lodge and *before* a vision quest. The idea is to include a naming with another ritual.

> *"Some boys have already gone to a sweat lodge to see what the Great Fathers had to say to them and give some of them their Spirit Names. The Great Fathers are the hot stones that heat up the sweat lodge. I know an elder who did 24 Great Fathers! That is a lot of heat, and the Great Fathers' message was then strong. Part of becoming a man is to stand more and more heat.*
>
> *"I don't have a spirit name. Yet. I've been initiated through the streets, until I was arrested for assault and battery. In treatment I met up with my first Indian Medicine Man. He saw in me the man I could be. He's worked with a lot of lost teens—of all backgrounds. Soon I hope to be ready to do my first sweat and listen to the Great Fathers. This will be a very important day for me."*
>
> —DAN, OGLALA SIOUX, AGE 18

Below are two examples of finding one's Spiritual or True Name (what some refer to as our Natural Name). The first naming ceremony is borrowed from Native American traditions and facilitated by an Oglala elder. The second is a story of a young woman who empowered herself by giving herself a True Name.

How I Came to Be Named Flaming Rainbow Woman

To be honest, I went on my first vision quest and naming ceremony on a whim. I wasn't even sure what I was getting myself into. A friend mentioned to me that a group was headed to Bear Butte Mountain with Eagle Man (Ed McGaa), and would I like to come? Sure, I thought, I could use some help. So, I quickly made arrangements and packed up some clothes and a sleeping bag.

We were asked to fast on our way there, an entire day's trip, and to find our *Wotai* stones first thing the next morning. Fasting is intended to make you more receptive to a vision and more likely to achieve some insight. Like emptying out a vase, making room for an arrangement of new flowers. A little hungry and curious, we went to a nearby creek and searched for our stones. The Oglala believe there is power inherent in the Wotai stones, thus they are very sacred to them. Eagle Man told us to let our eyes move slowly over the stones, allowing our *Wotai* stone to "appear" to us. I found it difficult to find one, but then one seemed to find me. The stone is symbolic of the healing we need at the time, and the power we can carry with us into our vision quest and beyond.

There were about eight of us on the trip, plus Eagle Man. He and one other young man placed the large fieldstones on the fire to build up the heat in the sweat lodge. I was nervous but mostly excited. What would this experience unlock inside of me? What do I really believe about all this? I was open, yet held on to some skepticism. Can such a ceremony really offer a young white woman anything real?

During the sweat, I thought I saw a spirit pass outside the lodge. My heart leaped, until I realized it was just someone placing more stones on the pile. I felt myself getting hotter and more uncomfortable. My thoughts were jumping around, until Eagle Man said that some in the group were meant to receive their Natural (Spirit) Name. I listened as he spoke, in the Oglala language, names for several others . . . and then he called my given name and repeated over and over in Oglala: you are

Flaming Rainbow Woman. *Flaming Rainbow Woman.* I took it in and wondered what did it mean for me, this Natural Name?

Then, when the sweat was finished, we prepared to go directly up Bear Butte Mountain to seek our vision.

Visions, I was told, could come in the form of a dream, an encounter with nature, insights, or intense emotional states. So, about an hour or two of walking up the mountainside (we were not to take any watches with us), I left the side of my friend and found a place to lie down. Not too far off were the others in search of their place and vision. But as the dark came, the distance between me and the others seem to grow. I held no specific question in my mind; rather I opened myself up for general guidance from Spirit. I wanted most to experience something "real" with the spirit world. I laid awake the entire night, looking up at the sky. I thought about my new name and what it might mean to me. Some time into the night I noticed storm clouds approaching the mountain and heard the THUNDER. The lightning and thunder moved in closer and closer. I didn't move, but I wanted to. I began to question the safety of the entire experience—I could be home safely in my bed! All night and morning I watched the storm with its thunder and lightning. It flamed around the mountain, and kept threatening us with danger. . . .

It wasn't until we descended down in the early hours of light that the storm actually covered the mountain and released its rain on us.

So, what was my vision? For me, I left that mountain with a truer name—a name for my spiritual self, the Spiritual Warrior. *Flaming Rainbow Woman.* I left that mountain stronger and braver—flaming with curiosity and purpose about life and my place in the circle of life. I later journaled that "it often seems to appear as though a storm is going to blow me off my mountain when all it does is give me a greater sense of myself (and a good scare). I *am* Flaming Rainbow Woman. And I carry that Name out into the world now." And I will spend my life living up to that name—and that is its true power for me, this desire to live up to what it means to me to be Flaming Rainbow Woman.

"Every Oglala who believes in the omnipotence of Wakan Tanka (Great Spirit) wears or carries a small, spherical stone carefully rolled up in a wad of sage and deposited neatly in a miniature buckskin pouch no more than an inch in diameter. . . . It is not necessary to carry these stones on one's person every day, but if one is to embark upon some important mission, or if one wishes to invoke the aid of the supernaturals, one carries the stone with him."

—ED MCGAA, EAGLE MAN, FROM *RAINBOW TRIBE: ORDINARY PEOPLE JOURNEYING ON THE RED ROAD*

Finding My True Name

by Tatiana Katara, artist and Spiritual Warrior

When a butterfly comes out of its cocoon and flies for the first time, it will never wish to be a caterpillar again. Much like this, when we pass through our Thundering Years, we cannot be a child again.

Changing my name was one of the most life-altering things I have ever done. I was really just running away . . . from my father's name, from my past, from my family, and from who I thought I had been. My birth name was Tanya Leach. I didn't mind the first name, but "Leach" was too much to handle. I was teased a lot in school, called "lurch" and "bloodsucker" and "worm" and probably a lot of other names that I have been trying to forget until now. When I reached my "Thundering Years" I was probably between 12 and 14. I was sexually active, rebellious, into smoking pot, stealing, drinking, and willing to try just about anything once. I had nothing to lose because my father would never accept me no matter how good I was, and people had already decided who they thought I was. They were wrong, and I was wrong to believe them. But this I am still learning.

Changing my name was my way of removing my train cars of baggage and letting them roll downhill to crash and burn without me. It worked. . . . I moved to a new city, and I became *Tatiana* (the formal Russian name for Tanya). The last name I chose was made up. I sat down with a pen and started writing names I liked or that seemed familiar to me. Kitaro was some music I really liked at the time. My boyfriend had a Katana motorcycle. I wrote every combination I could think of . . . Kitano, Kitara, Kataro, Katara . . . that was it, I chose Katara. So I am now *Tatiana Katara*. I later found that Tatiana means queen of the fairies and Katara is the fire in the lotus. (Or so I've been told. I was also told it means great dagger.)

The power of changing my name was in being able to *re-create myself*, to become my own ideal person. Or at least strive to be that. It was easy to hear my new name and respond. I loved hearing others say it, and I was proud to introduce myself. People always seem to comment on my name, and they rarely forget it, because it's unusual. As I felt myself in my new name and new city, I automatically became a different person. I knew that Tanya was a thief and liar and had done a lot of "bad" things, and I knew that Tatiana was beautiful and natural and peaceful and honest. I knew this because she was a character that I created in my mind . . . a vision of who and what to step into. Day by day I evolved into Tatiana, making decisions that were responsible and honest. Instead of figuring out how to "screw someone over" who had betrayed me, I dealt with situations in a peaceful way. This had its own ripple of problems because I seemed to attract people who would hurt me, but that was all part of my initiation into adulthood.

For me, the initiation is still happening. I am still becoming and will always be transforming into the Tatiana I create. I don't have to be the person my parents labeled me as. I have made my own creation of myself and can continue to do so. I am my highest self, and I believe I have chosen the name that my soul wishes to be called.

Many, many times our parents choose names from baby books and popular lists, not knowing that we have a spiritual name, a soul name. Sometimes those names don't exist in our language. The most powerful name you can choose is not the name of someone who was popular in school or on TV. The most powerful one you can choose is the one you can slip into and really become, your TRUE name, your spirit name. You can find this by looking through books of names and listening for things that sound familiar to you. Sometimes it's a word that you see written and it just looks right. It's like a secret map. Follow the signs, coincidences, names that "ring" true for you somehow, and you will come to it. There is no hurry in choosing a name, for this name will be yours only when you find it. There's nothing wrong with trying on names with yourself and/or close friends, and there's nothing wrong with discarding a name that doesn't fit. EVEN IF IT'S YOUR BIRTH NAME. Even if your parents don't understand. Our society can make us feel like criminals when we want to change our name. They make us pay money, go to court and ask a judge's permission, and explain WHY. It's nobody's business why you change your name, unless you choose to explain. In other cultures and countries a young person is given a ceremony when they become a man or woman. They enter adulthood with a new given or chosen name, and from that moment on, they are responsible for their actions.

We are missing the initiation rituals into adulthood that acknowledge our transformation. But you can initiate yourself with just as much power and determination, by finding your own True Name.

Think about all of the famous people in the world who changed their names BEFORE they became famous. Did changing their name help them to transform into that dynamic or charismatic person and allow them to become famous? Many of the famous names we know are created by that individual, just like I came up with my True Name.

There is something quite powerful in finding out our True Name or adopting a Spiritual Name, if the one we have isn't enough.

Releasing Anger Ritual

"I don't think that anyone really understands the tension in us."
—KEITH, AGE 22

This ritual was created by Ellen Hufschmidt, ritual consultant, to provide "a safe, symbolic, and thoroughly satisfying way to release anger from the body and mind."

What you will need for this ritual:
- clay pots that you can hold in your hand (three or four per person)
- magic markers for writing on the pots
- clay and some utensils to shape the clay
- a large sheet (at least large enough to fit a twin-size bed)
- a board (to strike the pots against) or, if outdoors, a large flat rock
- a large plastic sheet
- objects for altar that symbolize your anger
- drums, rattles, sticks, and other noisemakers
- food to eat after the ritual

The time needed for this ritual varies, depending on the size of the group. Eight to ten participants are recommended. Allow for at least three hours for this ritual, with an hour for eating time afterward.

For the Altar

Bring objects that represent what you are angry about and other objects of significance. The altar can be a simple cloth on the ground, or a table may be used.

Heart of the Ritual

After setting up the altar, create the ritual space as described earlier in this chapter (see page 101). A good meditation for this ritual would be the Sacred Tree Meditation found on page 160. Following the meditation, each participant can share the meaning of what they brought to place on the altar. This will give each person a chance to say something about the anger they feel. It will also emphasize that our anger and hurts can be expressed and contained within a sacred circle. If you so choose, everyone can write what they are angry about on the clay pots with magic markers. This will add another dimension of bringing the anger to the surface and can enhance the ritual breaking of the pots.

Then to *raise up the energy* and to get everyone to bring up their emotions of anger, shout, move, and drum. The larger the group, the easier it is to get lost in all the uproar. Beat on the drums, make lots of noise, move and flail and stomp, shout out your anger. Two or three people can be considered the "noisemakers" or "containers of the energy" and their role is to keep the drumming and shouting going. This part will go on for as long as the group needs or wants. Here is where spontaneity is valuable, allowing people time and space to release their anger, getting to the point where breaking the clay pots will be easy.

Then the group will make a circle, holding on to the sheet. Underneath the sheet, in the center of the circle, lies the wooden board or rock. Each person takes a turn throwing a clay pot into the center of the sheet, smashing it against the board or rock. Those holding on to the sheet need to look away so as to not

> "A tree does not move unless there is wind."
>
> —AFGHAN PROVERB

123

get any clay pieces in their eyes. (Clay pots break easily without much shattering. Do not use glass or porcelain/china.)

When you throw the pots down yell out who or what you are angry about. The others can then shout and holler their support. The "noisemakers" can keep the responses of shouting going. Do this until everyone who wants to has broken one or several pots.

When everyone is finished, or all the pots are broken, have each participant take hold of the sheet, so it can be held up with all the shards of clay in the center. Begin to toss up the shards of clay slightly into the air, having them land within the sheet. You will quickly notice that the sound of the broken shards is like wind chimes. Already you and the others are experiencing the way anger can be transformed into something new. In this case, the sound of anger is *symbolically* transformed into the sound of pleasing wind chimes. Keep tossing the chimes up in the air, allowing those who want to speak about the sound of the "chimes" to do so.

The sharing of personal experiences, myths, and stories of anger being transformed into something more peaceful can take place at this time. Some may begin singing or chanting along with the sounds of the "wind chimes." As in all rituals, allow for spontaneity.

Next, each person takes some of the shards of the broken pots and makes them into a personal mandala. A mandala is art, thoughts, words, and emotions expressed in a circle. Use the soft clay to create the mandala's circular shape and use the broken shards to decorate it. You are taking the symbols of your anger and all the energy it took to break the pots and transforming it into something new. Your mandala symbolizes *your* ability to build your future from the past, even your anger. Remember it is not a contest of who is the best artist; instead, it is a simple expression of your transforming anger into something new. After you are done sit in silence as the others finish their mandalas. When everyone is done, take time to share your mandalas with each other. You can place your personal mandala on your altar at home.

"And we can rise with the fire of freedom,

Truth is the fire that burns our chains.

And we can stop the fire of destruction,

healing is the fire running through our veins."

—RITUAL SONG BY STARHAWK, RITUALIST, PEACE ACTIVIST, AND AUTHOR OF *THE SPIRAL DANCE: A REBIRTH OF THE ANCIENT RELIGION OF THE GREAT GODDESS*

End the ritual by thanking all the spirits you have invited to participate, sending them back to their "homes." Make a statement of gratitude about the passion of anger.

The ritual is now over and the eating can begin!

Celebrating the Changing of the Seasons

The following rituals are designed to celebrate the changing of the seasons and to better connect us with the natural world. Through these rituals we can tap in to the natural energies alive within each season, such as the heat and passion of summer or the cold and restfulness of winter. Seasonal rituals are also a way to accept and acknowledge the dependence we have on the health of our planet. This is important because we are totally dependent on this earth for our very lives. To ignore this dependency is causing all of us a lot of damage, resulting in toxic wastes in drinking water, pollutants in the air from factories and automobiles, and untimely plant and animal extinctions. We have a history of ruining entire ecosystems, destroying habitats and the life that is dependent upon them. Seasonal rituals can offer us a way to give back to the earth by acknowledging our dependence on and appreciation for all that nature gives us. You will likely discover, as I did, how ritual offers you a better understanding of the natural world and our place in it.

We are also intimately connected to the changing of the weather and the seasons and the various holidays that each season holds for us. These seasonal rituals are meant to be enjoyed as well as give us a way to listen to our inner clock that is always tuned in to these natural cycles. The seasonal rituals are best done outside—where we get in touch with this energy more. (If you live in the city, you can contact your nearest state or federal park and reserve a campsite. The cost is minimal for a group site fee.)

> "I wish for you a life full of ritual and community."
>
> —FLAMING RAINBOW WOMAN, SPIRITUAL WARRIOR

Winter Solstice Ritual (December 20–23)

For those living in the Northern Hemisphere, the Winter Solstice marks the longest night of the year. It is the day when the sun is at its lowest point in the sky. After the dark night of the solstice the sun is returning and the days begin slowly to hold the light longer. A ritual around this time can acknowledge that "this is as dark as it gets." There are times in each of our lives where it seems to be so dark we start feeling hopeless and helpless. This ritual brings us hope as we remember that there is always a limit to the dark times! It can also be a way to remember that much takes place in the dark that is beneficial to us: the growing of a fetus, seeds sprouting in the dark earth, and a peaceful night's sleep. The Winter Solstice is a time to dream and make plans for the future.

What you will need for this ritual:

- candles, menorah, and other sources of light
- mistletoe, holly, and other herbs of the season
- large ceramic or metal bowl
- small thin strips of paper
- objects that represent light and the new year approaching
- ritual fire (outdoors in fire pit or indoors in fireplace)
- Solstice tree

Altar

You may want to include mistletoe, holly, or other herbs and objects that represent the new year (light) approaching, as well as your hopes for this coming year. Instead of an altar, you may decorate and light a Solstice tree. Make sure in your planning that everyone brings a candle and a candleholder if you are going to light candles.

Heart of the Ritual

The ritual can include letting go of the darkness that is passing. What would you like to let go of that has caused you pain, sadness, or hopelessness? Sit quietly together in a circle during the darkest moment of the solstice (your local newspaper will tell you when this is). Think about what you want to let go of as the darkest moment passes. Then, when the time has passed (about three to five minutes) have someone light a candle in the center of the circle. Have a large ceramic or metal bowl next to the candle. Write down those things you want to release on a small, thin piece of paper. Then either tear up or burn the small strips of thin paper, and release what's left of them into the bowl. You can announce to the group what you are letting go of, or you can release it in silence. If the ritual is done outside, you can release the paper or other symbolic objects into a fire. The fire should be lit after the period of darkness and meditation is over.

When everyone is done releasing the old, it is time to bring more light into the ritual and into your lives.

This part of the ritual will be a way of celebrating the light. You can turn on the lights of your Solstice tree, light candles in the room, or carefully light candles on a traditional Solstice tree. As you light a candle announce out loud a prayer or hope you have for yourself and for others. There's great strength felt in sharing a prayer with people who care for you and want your prayer to come true. You then have several others carrying this hope for you in their hearts and minds.

Spring Equinox Ritual (March 20–23)

Spring Equinox is a time when the day and night are *equal* in length, when plants begin to burst forth from the earth, when leaves appear on the trees, when the earth around us begins to warm up. Spring is a time to celebrate renewal and joy! Most people feel surges of creative energy during this time of year. It's the season many people claim to fall in love. You can tap in to this energy through this ritual. Look at all the plant life that is coming alive; notice how the sun is warmer and the days are longer. Everything in nature taps in to the energy of this season, and you can too.

The celebration of Easter occurs close to the time of this equinox. Easter was named for the goddess Eostre (also Ostara, Astarte), whose aspects have to do with spring, dawn, and rebirth. The egg is used as a symbol for Eostre as it represents birth and the life force of all of nature. *Ostara,* a feast of the goddess Eostre, celebrates the power of fresh beginnings. Everything in the natural world, including us, experiences rebirth. The day or night before your Spring Equinox celebration is a good time to do some type of cleansing to prepare for the rebirth of your body. A cleansing can be fasting for a day, taking a bath, drinking an herbal cleansing tea, attending a sweat lodge, or meditating on what you need to release. To bridge with the dreams and planning done during the Winter Solstice, the Spring Equinox can be the time to clear away blocks to achieving your goals, much as a gardener begins to get the soil ready to plant seeds.

What you will need for this ritual:

- fresh candle
- spring flowers
- bowl of water
- cornmeal
- objects that symbolize creativity, personal growth, and springtime
- drums and other noisemakers
- costumes for dancing
- food to eat after the ritual

Altar

Include some spring flowers, a new candle, and a bowl of water. The water can symbolize the cleansing that you are going through for your rebirth. Place objects that acknowledge your creative energy, perhaps something that is in its growth stage (some project that isn't finished yet). Pictures of friends and family are often added to the altar at this time.

Heart of the Ritual

Sit in front of the altar (if alone), or in a circle around the altar if in a group. Have someone read through the Sacred Tree Meditation (see page 160). Then read this to yourself or have someone in the group read it *slowly* aloud:

Feel the energy of springtime in your body. Invite every cell, every molecule, every atom of your body to be infused with the energy of spring. Let your breath flow naturally . . . like the tree that breathes in the heat of the spring sun.

The cold of winter is broken and now the warmth is moving in. Feel the coldness move out of your body and the warmth, the vibrancy, move in and throughout your entire self. You are being filled up with the same creative energy that fills all creatures and plants at this time. Feel it fill and excite you.

What do you want to do with this intense, vibrant energy? And what does this energy expect of you?

As in the Releasing Anger Ritual, have some designated "containers of the energy" begin to hit drums, shake rattles, or sing a song or chant while everyone gets up and begins to turn the altar into a mandala, a circle of spring objects. Use everything on the altar and anything else you want to add to it. If you are at a park, include things on the ground: sticks, rocks, debris—whatever attracts your attention. The mandala is like a painting, only the "paint" is the objects and the "canvas" a circle you have made on the ground. The circle itself can be made of stones, cornmeal, sticks, or whatever you and your group come up with. Have everyone help with the creation of the spring mandala. In your planning of the ritual you can remind everyone to bring special objects to contribute to the mandala. With the help of the drummers and noisemakers, continue adding to the mandala until everyone feels it is finished.

When the mandala is completed everyone can begin to shout, beat on the drums, shake noisemakers, and jump and dance around your sacred mandala.

Or, you may have a planned song to sing or music to play on a boom box. The mandala you have made is an expression of your creativity and how easy it is for you to tap in to this part of yourself. Mandalas are considered very sacred and are believed to have the means of generating more energy. As you dance and shout, imagine pulling the energy from the mandala into your body and mind. Use the power of your imagination and intensity! It is important here to keep the drumming, dancing, and shouting going. You want to dance long enough to work your way into an altered state of excitement and enthusiasm.

When it is time to stop, take about five minutes to sit around the mandala you created together. Stay tuned in to the energy you stirred up in yourself and in the group. If anyone feels like speaking up, this is a good time to do so. Participants may express what the mandala represents to them, or what feelings and thoughts came up during the dance. This is a great ritual to do wearing costumes that make it easy and fun to dance in! (This too can be decided at your planning of the ritual.)

Then, when you feel ready, begin to dismantle the mandala, returning whatever you borrowed from the park back to the ground. Have the entire mandala put away and stand in a circle silently around the bare ground for a few moments, perhaps thinking about how you are going to take your creative "spring" energy out into your daily life. End the ritual by thanking all the spirits that were called upon to assist in your ritual and then prepare to have an abundant feast. You will be hungry after raising all that energy! At one such ritual we left the circle of cornmeal on the ground with birdseed in the mandala as a way to symbolize our gratitude to the earth and its wildlife. You too may want to leave behind something edible for the wildlife.

Summer Solstice Ritual (June 20–23)

This ritual can also be used at other times of the year as a Gifting Ritual, a time when you or others are given gifts in recognition of your value and worth to the community. The Summer Solstice is the time of year when the light reaches its

"Genuine, heartfelt ritual helps us reconnect with power and vision as well as with the sadness and pain of the human condition. When the power and vision come together, there's some sense of doing things properly for their own sake."

—PEMA CHÖDRÖN, BUDDHIST NUN, AUTHOR OF *THE WISDOM OF NO ESCAPE AND THE PATH OF LOVING-KINDNESS*

peak and the earth is abundant with life! Everything is manifesting its intent—the plants are bearing fruit, the grass is high and green, the river warm and full of life, the sky full of songbirds. You, too, are in the season of manifestation—the season of "showing off" the gifts and talents you have to offer.

What you will need for this ritual:

- summer flowers, summer fruits, and other symbols of summer
- body paints, henna tattoo art, and/or mud
- objects that symbolize personal empowerment
- large towel or sheet
- gifts for other participants in ritual
- drums and other noisemakers
- food to eat after the ritual

Altar

Decorate the altar with symbols of personal empowerment. What symbolizes your power or gives you the sense of power? Place on the altar examples of your talents and gifts. Include summer flowers (wild ones, if you can find them), summer fruit, and other signs of summer.

Heart of the Ritual

This ritual is best done outside, but it can be done indoors as well. Either bring body paints, henna tattoo art, or a large bowl of mud. After creating a ritual space, sit in a circle with a large towel or sheet in the center.

Sit comfortably in a meditative posture and have someone slowly read the following meditation aloud:

Bring your awareness to your breath. Feel the breath as it moves in and out of your body. Let the breath flow by itself . . . feeling the breath of life move through you. Breath is a natural part of life. Breath is life. Feel this life, allowing it to move in and move out; watch it with your inner eye as it moves in and moves out. In and out . . . in and out . . . in and out . . . in and out . . .

You have a reason to be here. Everyone has a reason to be here. Right now nature is abundant in all its reasons. Birds are feeding their young, fields are full of crops, the sun is high in the sky. You too are here to create, to be someone special. You are meant to be here. What's your name; who are you? Why have you come to us? . . . Let the images come to you, naturally.

Play with the images or thoughts for a while, letting the breath flow by itself. Why did you come to us?

We are all glad you came, that you are part of our life. We want to know your name, who you are.

Now, open your eyes and look around you. In silence, look into each other's eyes and offer a welcoming look or smile to everyone.

Each one will then take turns sitting in the center of the circle and sharing with the rest of the group who they are. This is the time you will share what came to you in your meditation. Perhaps an image of an animal came to you. How are you like this animal? What might it mean to be a tiger, a bear, or a turtle? You may have had a word come to you such as "biologist" or "writer," or "friend." You may simply want to announce your given name and be gifted and recognized for this. Share with the others characteristics you like about yourself. Tell others accomplishments you had over the past year (what you have manifested). This can be anything—even a change in attitude or an awareness you've had recently. Or, it may be an award you won or some change you've made. Don't be modest. Boast of yourself, like everything else in the summer that is boasting of itself with color, fragrance, and song!

In response, everyone in the circle will reply to your sharing with their praise and gifts. Each one will step up to you and offer you praise and recognition and a small gift. The gift can be something that symbolizes their support of you.

(The type of gift will be decided at the planning meeting.) It is best if the gifts are unwrapped. The gifts can be something that you have made or taken from possessions you already have and want to give to another. Choose something that symbolizes the importance of this person in your life and community. Each of you then can have these symbols as reminders of the affection and esteem others have for you.

After everyone has been gifted and honored, it is time to celebrate your abundance, and the abundance of summer. Have the chosen noisemakers begin shaking rattles, singing a song, and/or beating on drums. Take turns using the body paints, henna, or mud to decorate each others' face and arms. You'll want to make sure you have enough mud or paint ready so everyone can get painted. If it is a warm summer day, you may want to wear swimsuits beneath your clothes and paint yourselves all over. Some do this ritual near water and go swimming later to wash off the mud or paint. Keep the drumming and shouting going until everyone is painted. Feel free to raise as much of this energy as you like by dancing and drumming and getting "decorated" by the mud or paint. Let yourselves be silly and have fun.

When everyone is painted and it feels right, end the ritual.

The food for this ritual can include roasted marshmallows, s'mores, fresh fruit, hot dogs, salad—all your favorite summer foods.

Fall Equinox Ritual (September 20–23)

This is the time of harvest and thanksgiving. Most of us already engage in a yearly thanksgiving ritual of eating big meals with family and friends. Sometimes we add our own special way of acknowledging what we are thankful for, such as sharing in conversation what we appreciate about the past year. You and your family or friends may want to add some or all of this Fall Equinox ritual to your Thanksgiving tradition.

The Fall Equinox ritual acknowledges all the blessings and abundance we have in our lives. Its intent includes eliciting feelings inside you of gratitude and thanksgiving. These powerful feeling states can have a positive impact on your mental, emotional, and spiritual well-being. And practicing having such feelings and thoughts gives you the ability to bring them on at other times in the year when perhaps you are feeling less grateful. Each ritual's impact, as you will discover, goes beyond the hours put into the ritual itself. To learn to bring gratitude into your daily life is a great reward.

Sometimes our abundance is great, while at other times it is quite slim. But the little we have can signify a lot and a little can be built upon. This is so because when we acknowledge what we have and what we are grateful for, we often find ourselves receiving more. Much like when we thank someone for a gift they have given us, they are likely to offer us more gifts because our gratitude made it more fun for them to give. Don't you feel good when someone thanks you for something? This is also true of the spiritual world. When we show our sincere gratitude for what we *have,* we are given more. And when we are thankful for what we have, we feel better because our focus is on what we *have* rather than what we *don't have.*

Too often we want more—to get more, achieve more, have more, without slowing down enough to truly appreciate and enjoy what we have in our lives. So, this ritual is also about appreciation for what has come into our lives. The summer ritual is about showing off our talents and whatever we have manifested this year; in the fall ritual we acknowledge what the earth, our Creator, Spirit, and others have brought to us. Sometimes to do this we must let go of what we feel angry and hurt about. When our focus is on our hurts and what we lack, we tend to forget what we have. We are then held back by our hard feelings, not letting ourselves enjoy what we do have. That is why we begin our thanksgiving ritual by "banishing," or casting out, the hurts we are holding on to.

"Our food comes from the super-market, but it originates in nature, springing from the soil and waters as living creatures."

—JAMES A. SWAN, PH.D., ECOPSYCHOLOGIST AND AUTHOR OF *THE POWER OF PLACE: SACRED GROUND IN NATURAL AND HUMAN ENVIRONMENTS*

> **What you will need for this ritual:**
> - fall fruits, fall flowers, grains, and corn
> - objects that symbolize what you are grateful for
> - drums and other noisemakers
> - favorite fall foods for ritual meal

Altar

You may want to decorate the altar with fall fruits, flowers, grains, and corn. Include objects that symbolize all that you are grateful for.

> *"My altar is full of pictures. When I'm depressed I look at all the pictures, all the good times and faces. Everything on my altar has some positive meaning for me."*
>
> ERIN, AGE 17

You may want to keep such objects of gratitude out on your altar year round, changing them each fall.

Heart of the Ritual

After you have created a ritual space, have the group sit in a circle and begin with a five-minute breath meditation (see page 146). When you are done with the meditation, have everyone slowly stand up. Have the designated noisemakers begin hitting the drums and sticks, with the group moving in a *counter*clockwise circle. Now do what is sometimes called the "Banishing Dance." Moving in this circle, each one shouts out something that has been holding them back, something or someone that has hurt them. Shout it out loud! The others will take it up and echo it back, shouting it out, loosening its hold on you. Hearing what you feel stuck in shouted back over and over again has the effect of dismantling its negative influence. (You will find this out for yourself when you do this ritual.) Then someone else shouts out a phrase, which is picked up and echoed back by the rest. Do this until everyone has at least shouted out one way they are being held back, one hurt that they are focusing on. After a period

"All ceremonies are ceremonies of thanksgiving."

—GKISEDTANAMOOGK, CITIZEN OF THE WAMPANOAG NATION, FROM *ANOQOU: CEREMONY IS LIFE ITSELF*

of silence, a designated person can simply ask, "Are there any hurts left to be said?" Here are just a few examples of what I have heard shouted in this ritual:

"I think I am stupid!" someone shouts. The others shout back several times: "I think I am stupid! I think I am stupid!"

"I am always worried about what others think!" The others: "I am always worried about what others think! I am always worried about what others think!"

"My relationship ended!" The others: "My relationship ended! My relationship ended!"

Once a young woman shouted, "No one really likes me; everyone is just pretending!" The group shouted this back for a long time (maybe others felt this way too), until everyone was either crying or laughing. Remember to let out your emotions when you are doing these rituals.

When everyone is finished "banishing" the bad, walk for a while in the same circle in silence, letting go silently of anything else you feel is holding you back.

Since the feast is an essential part of the Fall Equinox ritual—occurring *within,* not after, the heart of the ritual—enjoy a festive meal of all your favorite fall foods. During the meal, have everyone talk about what they are thankful for in their lives. Eat your food slowly, focusing on the abundance you are experiencing with the meal. In many traditions one plate of food is put out for the spirits who have been invited to the ritual.

When the meal is over, the ritual is over. In this and all rituals, remember to thank the spirits that were invited into the ritual.

Hunting Ritual

Another fall ritual can be for those of you who hunt animals and other natural foods in the wild. Such a ritual is often used as part of a coming-of-age for boys and girls in today's culture. Many young adults look upon their first hunting experience with their parent or mentor as an acknowledgment of their maturity.

A hunting ritual can be for those who hunt animals in the wild or appreciate such an experience. A hunting ritual is particularly valuable because it acknowledges that the food we eat (fruit, vegetables, meat, even grains) are *living things* that come from the earth. Eating a fast-food burger or getting our food out of a package puts a great deal of distance between us and the earth in which this food originated. When we are out of touch with where our food comes from, it creates a greater distance between the natural (and wild) world and ourselves. As in all the seasonal rituals, the hunting ritual helps to deepen our relationship with the earth we are dependent upon. If you do not eat meat, your hunting ritual can be about hunting for wild berries, asparagus, or even hunting in the woods to *watch* wildlife.

> **"Hunting stories represent a touchstone of honesty in a largely sanitized world. It is healthier for the soul to be biologically honest than to be politically correct."**
>
> —JAMES A. SWAN, PH.D., ECOPSYCHOLOGIST, FROM *IN DEFENSE OF HUNTING*

A Calling to the Hunt

by William E. Ishmael, wildlife biologist and mentor

We called friends who hunted and ones we knew appreciated the results of a good hunt (in this case the venison). Friends from the city (who never or seldom hunted) and the country (who held the yearly tradition of hunting) participated in our first hunting ritual. The purpose of the ritual was to acknowledge what we valued about the animal being hunted and the hunting experience. We borrowed from the Native American tradition of "calling" the animal to the hunter. Calling an animal to the hunter means the animal is being called to give its life to the hunter. Animals are hunting each other all the time. Buffalo gives its life to wolf, mouse gives its life to hawk, deer gives its life to man (and to coyote, crow, and wolf). The "calling" is about showing respect for the animal that you are about to kill. It is also a way to recognize that you are about to have a very intimate experience with this animal and with the great outdoors.

We set up our ritual site, which had a fire in the center of it. We all planned on bringing something to the ritual that symbolized what hunting meant to each of us. As the fire heated up we took turns telling our hunting stories and presenting the symbolic object to the group. As in many of the seasonal rituals, this ritual helped us value a tradition that people have been involved in for thousands of years—hunting. As each one spoke, my respect for the hunter and the hunted deepened. After everyone finished sharing, we called in the deer to each hunter by pounding drums and sticks and shouting out. Dinner followed, which was a venison stew and wild turkey chili.

"Hunting is a great teacher of life. It is a way of harnessing natural passions, that intensity of experiences during the Thundering Years. Learning to guide our passions with ethics and values moves us into adulthood. When you learn to hunt in an ethical manner, showing respect to animals, eating what you kill, taking only what you need, and giving back to nature by helping preserve wildlife habitat, preventing pollution, and reporting poachers, you will not only be a good hunter, you will be a good *citizen*, whose values will inspire other people to care about nature.
Mastering a lethal weapon—gun or bow—
is a sign that you are a responsible person."

—JAMES A. SWAN, PH.D., ECOPSYCHOLOGIST AND
AUTHOR OF *THE POWER OF PLACE: SACRED GROUND IN NATURAL
AND HUMAN ENVIRONMENTS*

Whatever time of year or life it is, now is the time for you to find your way outdoors—to the woods, a mountain pass, the river, or the prairie—to have your ritual with nature, Spirit, and community. Or, perhaps to make up your first altar, with your message to the natural or spiritual world.

Books, Resources, and Wisdomkeepers Related to This Chapter

ANOQCOU: Ceremony Is Life Itself, by Gkisedtanamoogk and Frances Hancock (Astarte Shell Press, 1993). A valuable book about ceremony and the importance of our respecting indigenous traditions while we borrow from their ceremonies. To order the book contact:

Astarte Shell Press
P.O. Box 10453
Portland, ME 04104

Boy into Man: A Fathers' Guide to Initiation of Teenage Sons, by Bernard Weiner (Transformational Press, 1992). This book is a guide for boys who want help putting together their own coming-of-age ritual. The young boys who participated in this ritual give their personal accounts, and one chapter explains the mother's role in such a ritual. Highly recommended.

Celebrating the Great Mother: A Handbook of Earth-Honoring Activities for Parents and Children, by Cait Johnson and Maura D. Shaw (Destiny Books, 1995). An excellent resource of rituals, dreams, and meditations honoring the earth, with special emphasis on seasonal rituals.

Seasons of Magic: A Girl's Journey, by Laurel Ann Reinhardt, Ph.D. (Llewellyn, 2001). A delightful book about a year in the life of a 12-year-old girl and her spiritual journey. Takes younger teens through seasonal rituals.

Of Water and the Spirit: Ritual, Magic and Initiation in the Life of an African Shaman, by Malidoma Patrice Somé (Penguin Books, 1994). A sharing of living African traditions, offered as a supportive guide for those needing strong messages of Spirit.

The Return of the Tribal Body Adornment Kit (Park Street Press, 1998). Useful kit for rituals and rites of passage. Contains a 64-page book and 5 different styles of body adornments.

Ritual: Power, Healing and Community, by Malidoma Patrice Somé (Swan-Raven & Company, 1993). Malidoma Somé was raised in a village in Burkina Faso, West Africa. He is initiated in the ancestral tribal traditions and is a medicine man in the Dagara pattern. This book shares his story of the Dagara traditions and how we might benefit from them.

The Sacred Pipe: Black Elk's Account of the Seven Rites of the Oglala Sioux, by Joseph Brown (New York Penguin, 1971). Describes rites of the Oglala Sioux.

The Spirit of Intimacy: Ancient Teachings in the Ways of Relationships, by Sobonfu E. Somé (Berkeley Hills Books, 1997). An easy-to-read book about ritual, community, and relationships. Helps give purpose to our rituals.

The Teen Spell Book: Magick for Young Witches, by Jamie Wood (Celestial Arts, 2001). This book is written for teens who are wanting to add some spell-magick to their lives and rituals. It draws from Wicca—an earth-based religion—and includes spells such as "Banish Self-Destructiveness." A most wonderful companion to any ritual.

Rites of Passage Experience (ROPE)
The Center for the Advancement of Youth, Family, and Community Services
P.O. Box 816
Glastonbury, CT 06033
(860) 633-5349
e-mail: TheCenter@rope.org
www.rope.org
ROPE students learn about their potential and gain self-confidence and problem-solving techniques. For further information see online resources below.

Selena Fox
Circle Sanctuary and *Circle Magazine*
P.O. Box 219
Mt. Horeb, WI 53572
e-mail: circle@mhtc.net
A resource on rituals, primarily on Nature Spirituality. *Circle Magazine* offers ideas, contacts, and articles on Pagan rituals. Circle Sanctuary also offers information and help on coming-of-age rituals, medicine walks, and shamanism.

Malidoma and Sobonfu Somé
Echoes of the Ancestors
4400 Keller Avenue, Suite 260
Oakland, CA 94605-4505
(510) 639-7637 Fax: (510) 482-1097
www.malidoma.com

Malidoma and Sobonfu offer lectures, workshops, a newsletter, and books and tapes on ritual. See online resources below for Web site information.

Ellen Hufschmidt
Ritual Consultant
3937 21st Avenue South
Minneapolis, MN 55407
(612) 721-1021
e-mail: Ritualink@aol.com
Ellen guides individuals, families, and classes through ritual. She has worked in many schools teaching ritual to students and teachers. She is especially interested in working with adolescents and helping with rites-of-passage rituals and conducts rites of passage for young women and their mothers.

Online Resources

African Centered Rites of Passage
www.mawasi.com/RoP/RoP.html
This site is full of information centered around African and African American traditions and rites of passage, with research papers, resources and lists of organizations, and people interested in and writing about ritual rites of passage.

Echoes of the Ancestors, Inc.
www.malidoma.com
Echoes of the Ancestors, Inc., is a nonprofit group headed by Malidoma Somé and Sobonfu Somé. It is "dedicated to the preservation of the Wisdom of the Dagara and other indigenous tribes of West Central Africa." The purpose of this group is to bring the wisdom of Africa to the West. The site

contains information about the projects of Malidoma and Sobonfu and links to audio files of talks about African rituals and the African Wheel.

Life Rites

www.liferites.org

This is the site for the Life Rites organization, which "provides practical advice and guidance on Rites of Passage and Life Celebrations, empowering people to do things for themselves." It includes a special page on puberty rituals and a link to the Rites of Passage WebRing.

The Hero's Journey

A Modern Day Rite of Passage for Boys and Girls
Raphael Peter
P.O. Box 3261
Asheville, NC 28802
(828) 274-7223
e-mail: douglas@caseinc.net
Offers workshops for groups or schools. The mission of The Hero's Journey is to offer young people a series of experiences that will provide healthy, empowering choices in diverse settings.

Rites of Passage Experience

www.rope.org

This is a very informative site of the Center for the Advancement of Youth, Family and Community Services, Inc. The page says ritual should be used to reconnect people with their essential beliefs, help them through periods of stress and transition, provide social connection, and provide a healthy transition to adulthood. The site walks you through the process of contemporary rites of passage.

Ritual Arts

www.ritualarts.com

This site tells us that our souls are hungry for ritual and the importance it can bring to our lives. A discussion of reviving ritual for the healthy coming-of-age and the psychological initiation of young people into manhood and womanhood is included in the text.

Thundering Years

www.thunderingyears.com

This site offers you the opportunity to link to others who are practicing ritual and to share your experiences.

How joyful to look upon the Awakened
and to keep company with the wise.

Follow then the shining ones,
the wise, the Awakened, the loving,
for they know how to work and forbear.

But if you cannot find friend or master
to go with you,
travel on alone—
like a king who has given away his
kingdom,
like an elephant in the forest.

—FROM THE *DHAMMAPADA*
(SAYINGS OF THE BUDDHA)

Chapter Six

Meditations for the Mindful Warrior

"The path of the mindful-warrior
involves much sitting
—without falling asleep.
Just as the eyes grow heavy
—a clap of THUNDER!
A rush of cleansing tears
Hoof beats
Hard rain
Brings shining new worlds
Seeds push up
Much to do!"

—SHANNON KING, POET

"Mindfulness is the basis of happiness."

—THICH NHAT HANH, VIETNAMESE ZEN MONK

I N TRADITIONAL CULTURES meditation was part of daily life. Today more and more people are taking up a meditation practice. Why? Why is meditation considered so valuable? For many, it is to hear the "still voice of God." For others it is to tap in to their inner wisdom, to heal themselves of anxiety, and to bring more peace and happiness into their lives. Each of us will have our own reasons.

One aspect of living the Warrior's life is to live in the present moment and to learn to appreciate each day on its own terms. A meditation practice can help you do this. Meditation is simple, yet you can have a variety of powerful experiences with a meditation practice. Through the practice of meditation you can learn to use your Thunder-energy in a genuine and creative way.

A meditation practice provides simple but powerful insights and strength needed for the journey into adulthood and beyond. It is a way to cultivate more courage, more love, and more gratitude in all areas of our lives. The central objective held within the practice of mindfulness meditation is an appreciation for the present moment. Rather than ignoring the present experience through constant worry, planning, or seeking the future, we are given a simple tool to bring ourselves back to the "here and now."

Chögyam Trungpa in his book *Shambhala: The Sacred Path of the Warrior* writes: "Our life is an endless journey; it is like a broad highway that extends infinitely into the distance. The practice of meditation provides a vehicle to travel on that road." He goes on to describe the importance of meditation on the spiritual path of the Warrior and how "sitting" in a meditative posture is a way of expressing our warriorship and our courage. Jack Kornfield, another well-known meditation instructor, describes a meditation practice as one of the most important acts we can do to improve our own well-being and the well-being of the entire planet. A meditation practice offers us what is called "direct experience"—we open up more and more to experiencing our lives more fully, more creatively, and more sensuously. We accomplish this by practicing attentiveness to the moment. We become more aware of the *present* experience, whatever it may be, and thus have a more *direct* experience. Most of us, however, are running around worrying, planning, or judging what we are do-ing—all of which take us away from direct experience.

We can derive many benefits from meditation, including peace of mind, bet-ter skill in athletic achievements, ability to concentrate, calmness, increased creativity, more enjoyment of life's experiences, loving-kindness to ourselves and others, and more acceptance and tolerance of the difficult times in our lives.

"I began meditating because I experience social anxiety. It was getting worse and worse, so in my junior year of high school my parents found me a therapist who teaches mindfulness meditation. I'm still working at being less anxious and the meditation really makes a difference. On days I meditate I always notice a better feeling I carry around inside of me. When I don't meditate the peacefulness and good feeling are so much less. Meditation is going to be part of my life, I know this. That good feeling I get tells me that someday I will be free of my anxiety."

CECILIA, AGE 16

The Practice of Meditation

"The Kingdom of God is within you."

—LUKE 17:12

"The same energy that moves thoughts through the mind, moves the stars across the sky."

—STEPHEN LEVINE, MEDITATION TEACHER
AND AUTHOR OF *A GRADUAL AWAKENING*

A meditation practice begins with sitting down. You can either sit in a chair with your feet on the floor or sit on the ground in a meditative posture. A medi-tative posture is one in which your back is not fully resting against anything (unless you have back problems). So if you choose a chair, rest your lower back (not the entire back) softly against the chair's back, or do not rest your back at all. Sitting on the floor, you can sit with your knees crossed, resting your buttocks on a pillow or a meditation cushion. You can have only one knee crossed, if this is most comfortable for you. In both positions it is important to have your back straight but not stiff or arched. This is known as an "alert" spine, one that is straight but not too stiff or too relaxed; it creates the best body posture for a meditation practice. You should be comfortable but not so comfortable that it is easy to fall asleep or to drift into daydreaming.

Meditation teachers suggest that we imagine ourselves a mountain, sitting up proudly, with our lower spine reaching down to the earth and the crown of our head opening to the heavens. While being aware of your "body sitting upright," allow your jaw to relax open and your tongue to rest naturally at the roof of your mouth. This makes breathing through the nostrils easier, and more natural. Once in the posture, gently close your eyes.

> "You sit simply, as a warrior, and out of that, a sense of individual dignity arises."
>
> —CHÖGYAM TRUNGPA, TIBETAN LAMA, FROM SHAMBHALA: THE SACRED PATH OF THE WARRIOR

Mindfulness Meditation: Finding the Breath in your Meditation

> "Student, tell me what is God? He is the breath inside the breath."
>
> —KABIR, INDIAN MYSTIC AND POET

Breath is commonly associated with power and wisdom. The Bible refers to "the *breath* of life." In the Pawnee story of *Bear Medicine Woman*, breath is the means to exhibit power. The Zuni believe the human spirit *(pinanne)* resides in the breath. Breath is considered the life principle—without it there would be no life. The connection between breath and Spirit is part of Western and Eastern traditions. Controlled breathing is part of Muslim spiritual experience and Tantric meditation, and it is most developed in the Hindu system of Yoga, where breathing aligns you directly with Spirit. Many traditions view breath as a Divine gift, which is returned to the "Giver" at one's time of death.

In mindfulness meditation, it is the breath that brings us into the moment, and where we find our peace and courage. So, as you sit in your "mountain"

146

posture, bring your attention gently to your breath, while you simply and naturally breathe in and breathe out. With your eyes closed, practice finding your breath. Are you drawn to the breath as it rises and falls from your belly? Or can you feel the sensation of your breath as it moves in and out of your body, softly brushing the top of your nostrils? After a few breaths, choose to have one of these locations be the place you focus on your breath.

Once you choose a focus point, either the rising and falling of the belly or the brush of air as it moves in and out of your nostrils, keep your attention there. Keeping your focus on one place—this alone helps calm the mind.

> *"My meditation technique is to sit in front of my altar and light all my candles. I sit on the floor and stare softly at the candles. Sometimes I sit for five minutes, sometimes for half an hour. When I have a big problem I'm dealing with, my meditations can be longer. I've been doing meditation and ritual since I was a little girl. It comes naturally to me."*
>
> ERIN, AGE 17

"Be still and know that I am God."

—PSALMS, 46:10

You can record the following in your own voice or have a friend read it slowly out loud. I recommend you read through it a few times before you actually practice it. After a few practices, you will have the basics down so you will be able to meditate without this reminder. However, some find it helpful to listen to this meditation guide every time they meditate.

Continue to sit comfortably, yet alert . . . holding your body in the meditative posture, like a mountain . . . alert and tall. Slowly close your eyes and begin to let go of the experiences, thoughts, and expectations you brought with you. . . . Let go . . . softening around the moods, experiences, and thoughts. Let them come . . . and let them go . . . like waves of an ocean. Allow yourself to be fully present for this practice of meditation, letting go of worries you may have been carrying with you. As you notice what's present—the thoughts that are on your mind, or the physical sensations that are rising and falling in your body—let them come and go as they will. Get a

sense of the container called "the body." Notice the physical sensations of this meditating body. Get an overall sense of this body sitting. Try to not hold on to any thoughts, but let them go. As you do this, become aware of your breathing.

Notice that in the middle of all these thoughts and feelings there is a soft sensation of breathing. Now bring your attention to this breathing. . . . Letting the breath flow by itself, notice the physical sensations of breath, the coolness of the in-breath brushing against the top of your nostrils, or the rise and fall of your belly as you breathe. Notice the physical sensation of breath as it moves in your body. Let yourself feel your life-giving breath. Rest in the breathing. Rest in the meditating body. . . . Bring your awareness gently to it. . . .

Keep some of your awareness on the body as it continues to sit alert and tall. Be aware of this body meditating. Maintain some of your awareness on the body as you bring most of your attention to your breath. . . .

After just a few breaths you will notice that a thought carries you off on its own wave of experience and feeling. Notice where this wave of thought has taken you, let your awareness go there, then gently return your awareness back to the breath, and to this meditating body. Rest again and again in the breath by gently focusing your attention on the physical sensations of your breath . . . letting the breath flow through you, naturally. Hold a mindful attention on your breath, noticing when your attention moves away on another wave of thought or physical sensation, returning your awareness to the sensations of your breathing and the body meditating.

Now, when you are ready to stop meditating, gently bring your awareness to your entire body. Feel the body sitting in its upright, meditative posture. . . . At this time you may say a prayer of dedication (see page 151) as you gently open your eyes and refocus your attention on your environment.

Taming the Wild Mind

You will quickly discover that your attention wanders away from the breath many, many, *many* times during your meditation practice. This is quite common. Those who have been meditating for more than forty years talk about how their attention still wanders away from the breath! Jack Kornfield reminds all his students that much of the meditation practice even for him is "returning his awareness to the breath." He also tells us "every moment of sitting brings you closer to happiness." *No time in meditation is wasted,* even if your attention is on the breath for only a minute. However, since the object of your meditation in mindfulness practice *is* the breath, you want to return your attention to the breath whenever you find it has moved away from it.

This is part of the meditation practice—to be aware of where your mind is! When you find your mind has wandered off the breath, return your awareness back to the breath, *gently*. Be kind to yourself, not judging yourself or your practice. Returning your awareness again and again to the breath is often called "bringing the mind home." It is a process of slowly and gently taming the mind. Do you ever notice how your thoughts seem to boss you around? A worry or a negative thought gets hold of you and it just doesn't seem to want to let go? How about those days when everything is going great, then one minor bad event and, *crash,* you're swimming in negative thoughts! One thing is for certain, you have lots of company. Unless we have a meditation practice of some kind where we learn to tame our minds, our minds seem to get out of hand quite often. The mind is busy—wondering, worrying, fantasizing, guessing about the future—until we tame it and bring it home. Home to the breath. Home to the present moment.

Learning how to bring your mind back to the breath in meditation gives you tremendous power to bring yourself to the moment at other times in your life. This can be great for athletes, for example, helping them "keep their eyes on the ball." Artists and writers often speak of how mindfulness meditation helps them focus on their creativity. Those addicted to drugs or alcohol speak of how

> "If your mind isn't clouded by unnecessary things,
>
> This is the best season of your life."
>
> —WU-MEN, ZEN MASTER

149

meditation helps them stay clean. Those suffering from social anxiety or panic attacks speak to the healing effects of meditation.

To help you tame your mind you can use a technique called *labeling*. When you notice that your awareness has moved to a thought you can simply label it "thinking, thinking." Then, again return your attention to your breathing, resting with the meditating body. Any time you find your mind is on a thought during your meditation practice, simply label it "thinking, thinking," instead of following that thought to its conclusion or building upon it like a story. *Always return to the breath, gently and kindly.* Labeling thoughts during meditation frees you from getting caught up in anxious worries or fantasies. This gives you the power to decide how you are going to use your mind.

Another technique to help you bring your attention to the breath is to *count* the breaths. As you breathe out, you are letting go, and as you breathe in, you count the breath, up to *ten*. It is important to use the *counting* as a way to bring your awareness to the *physical sensation of breath* and not to meditate on the counting. Labeling and counting are ways to help you bring your awareness to the breath.

Remember, simply sitting quietly and softly listening to your breath is enough to experience the many benefits of meditation.

> *"I felt my body become like a soft rubber band that went down into the earth. It didn't seem to stop. It was a sensation I enjoyed, so I just sat in it for as long as it lasted, focusing on my breathing."*
> —SADIE, AGE 18

You will experience many sensations ranging from deep emotions to perfect stillness as you meditate. *There are no wrong or right ways to feel in meditation.* The key is to simply allow the feelings and sensations to arise as you rest in your breathing. Sometimes you will experience "highs" during your meditation, while other times you may feel sad, quiet, bored, or agitated. Whatever the emotions that arise, practice sitting upright like a mountain until your meditation time is complete.

"For one who has conquered the mind, the mind is the best of friends. But for one who has failed to do so, his very mind will be his greatest enemy."

—*BHAGAVAD-GITA*, HINDU SCRIPTURE

If you are just beginning to meditate, sit for five to ten minutes each day. The benefits of only five minutes of meditation on a regular basis are vast. After about three months of the regular practice of meditation you will be ready to sit for fifteen to twenty minutes at a time. *It is much more important to be meditating in twenty years than to do long sits at the start.* This is not a contest to see who can sit the longest. The benefits come from a regular, consistent practice of meditation. Much like practicing a sport or musical instrument, it's the commitment that results in its many benefits.

Dedicating Your Meditation

May my mind remain always steady and firm,
unswerving and unshaken;
May it become stronger every day. May I bear and endure with patience the
deprivation of dear ones and occurrences of undesired evils.
May universal love pervade the world and may ignorance
of attachment remain far away. May nobody
speak unkind, bitter, and harsh words!
May disease and pestilence never spread, may the people live in peace,
may the highest religion of ahimsa (noninjury) pervade the
whole world and may it bring universal good! Amen.

—JAIN PRAYER*

"As the web issues from the spider, as little sparks proceed from fire, so from the one soul proceed all breathing animals, all worlds, all the gods, and all beings."

—BRIHAD-ARANYAKA
UPANISHAD, HINDU
SCRIPTURE

All spiritual traditions have dedication prayers, used to dedicate one's practice and spiritual efforts to benefit others. Part of the power of all the practices mentioned in this book is that they also intend to benefit the community or planet as a whole. They recognize that we are all part of the same web of life.

A dedication prayer following a time of meditation is a testimony that our meditation practice not only benefits us as we sit, but benefits everyone. As we

---

*Jainism is an Eastern Indian religion with non-harm as its central code. It was the religion of Mahatma Gandhi, and there are more than 50,000 Jains in the United States.

improve upon our own well-being, everyone we come in contact with is positively affected. You have likely heard of Chinese hermits, Tibetan monks, or Christian monastics who spend months to years of their lives in meditation. They are meditating for us all, to help bring more peace and compassion into this complex and hurting world of ours. Some monks and nuns dedicate their entire life to a meditation practice for this purpose. But we don't have to go sit in a cave or a monastery to benefit others through our meditation practice. It takes great courage and discipline to practice mindfulness meditation amid all the distractions of our everyday world! And every time we practice mindfulness, we are bringing a little more peace and sanity to this chaotic and busy world of ours.

Here is a variation on a common dedication prayer:

> *Through the power and truth of this practice,*
> *May all beings have happiness and the causes of happiness;*
> *May all be free from suffering and the causes of suffering;*
> *May all be happy.*
> *May we all live in harmony,*
> *Without too much attachment and too much bitterness,*
> *And live believing in the beauty of all living things.*

By dedicating our practice to others we are asking for *all* to be free from suffering and pain. Our efforts then in meditation are extended beyond just ourselves and become far reaching. "May we all live in harmony" means not being hard on ourselves or others, or not being too caught up in the troubles of our lives. We ask to live "without too much attachment," because when we are too attached to something we suffer, feeling "we gotta have it." Meditation teaches us to feel our wholeness without so much attachment to what we have (or bitterness about what we don't have). In our dedication, we wish this nonattachment and peace of mind for everyone. Finally, we are dedicating our meditation to everyone's well-being, "believing in the beauty of all," believing that everyone and every living creature has a right to life and happiness—even those who anger us.

"Just as the great oceans have but one taste, the taste of salt, so too is but one taste fundamental to all true teachings of the Way, and this is the taste of freedom."

—THE BUDDHA

You can create your own dedication or even use The Lord's Prayer (Christian) or the Shema Yisrael (Jewish) to dedicate your practice. "May my practice benefit all who are in need of peace," is a prayer of dedication that one young man says after each of his meditations.

Exploring Your Anger and Thunder with Mindfulness Meditation

> "Freedom is born out of our capacity to work with any energy or difficulty that arises."
>
> —JACK KORNFIELD, MEDITATION INSTRUCTOR AND AUTHOR, FROM *A PATH WITH HEART*

> "The happiness of your life depends on the quality of your thoughts."
>
> —MARCUS AURELIUS, ROMAN EMPEROR

Meditation and sitting quietly with oneself can be helpful in dealing with anger and other intense emotions, such as jealousy, grief, and anxiety. Here's a simple meditation that allows you to explore your anger or other intense emotions. Anger is a valuable emotion to listen to because when we are angry we are angry *for a reason.* But too often we get so caught up in the feelings of anger we lose sight of what we are angry about. Then we often misuse our anger to hurt ourselves or others. Getting angry about something can trigger more anger that we may have bottled up—so we can easily become "blinded" by our anger. Taking ten minutes to sit quietly, giving your attention to your anger, can give you the power and freedom to do something meaningful with this emotion.

You can record this meditation yourself and play it back or have it read slowly by a friend.

Sit quietly in an alert, yet comfortable, meditative posture. Begin by finding your breath, slowly closing your eyes, and practicing a few minutes of the mindfulness meditation. Listen to the rhythm of your breathing by bringing your awareness softly to your breath. Just let the breath flow by itself and for ten in-breaths and ten out-breaths listen to the breath's rhythm. . . . Begin to open up to your anger, instead of tightening around it. Use the image of

153

opening your hand, rather than tightening your grasp into a fist around something . . . open up to it, loosen to it . . . breathe into your feelings. Make room for your anger. . . .

Where in your body does your anger arise? Be curious rather than caught up in the anger. What physical sensations accompany your anger? Does your body feel as if it wants to jump out of its skin? Do you feel tense anywhere? Is your body tingling or jittery? Be like a curious detective and simply observe with your own inner awareness what sensations are in your "angry" body. As you do this, continue to have some of your awareness on your breath. Use your breath to keep yourself focused on the meditation if you find your thoughts wandering off to other things.

Now bring your attention to what you are angry about. What fantasies or plans go with this feeling of anger? What might you want to destroy? Who or what do you see as the cause of this anger? Do you hold any intent to harm anyone, including yourself?

Notice how the anger affects your body, heart, and mind. Listen inwardly for the answers to the following questions. (After your meditation, you may want to write in your journal the answers that come.) While still experiencing the many sensations, thoughts, and feelings that accompany your anger and intensity, use the following questions to gain more understanding and help. Answer each question for yourself. The one you may want to skip may hold the most potent insight. Again listen inwardly for the answers to these questions:

What do I usually do when I am angry?

How have I caused myself or others harm with my anger in the past?

What could I do differently this time?

What in this situation is simply unavoidable and needs my acceptance?

What can I learn from this situation and from my anger?

When you are ready, slowly open your eyes and refocus your attention on your surroundings.

> "He then sits and meditates as long as he deems proper and then he rises and calls on the Spirit of the Winds and of the Clouds and of the THUNDER to help him, and makes an offering of smoke to these . . ."
>
> "PREPARING FOR A SUN DANCE" FROM *LAKOTA BELIEF AND RITUAL*

When taking the time to meditate and reflect on our anger we often find a hidden gem among the ruins of our feelings and experience. Most often, the help we seek is *within the problem or situation* that is causing us to feel angry. This means that underneath all our anger, jealousy, or anxiety is often the answer we need. So, *slowing down* and becoming mindful of our anger may be all we need to do to find a solution to our pain. Then we experience the freedom Jack Kornfield refers to earlier. The freedom in not letting our anger dominate us. Please remember that an important part of our meditation practice is to be gentle and kind with *ourselves*. Let the anger and intensity arise without becoming hard on yourself or others. This is a great accomplishment itself!

"I constantly thought about death. So much so, I found myself talking about it a lot to my friends and family. When I would watch a show on television about someone's sorry life, my response would always be 'I would just kill myself.' Everyone got scared when I actually attempted suicide. It seemed to just happen. I was angry with my younger sister again, so I just grabbed a bunch of pills and swallowed fast. I got really freaked out and told my sister, who then called 911. I ended up in the hospital where they told my parents I needed counseling. My counselor taught me to meditate and to get a better understanding of myself. I've come to understand that my thoughts about death are my way of handling my anger. Now I'm learning to find different ways to react to bad news. I am feeling a little more hopeful about myself. And I've noticed that when I take the time to meditate I always feel better."

—MERRA, AGE 16

"Do you have the patience to wait till the mud settles and the water is clear? Can you remain unmoving till the right action arises by itself?"

—LAO-TZU, ANCIENT TAOIST SAGE AND AUTHOR OF *TAO-TE-CHING*

Loving-Kindness Meditation

"The practice of loving-kindness is revolutionary because it has the power to radically change our lives, helping us cultivate true happiness in our ourselves, and genuine compassion for others."

—SHARON SALZBURG, MEDITATION INSTRUCTOR AND AUTHOR, FROM *LOVING-KINDNESS: THE REVOLUTIONARY ART OF HAPPINESS*

We all long to be loved. We all want to fall in love and find happiness. We all want to belong to something worthwhile and be recognized for our own worth. Throughout our lives, we long to feel good about ourselves and find a greater sense of connection with Spirit or the Divine and others. In fact, all of these longings are part of our willingness to be on a spiritual path. Our commitment to the life of a Spiritual Warrior comes through listening and responding to these universal longings. The meditation practice of loving-kindness helps cultivate happiness in our lives and in the lives of others. The beautiful thing about this meditation is that it encourages us to accept and love ourselves *as we are*, rather than withholding such good feelings *until* we are thinner, smarter, popular, and so on. It is about opening our hearts up to ourselves and to others, however we are.

"Thoughts are like arrows: once released, they strike their mark. Guard them well or one day you may be your own victim."

—Navajo proverb

Spiritual practices throughout time and around the world call for us to love ourselves and each other.

Jack Kornfield, in his book, *A Path with Heart*, expresses this universal truth that "all other spiritual teachings are in vain if we cannot love. Even the most exalted states and the most exceptional spiritual accomplishments are unimportant if we cannot be happy in the most basic and ordinary ways, if, with our hearts, we cannot touch one another and the life we have been given." The teachings of both the Buddha and Jesus were founded on the practice of love.

If I speak in the tongues of men and of angels, but have not love, I am a noisy gong or a clanging cymbal. And, if I have prophetic powers, and understand all mysteries, but have not love, I am nothing. If I give away all I have, and if I deliver my body to be burned, but have not love, I gain nothing. . . . So faith, hope, and love abide, these three; but the greatest of these is love.

—1 Corinthians 13:1–3, 13

The thought manifests as the word
The word manifests as the deed;
The deed develops into habit;
And habit hardens into character;
So watch the thought and its way with care,

And let it spring from love
Born out of concern for all beings . . .
As the shadow follows the body,
as we think, so we become.

—FROM *THE DHAMMAPADA* (SAYINGS OF THE BUDDHA)

When we sit and meditate on love, we bring on the feelings and experience of love. We cannot be sitting and thinking of hating someone or ourselves and at the same time be meditating on love. That is how the Loving-Kindness Meditation works and why it is so powerful. As you sit and meditate on love, *love comes to you.*

> *"I spent a few years learning mindfulness meditation from many Buddhist teachers. Many times I would be sitting in a ten-day retreat in silence beating up on myself! I would be thinking how I should be doing better, or I would silently compare myself to others. The teacher would then talk about loving-kindness and how important it is to bring the feelings and attitude of love and kindness to whatever our thoughts and emotions are at the time. So, I would practice bringing love to my judgmentalness, and sooner or later the harshness would melt and the feelings of love, generosity, and kindness would find their way to my heart and mind. It is always about practicing. Like, practicing the piano. When we practice, we are actually playing the instrument and, at the same time, we are getting more skilled at our playing. It is the same with the Loving-Kindness Meditation. We practice it and each time we practice it we notice that love and kindness toward ourselves and others increase. Then, as we go out into our daily life, we feel more of this love and kindness toward ourselves and others. We also find we can bring the loving-kindness practice to situations that are difficult."*
>
> —ANNETTE, AGE 24

This meditation too can be recorded in your own voice or read aloud slowly by a friend:

Sit comfortably and slowly close your eyes. Let your body relax more than

"All spiritual traditions speak of the importance of greeting negative circumstances with love."

—SHINZEN YOUNG, BUDDHIST MEDITATION TEACHER

"As he thinketh in his heart, so is he."

—PROVERBS 23:7

you would in the breath meditations. Let yourself be comfortable and rested. As best you can, let your mind rest, letting go of your worries or the planning that often goes on. Take a few minutes to bring your awareness to your breath . . . bringing your awareness more and more into this time of meditation. Notice the various sensations in the body, and continue to relax and bring your awareness to your breathing and body.

Now imagine breathing into your heart. On each breath imagine your heart softening and opening. And say quietly to yourself:

> May I be filled with loving-kindness;
> May I be strong and happy;
> May I feel good about myself;
> May all my dreams come true.

Imagine each cell, molecule, and atom in your body filling up with the meaning of these words. Repeat these phrases again and again, letting the meaning fill you up. Continue to breathe in and out, saying these words of love for yourself. Feel your heart open up to you.

Slowly begin to include others in the room, or others in your life you care about. Imagine your heart opening up and sending some of this loving-kindness and well-wishing to everyone near to your heart. Bring to mind all the people you love and care about. Say these phrases softly to them:

> May you be filled with loving-kindness;
> May you be strong and happy;
> May you feel good about yourself;
> May all your dreams come true.

Send them this love, while always keeping some for yourself. This keeps you replenished. Include friends, neighbors, teachers, animals, people you know who are suffering and need your loving thoughts.

Imagine sending it anywhere and everywhere.

"The habit of ignoring our present moments in favor of others yet to come leads directly to a pervasive lack of awareness of the web of life in which we are embedded."

—JON KABAT-ZINN, PH.D., MEDITATION INSTRUCTOR AND AUTHOR OF WHEREVER YOU GO, THERE YOU ARE

Try including someone you're angry with. How does it feel to send them these kind thoughts and loving feelings?

Now sit softly in your breath for a while as you fill yourself and the world with your love and kindness. When you feel ready, slowly open your eyes.

As you practice this meditation you will experience a deeper and deeper connection to yourself and to others. At first, it may feel awkward or difficult—this is quite common. Keep practicing it, and soon you will find yourself feeling more love for yourself and for others. As Buddhist meditation teacher Shinzen Young reminds us: "There are two main goals in the spiritual life. One is to have a sense of complete freedom and fulfillment for oneself. The other is to be a source of love and goodwill to others. If you can experience negativity (anger, hate, jealousy) as *energy*, and 'recolor' that energy as love and goodwill, and let it spread out from you, then you will be simultaneously achieving those two goals. With practice, any person can experience a freedom through such a practice."

And finally, our meditation practice isn't about becoming something better because we feel we are something bad. It is about opening up to ourselves as we are, accepting and making room for all that is inside us—the goodness, the creativity, and the messiness. If we do this practice trying to force ourselves to be a "perfect spiritual human being," we will only hurt ourselves. Meditation practice is about becoming better friends with ourselves and the world around us. A friend accepts us as we are, while we continue to grow and change.

> **"The ills from which we are suffering have had their seat in the very foundation of human thought."**
>
> —PIERRE TEILHARD DE CHARDIN, JESUIT PRIEST AND AUTHOR OF *PHENOMENON OF MAN*

A Journey into Guided Meditations

"We increase concentration and memory skills, improve academic learning, and excel in sports through the use of imagery."

—MAUREEN MURDOCK, ARTIST AND EDUCATOR

Guided meditations are used with the specific intent to create certain experiences. In the Sacred Tree Meditation the purpose is to connect us more with the groundedness of the earth and the expansiveness of the heavens, of which

we are all a part. The Ancient Scroll Meditation helps us reach inside ourselves for the deeper wisdom and intuition we hold. We can go inside for such guidance, especially when we are getting mixed advice from others. A guided meditation takes us beyond focusing on the breath to bringing forth a particular experience.

Guided meditations use our imagination to help us get what we want out of life. But guided meditations alone won't make things happen. Ultimately, we need to have the confidence and courage to go out and do things for ourselves. Guided meditations can, however, help build up our confidence and courage. Such meditations are a way to give time and attention to parts of ourselves that strengthen us. What we give time and attention to in return gives time to us— when we meditate on our strengths, we become stronger.

When doing a guided meditation it is very important to *breathe*. Sometimes when we concentrate on something, such as focusing on an idea, we hold our breath, or do shallow breathing. *Begin each guided meditation with a few minutes of mindfulness meditation.* Then as you move through your guided meditation, you can always return to the breath to help you stay focused on your meditation.

Sacred Tree Meditation

> "It may be that some little root of the Sacred Tree still lives. Nourish it then, that it may leaf and bloom and fill with singing birds."
>
> —BLACK ELK, OGLALA SIOUX HOLY MAN

This meditation is a favorite among many young people. It helps connect us to the great earth, nourishing the "little root" from the Sacred Tree that lives inside each of us. It also opens us up to wisdom from above, so we "bloom and fill" ourselves "with singing birds." Those who favor this meditation speak of a sense of strength, courage, and "groundedness" during and after the meditation.

You can record this meditation for yourself or have a friend slowly read it to you:

Sit in a chair with both feet on the floor. Close your eyes and softly focus on your breath for a few minutes, allowing your attention to come into the moment. Let go of concerns. . . . Bring your awareness to your breath as you breathe in . . . and out, naturally.

Have your awareness go to the bottoms of your feet. Feel your feet on the floor. Imagine roots coming out the bottoms of both feet. Have the roots move down through the floor and through all the layers of earth, rock, and water. With little effort, and remembering to breathe, imagine them moving down, down, until they reach the center of the earth. Once they reach the center of the earth imagine your roots pulling up energy and nutrients from the earth's center. Draw this energy all the way up through your roots into your feet, up your legs, and up into your solar plexus area, above and behind your navel. Let the earth energy move all around in this area and then go down and out through the same roots, so you have a continual cycle of earth energy moving up and down. You are the Sacred Tree; your roots still live.

Now, like the great Sacred Tree, open the top of your head and let your branches reach up and out. Imagine the sun's energy coming down into the top of your head, traveling slowly down your spine until it meets up with the earth energy in your solar plexus. Have the two energies mix together, as trees mix the energy of earth and sky. Sit as a Sacred Tree, receiving all the nutrients from the earth and all the strength and wisdom from the sun and sky. Feel your sacredness. You are the Sacred Tree. Feel your strength and wisdom. You are the Sacred Tree. You are the Sacred Tree. Feel the groundedness from the earth and the vision from the sky. You, my friend, are the Sacred Tree.

When you feel finished bring your awareness back to your breath. Rub your hands together and gently touch the palms of your hands to the ground as you slowly open your eyes.

"Whoever sits under the tree receives and shares this circulation of power and cleansing energy. Feel your whole body as part of this network of life, tradition and energy."

—CAITLÍN MATTHEWS, WRITER AND SINGER, FROM *THE ELEMENTS OF CELTIC TRADITION*

You may do this meditation sitting up against a favorite tree, imagining yourself becoming like the tree. When you are done, you may want to sit and remember the experience or write it down in your journal. If there is a group sharing in the meditation, you may want to tell your experiences to each other.

The Ancient Scroll Meditation

"Earth and heaven are in us."

—MAHATMA GANDHI, INDIAN NATIONALIST AND SPIRITUAL LEADER

"Your imagination is your preview of life's coming attractions."

—ALBERT EINSTEIN, PHYSICIST

An Ancient Scroll is a "manuscript," or book, believed to contain all the wisdom of all time within it. It is not a book one checks out from the library. Instead, it is available to each of us through the power of our imagination. This Ancient Scroll Meditation allows you to get in touch with a place *inside* yourself that holds this wisdom. When in need of guidance or ideas, go to *your* Ancient Scroll through this meditation. It's important to do this (and every guided meditation) slowly, and to *trust what comes*. If you have concerns or questions about what you receive in this or any other guided meditation share it with someone you trust, or contact the author (see chapter resource list).

"You give birth to that to which you fix your mind."

—ANTOINE DE SAINT-EXUPERY, AUTHOR OF *THE LITTLE PRINCE*

You can record this meditation for yourself or have a friend slowly read it to you:

Close your eyes and focus on your breath for a few moments. Send your roots into the ground and open your head to the sky as you do in the Sacred Tree Meditation. Continue to breathe freely. Imagine yourself walking down a path. This path represents the path of your life. As you walk, you have a destination in mind. You are going to the place on your path where your Ancient Scroll is kept. This scroll is your "book of life," and it can help you with questions you might have about what is going on in your life at this time. Continue walking down the path. In front of you now you see a container that holds your scroll. Your scroll may be inside a castle or simply placed under a tree. The container may be a chest, box, basket, or a vase. . . . Walk up to the container and open it. Bring out the Ancient Scroll, opening up to a page that has a message or answer on it for you. Read the message. . . . What is the message for you? . . . Let the message come to you easily. It may be a sentence or two or one word. It may be an image or a strong thought or feeling. It can even be a memory or a dream remembered. . . . Trust what you get. Remember what it says, or what you experience. Open up to it without trying to force something or put too much into it . . . simply allow for something to come to you. . . . Return the Ancient Scroll to its container and begin walking back up the path. Walk until you see a nice open field. Imagine yourself sitting down in the field in a patch of warm sunlight. Feel the sunlight on your face and body. . . . Now gradually return your attention to your breath, letting the breath move in and out by itself. Softly focus on the breath. Relax back into the breath. Rub your hands together and gently touch your palms to the ground. When you feel ready, slowly open your eyes.

You may want to write in your journal what message you received. The Ancient Scroll can be a group meditation in which you listen to each other's questions and messages in a supportive circle, giving each other feedback and support. Many times we need help understanding our message. You may want to look at the chapters on dreams or consulting nature, and use the same methods of interpreting your message as you would for your dreams or encounter with nature. You can also ask a meditation teacher, mentor, or adult friend who is skillful in meditation for help in answering any questions you might have about your experiences. If you have a therapist, he or she may even guide you through some of these meditations.

> *May you be filled with loving-kindness;*
> *May you be strong and happy;*
> *May you feel good about yourself;*
> *May all your dreams come true.*

Books, Resources, and Wisdomkeepers Related to This Chapter

Blue Jean Buddha: Voices of Young Buddhists, edited by Sumi D. Loundon (Wisdom Publications, 2001). Recommended for any teen who considers themselves a Buddhist or wants to know more about Buddhism.

Just Say OM!: Your Life's Journey, by Soren Gordhamer (Adams Media Corp, 2001). A great book to further your meditation practice, written specifically for teens. A perfect companion to this chapter.

Loving-Kindness: The Revolutionary Art of Happiness, by Sharon Salzburg (Shambhala Publications, 1995). An easy-to-understand book on loving-kindness meditations.

Wherever You Go, There You Are: Mindfulness Meditation In Everyday Life, by Jon Kabat-Zinn (Hyperion Publishers, 1994). An easy-to-read book on the techniques and philosophy of mindfulness meditation. Good follow-up to this chapter.

Lama Surya Das
Dzogchen Foundation
P.O. Box 734
Cambridge, MA 02140
e-mail: foundation@Dzogchen.org
www.Dzogchen.org
Offers books, video tapes, and resources on Buddhist practices and ethical teachings to Western audiences. Lama Surya Das is the author of the bestselling book: *Awakening the Buddha Within* and is available for workshops.

Julie Tallard Johnson
Flaming Rainbow Rites
P.O. Box 186
Spring Green, WI 53588
(608) 643-3649
e-mail: jewelhrt8@aol.com
www.thunderingyears.com
Will answer questions or concerns you may have about your meditation practice. Offers group and class instruction on a variety of meditation practices, as well as tape recordings of mindfulness and guided meditations. Web site includes articles, poetry, and rituals by other teenagers. You can submit your ideas and works to the site, too.

Insight Meditation Society
1230 Pleasant Street
Barre, MA 01005
(978) 355-4378
www.dharma.org/ims.htm
Offers information about insight meditation (mindfulness meditation). See online resources below for Web site information.

Jack Kornfield
Spirit Rock
P.O. Box 909
Wood Acre, CA 94973
Spirit Rock is a meditation center with information on retreats and instruction on meditation and Buddhist practices. Jack Kornfield, the director, is the author of *A Path with Heart: A Guide Through the Perils and Promises of Spiritual Life.*

Shinzen Young
Vipassana Support Institute
4070 Albright Avenue
Los Angeles, CA 90066
(310) 915-1943
www.shinzen.org
Offers retreats, cassettes, and resources on Vipassana (mindfulness) meditation. Shinzen Young is a leader in developing meditations for those living with chronic pain and meditation for athletes.

Warm Rock Tapes
P.O. Box 108
Chamisal, NM 87521
Offers cassette recordings of Stephen Levine's (author of *A Gradual Awakening*) guided meditations and talks.

Online Resources

Insight Meditation Society
www.dharma.org/ims.htm
Provides information about retreats for the practice of insight meditation and scholarships available for students. Includes links to Dharma Resources and teachers and centers on the internet to help us learn how to meditate.

Learning Meditation
www.learningmeditation.com
This site is an aid for beginners to learn the basic techniques of meditation and relaxation. Various meditation practices are included, such as a reducing stress exercise, and ways to fulfill our potential in life. Many practices are accompanied by an audio guide to make learning easy.

Shambhala International
www.Shambhala.org
A comprehensive site on Shambhala meditation practices—the sacred path of the Warrior. A great resource with links to all the Shambhala centers around the world. (Every center offers free meditation instruction.)

Teaching Tools for Mindfulness Training
www.mindfulnessclasses.com
This page is a mindfulness training school on the Web with great pages that include information on Zen Mindfulness, Shambhala Training, Meditation Practices, and links to science and spiritual resources. Buddhist, Jewish, Christian, and scientific approaches to mindfulness are included on this site.

The World Wide Online Meditation Center
www.meditationcenter.com
This site contains general information for the beginning student of meditation and techniques for the more skillful, such as inner light meditation and mindfulness meditation. The center provides suggestions for meditation tapes to buy to aid in our practice and links to other alternative and spiritual resources on the Web.

"What if you slept, and what if in your sleep you dreamed, and what if in your dream you went to heaven and there plucked a strange and beautiful flower, and what if when you awoke you had the flower in your hand? Ah, what then?"

—Samuel Taylor Coleridge,
English poet and journalist

Chapter Seven

Dream Weaving

by Dr. Laurel Ann Reinhardt,

psychologist and Dream Weaver

"Am I Chuang Tzu dreaming I'm a butterfly,
or a butterfly dreaming I'm Chuang Tzu?"

—CHUANG TZU, ANCIENT CHINESE PHILOSOPHER

"The future belongs to people who believe in the beauty of their dreams."

—ELEANOR ROOSEVELT,
FORMER FIRST LADY, ACTIVIST, AND HUMANITARIAN

"Dreaming liberates perception, enlarging the scope of
what can be perceived."

—CARLOS CASTANEDA, SPIRITUAL WARRIOR
AND AUTHOR OF THE ART OF DREAMING

LAUREL ANN REINHARDT is a Licensed Psychologist who has been dream weaving for several decades. She works with people of all ages, helping them overcome their fears and live their dreams. As a mentor to young adults, she guides and encourages them to go after their own dreams. Laurel is the author of *Seasons of Magic,* a book about a young girl's spiritual journey. The following text is based on Laurel's work with dream weaving.

Waking to Dreams

Why dreams? How can they be helpful—after all, they're not real, are they? Yet there are some cultures on the planet that actually believe our dream lives are more real than our waking lives. And there are some scientists who are beginning to think they might be right.

The truth is, no one really knows what dreams are. In fact, they might be many things, many layers of things. They might be related to yesterday's events or what you had to eat last night. But they might be so much more. They might be helping you to answer certain questions you have, or solve an upsetting problem, or heal a long-standing illness. They might be telling you about events to come. They might even be giving you information for some of your friends or the whole planet. I myself have had the experience of having dreams "for" friends who weren't remembering their own dreams.

But why remember or work with our dreams if no one really knows for sure what they are or how they work? Is it enough to know that every culture, every religion has made use of dreams in some way? The Aborigines of Australia live in what they call the "dreamtime"; in the Bible, Joseph used his dreams to help his people; counselors use dreams to help people heal from physical, emotional, mental, and spiritual pain; Native Americans are still watching for the signs from dreams their ancestors had. No one knows exactly what dreams are or why they come to us, but it is clear that they are powerful and can make a difference in our lives. But where to begin?

Remembering

"Those who lose dreaming are lost."

—AUSTRALIAN ABORIGINAL PROVERB

The place to begin is in remembering your dreams. And everyone is in a different place with respect to what they remember.

Some people have no trouble remembering their dreams at all—they wake up each morning with one or more dreams extremely clear in their mind's eye or ear, and they are shocked to hear that this is not true for everyone.

Some people claim they don't dream *at all*. These people can't ever remember waking up with a dream and therefore have concluded that they simply don't dream. The truth is that, as far as we know, *everyone* does dream at night, the only difference is in the ability to remember our dreams. (Research with people who claim not to dream has shown that these people, like everyone else, go through periods of REM [rapid eye movement] sleep, the kind of sleep that is most clearly connected with the experience of dreaming.)

The majority of people fall somewhere between these two extremes of remembering dreams every day and never remembering dreams at all. In fact, people seem to go through various cycles of remembering dreams. Girls/women may find their ability to remember is connected with their menstrual cycle. People also report their ability to remember being affected by such things as: the cycle of the moon, what they had to eat or drink the night before, the level of stress they are experiencing, or whether or not there is something in their lives they just don't want to look at.

"I dreamed for years of escaping my house. But it never looked like my house. Sometimes it was a jail or dungeon. Sometimes it was some dark evil place. But I knew it was my house. I would usually get away but it took a lot and someone was usually chasing me. I took myself to a counselor when I found out I was depressed. We used my dreams to help understand my feelings. I was living in a

"I have never lost the sense that where my dreams come from is where I come from. And for that reason, they deserve serious study."

—ELIZABETH ROSE CAMPBELL, EDITOR OF *THE ROSE READER*

"The mind doesn't just wander around in sleep without a purpose. It wants to bring back shapes and angles, golden ratios, oceans, and mountains—it wants to make order out of chaos. It seems to be this: It wants to dream up stories."

—POPIE MOHRING, MASTER GARDENER

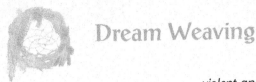

violent and alcoholic family. Yet I was pretending to myself and everyone else it was normal—that everything was really okay. But it wasn't. I wanted to escape."

—DEBRA, AGE 24

The question is, if you aren't remembering many, or any, of your dreams, are there things you can do to help yourself remember? And the answer is, "Yes."

How to Remember

The most important thing in being able to remember your dreams is *desire*—if you really want to remember your dreams, if this is important to you, then you are halfway there. This may seem like a little thing, but you'd be surprised how many people who don't remember their dreams simply don't care. Once you decide that you do want to remember them, the dreams often start coming. If you have already decided that you do want to remember them but they haven't started coming to you, don't worry. There are many more things you can do to help with this.

When you go to sleep at night, say to yourself (or to a spirit guide, guardian angel, or other helper), **"I want to remember my dreams in the morning."**

Don't eat or drink anything right before bedtime that could disturb your sleep or your ability to get to sleep. Going to bed with a full stomach will keep you from sleeping well, as will caffeine, which is found in chocolate, soda pop, coffee, and caffeinated teas. A little warm milk before bedtime, however, can be nice and soothing.

Try waking up without an alarm clock or radio or someone calling to you. Dreams are part of the night and seem to run away when confronted with anything from our waking lives. If you simply can't do this on a regular basis, try waking this way just one morning a week. Then, as you awaken, be gentle with yourself—don't open your eyes right away, move around slowly and gently, and just invite the dream images and memories to join you in your reverie.

Drink some "dream tea" before going to sleep, **or sleep with a dream pillow** under your regular bed pillow.

Making a Dream Pillow

Certain herbs can be helpful in promoting good, restful sleep, as well as dreaming or not dreaming by placing them in what are known as "dream pillows," bundles of herbs sewn or tied inside a small cloth bag. You put this "pillow" underneath your regular bed pillow to facilitate your dreaming process. The herbs recommended for dream pillows are very powerful and are not for daily or regular use; use them only when you are having a lot of trouble remembering your dreams or when you are making a particular request of your dreams. Use a tablespoon each of three or four of the following herbs:

> hops—for sleeping
>
> mugwort—for dreaming
>
> chamomile—for relaxing, calming
>
> roses—for relaxing, calming
>
> lavender—for relaxing, calming
>
> rosemary—for remembrance/to help stop nightmares

These herbs may be found at local health food stores.

Dream Tea

Four of the six herbs that are used in dream pillows can also be used in a "dream tea" that works in much the same way as a dream pillow. Since these herbs contain no caffeine, you can drink this tea right before going to sleep.

> hops—for sleeping
>
> mugwort—for dreaming
>
> chamomile—for relaxing, calming
>
> rosemary—for remembrance/to help stop nightmares

Again, herbs are powerful, so use only a small amount of each herb ($1/8$ teaspoonful) for the tea, and don't use it every night. Be forewarned—this tea will taste a little bitter, which is why a lot of people prefer using the dream pillow. However, there are some herbal blend teas on the market that have some of these same herbs in them, along with a few other things to make the taste more palatable. Ask someone at your local health food store to help you find these teas.

"Breezes at dawn have secrets to tell you

Don't go back to sleep

You must ask for what you truly want

Don't go back to sleep

People are going back and forth across the threshold

Where the two worlds touch

The door is round and open

Don't go back to sleep."

—Rumi, Sufi mystic and poet

Recording Your Dreams

Recording or remembering your dreams can be done in a number of different ways. One way is to write them down. If you want to do this place a piece of paper and a pencil (or, better yet, a special notebook or journal, decorated specifically with your dreams in mind) by your bed, ready to record any part of a dream that you remember upon waking. This might be in the middle of the night, so have the paper and pencil in a place that is easily reached, even with the lights off.

If you do wake up in the middle of the night with a dream but you don't have the energy or desire to turn on the light, let alone write down the whole dream, just record a single word or phrase that will prompt your memory of the entire dream in the morning. And don't worry—even if you can't remember any more of the dream in the morning, the one word, phrase, or image will be enough to work with. Dreams are *holographic*—meaning that each part of the dream can re-create the whole dream. I've worked with people who could get answers to some of their most important questions from a single dream image.

In addition to writing them down, you might want to record your dreams in other ways as well. Dreams are very sensual, especially visual. Drawing or painting them can be very satisfying, especially if you don't get caught up in judgments about your artistic skills—the point is simply to capture the dream in some way that has meaning or value for you. Certain scents can evoke powerful memories, so remembering the dream while inhaling a certain perfume or incense can be helpful. Making something out of clay also works. Getting up and moving, or dancing the dream, may also help you to connect with it more deeply, especially if you add some music you enjoy to the process.

Sharing your dreams with others whom you trust—whether they are people who live in the same household with you or whom you have to contact by phone, at school, or at work—is an especially nice way of remembering the dream. Once the dream is shared, there are others who will be able to help you remember it. And, they may find something valuable in it for you or themselves.

"When the state of dreaming has dawned,

Do not lie in ignorance like a corpse,

Enter the natural sphere of unwavering attention.

Recognize your dreams and transform illusion into luminosity,

Do not sleep like an animal.

Do the practice which mixes sleep and reality."

—TIBETAN BUDDHIST PRAYER

Hold a Dream Circle

"In some ways, your dreams may speak a universal language, and therefore, they belong not only to you but a larger community."

—LOUIS SAVARY, AUTHOR OF *DREAMS AND SPIRITUAL GROWTH*

There are records of a few cultures in which the community focuses on and is guided by the dreams that come to its people every night.

Choose to have six to twelve friends gather for a night of dreamwork. Start out by talking and possibly sharing in some activities, focusing your conversations and activities on dreams. You could talk about dreams you remember from the past, you could make dream pillows and dream tea together, you could look at art books together (a lot of art images come from people's dreams), or anything else you can think of that would put you in the mood for dreaming and remembering. There is a deck of cards called *The Dream Cards* whose images could be used to stimulate your dreaming process (see resources at the end of this chapter).

When you do go to sleep, everyone should be in the same room, lying in a circle with your heads all pointing toward the center. When you awaken, the first thing you do is share your dreams with one or more of your dreaming "partners." We are all part of the "circle of life," and this includes our dreaming. This means that your dreams are likely to have relevance—to be important—for those around you, maybe even for the entire planet. So share them with people who will honor them and treat them as the sacred gifts they are. In this case sit around over breakfast and share your dreams. Are there any common messages or images?

Next, look for similarities between your dreams and your waking (day) life. Don't be too literal with this. If you dreamed about wild animals of some kind, notice if any "wild" animals cross your path that day. A "wild" animal could be an unruly dog, a fox or deer, or a friend who starts acting "wild." If you dreamed you were crying, see if something happens during the day to make you or one of your friends sad. Perhaps you hear a news story about someone losing their

Why does the eye see a thing more clearly in dreams than the mind while awake?

LEONARDO DA VINCI, PAINTER, SCULPTOR, ARCHITECT, ENGINEER, AND SCIENTIST

"Hold fast to dreams

For if dreams die

Life is a broken-winged bird

That cannot fly.

Hold fast to dreams

For when dreams go

Life is a barren field

Frozen with snow."

LANGSTON HUGHES, AMERICAN POET AND AUTHOR OF *THE DREAM KEEPER*

home or a child? Or, if you are given a gift in the dream, does something special happen to you during the day?

The Language of Dreams

This gets us into the question of dream language and interpretation. If you've ever checked out the dream section of your local bookstore, I'm sure you've seen the "dream dictionaries" that are available. The reason these books are called "dictionaries" is because dreams are actually a foreign language! This language has more to do with pictures and feelings than with words, and words are what we are more familiar with. So we need to learn the language of dreams. However, if you bought one of those dream dictionaries from the store, I encourage you to put it away, at least for now. The reason is that you have to learn to understand *your own* dream language, not someone else's. Yes, there are some symbols that are "universal"—that is, they evoke the same or very similar responses in most people. But even those symbols carry personal and unique significance as well. Let me give you some examples.

In the *Wizard of Oz*, Dorothy has an Auntie Em. So, when I say "Auntie Em" to someone who has loved that movie, seen it several times, and talked about it with friends, they will undoubtedly think immediately of Dorothy's Auntie Em. But they might also think of one of their own aunts who reminds them of Dorothy's Auntie Em. I think of my own Aunt Em, who really isn't anything like Dorothy's aunt at all, but her name is Em. On the other hand, someone who has never seen the movie won't have any idea of what an "Auntie Em" is.

Here's another example. When I ask a group of twenty people what the word *water* means to them, I usually get *at least* ten different associations to that word: lake, ocean, glass, drink, swim, deep, beach, running, river, blue, aqua, fluid, clear, tasteless, fish, ice—the possibilities are nearly endless. If water showed up in one of your dreams, I'd ask you what kind of water it was, and *your* relationship or associations to it. I wouldn't assume that I knew what wa-

"The dream itself is a rebellion against language—and against, ultimately, the restriction that any kind of expression seems to impose on truth."

—BRENDA MURPHEE, POET AND ESSAYIST, FROM *DREAMS ARE WISER THAN MEN*

ter meant for you. But this is just what dream dictionaries do. *So I recommend making your own dream dictionary.*

> ### Make Your Own Dream Dictionary
> Whenever a new image appears in your dream life, put the word at the top of a blank sheet of paper and then start free-associating to that symbol—two or three associations is sufficient. The next time that image shows up in a dream, go back to that page and add any new associations that came up. Over time, you will discover what that particular symbol, picture, or image means for you.

This doesn't mean you can't sometimes use a "universal" dream dictionary or, better yet, a regular dictionary or an encyclopedia, to help you figure out why something showed up in your dreams. A friend of mine once dreamed about a car. I asked her what kind. "A Chevrolet—an Impala." I asked her if she knew that an impala, besides being a kind of car, was also a kind of animal. She said, "No," then went and checked out impalas at the zoo. It turned out that the impala *animal* made more sense to her than the Impala *car.*

There will be times when things will show up in your dreams that you didn't know you knew about, just like my friend and her impala. Find out about them by looking them up or asking someone else.

Dreams also like to make puns, such as "Visualize whirled peas" (Visualize world peace). Have you seen that bumper sticker? It's one of my favorites. How about the word *dope?* If Dopey from Snow White and the Seven Dwarfs shows up in a dream, acting crazy and scary, is it really about a dwarf, or have you been acting a little "dopey" lately? Is it about that "dope" you tried the other day that made you act a little "DOPEY?" What about the word *do?* Was it really *dew* or *due?* Which one is it? Try them all out and see which one feels right or fits the best for you at the time.

What Do They Mean?

"A dream which is not understood is like a letter which is not opened."

—THE TALMUD, JEWISH SPIRITUAL TEACHINGS AND LAWS

Everyone wants to know what their dreams mean. After all, isn't that why we're bothering to remember them in the first place? Well, yes and no. But let's assume that that is why we're remembering them—the only reason we're remembering them—and start there.

"Dreams have always been an important part of my life.
I think that is true for most people who are searching for
spirituality and go out and fast. Dreams guide you;
they show you the way that you should be living, or the direction,
or give you signs to help someone else, and they are gifts."

—JACKIE YELLOW TAIL, CROW WOMAN

One way to find out what dreams mean is by playing with them verbally, as I was doing above. You start by making associations to the images, the "symbols" that show up in your dream.

A symbol or metaphor is something that represents—or stands in for—something else. "Auntie Em" can be a symbol for a person or relative who acts like a mother, who looks out for our welfare, but who sometimes doesn't fully understand us. Water can be a symbol for something that flows or something that has the potential for freezing and becoming blocked. After you come up with a bunch of associations you start linking them together and begin to make a story.

Let's go back to my friend with the impala. In the dream she was driving around in her father's car, which turned out to be an Impala. She began by making associations to her father (a nice man, kind of strict, not around very much), and to cars (a way to get somewhere; her father's car, in particular, meant that she was a passenger—someone else, her father, was in the driver's seat). This didn't seem particularly helpful—my friend couldn't come up with a

> "If modern physics is to be believed, the dreams we call waking perceptions have only a very little more resemblance to objective reality than the fantastic dreams of sleep."
>
> —BERTRAND RUSSELL, ENGLISH MATHEMATICIAN AND PHILOSOPHER

"story" that made any sense to her or fit with her life at the time. But when I mentioned that the impala was also a kind of animal, my friend got excited. And she was even more excited when she came back and told me about impalas: they can leap high and far to get out of danger, but they won't leap, even if they're being attacked by an enemy, *if they can't see where they are going to land.* This was exactly what was going on in my friend's life—she knew she needed to change jobs because her current job was draining her life away, but because she didn't have another job lined up, she wouldn't make the leap of quitting the job she had. And, it was her father's Impala because he had once not left his job when he really needed to. Amazing, isn't it?

But there are other ways of making sense of your dreams, too, such as drawing, painting, sculpting, and dancing. The very first time I painted a dream, I was nervous. I didn't consider myself an artist and it was a long, involved dream—how could I possibly capture the whole thing? Rather than try to do it all, I picked one scene to paint—I was in a car driving over an old, dried-up riverbed in which something was struggling to get out of the mud. Before painting the dream I had no idea what that struggling thing was, but as I painted, it emerged—it was a phoenix, a mythical bird of renewal and rebirth. I was stunned. It was so clear in my painting, and it had been so unclear when I merely wrote the dream down.

Sometimes acting or playing out the dream is very powerful, too. So, if in a dream you are dancing, you might want to go dancing and see how that feels. If you got together for lunch with an old friend, you might want to give that person a call. If you were on a train, maybe it's time to take a trip somewhere and see what happens. There are reasons for remembering dreams besides just "figuring them out." **Sometimes it's important to let the dream be a mystery and just let it guide you, let it take you where it wants to go. Like taking a trip—starting to drive somewhere without a planned destination—just to see what happens.**

"We are in a time so strange that living equals dreaming, and this teaches me that man dreams his life, awake."

—PEDRO CALDERÓN DE LA BARCA, SPANISH DRAMATIST AND POET, FROM *LIFE IS A DREAM*

Requesting Help from Your Dreams

> "The Dreamer sees things we can't see and answers
> the questions we don't know how to ask."
>
> —RALPH THORPE, AUTHOR OF *THE DREAMER: A VOYAGE OF SELF-DISCOVERY*

If you are going through a particularly difficult time, if you're having trouble with a friend or there is some question that is plaguing you, you can actually ask your dreams to give you help, guidance, and information about the issue at hand. Just before turning off the lights at night, ask for a dream to help you with the issue. (This might be a good time to use a dream pillow.) When you wake up in the morning, simply assume that any dream you remember is an answer to the request, no matter how unlikely that seems. Then start playing around with the dream in some of the ways I mentioned above (free-associating, dancing, drawing, acting out, or sculpting). Be sure to ask a couple of trusted friends for their opinions too.

Intensity

> "There is a Dream dreaming us."
>
> —AFRICAN BUSHMAN

Dreams can be a part of the intensity of life—sometimes a scary part.

> "I was at an all-girl's camp with my mother. I needed to cross a bridge over some water that was full of snakes, including a big boa constrictor. One could get across the bridge only by thinking. I started across, stumbled, and fell into the water, but somehow managed to get out. Then my mother offered to drive me across. I got in the backseat. My mother was very calm and natural, as though she knew exactly what was happening. She began driving across the bridge. Suddenly, I was no longer in the car, and I stumbled again, this time falling headlong into the water. The water was full of girls who were floating on the surface and

screaming. I was underwater but somehow able to breathe. The boa constrictor curled itself around my body and pulled me toward his head."

—ERIN, AGE 17

Do you find Erin's dream scary? (Would you be surprised to hear that Erin didn't find the dream scary, just very powerful and important?) Do you have scary dreams yourself? Would you call them nightmares? Do you have the same scary dream over and over again? Are you afraid to go to sleep at night because of these dreams?

Sometimes dreams are scary simply because we don't know their language; in these cases, getting to know our own dream language better will help. *Sometimes scary dreams are trying to get our attention.* Maybe it's actually the same dream as a previous, less scary version to which we paid little or no attention. I have often worked with people who have had repeating nightmares that have disappeared once the person shared and worked on the dream with me.

Working with your dreams can help. Using a dream pillow with herbs aimed at helping get a restful, "dreamless" sleep, can help. You might also use a "Dream Catcher," a sacred Native American tool that is used to help babies sleep. It is generally a circle made from a tree branch, with a webbing of sinew in the middle—it looks a lot like a spiderweb. In the center there is a hole, often with a feather placed nearby. The Dream Catcher is hung over the place in the bed where your head will be during the night and is meant to catch bad dreams. The "good" dreams go through the hole in the center, while the "bad" dreams get caught up in the webbing. The feather near the hole in the center moves when a dream goes through the hole.

One of the scariest dreams for people is a dream about death—either their own death or someone else's. The thing to remember is that, like anything else in a dream, death is usually a sign, a *symbol*. Rarely does it mean that someone is actually going to die. What you might ask yourself is, "What is dying in my

> "Some dreams try to loosen the hold of old fears and beliefs, to set us loose. Some try to hold us in place."
>
> —BRENDA MURPHEE, POET AND ESSAYIST, FROM *DREAMS ARE WISER THAN MEN*

179

life? What is coming to an end? What don't I need to hang on to anymore?" Then, look at the context—the other things in the dream surrounding the dying person—for clues about what that might mean for your life. If it was a friend who died, then maybe there are some changes happening in one or more of your relationships. If it was you who died, and you happened to be in a school, maybe it is time for you to move out of the role of being a student.

Enjoy Your Dreams

I've talked some about the sacredness of dreams, their intensity, and how they can be of help in our lives, but there is another very important aspect to dreams—they are fun. Where else can you go flying, take risks, lose your life and keep on playing? (I know in video games you get three lives just to start, but on the planet Earth, this time around, you only get one.) Dreams are great fun, talking about them is great fun, and painting them, making masks from them, and acting them out are great fun, too. It doesn't have to be totally serious—simply respectful.

Becoming a Dream Weaver

"The dream, then, is a way of remembering a possible future in time to choose [the right path]."

—Brenda Murphee, poet and essayist, from *Dreams Are Wiser Than Men*

"Iktomi, the great teacher, appeared as a spider. He taught the people to make webs to catch their dreams so they could reach their goals and make good use of their ideas, dreams, and visions."

—Oglala Sioux legend

There are some people, such as the physicist Fred Alan Wolf, who think that we weave the universe with our dreams. That is, we create our experience here on Earth through our dreams. At the very least, our dreams are part of how we make things happen. If we are dreaming the current crisis on this planet, then

"Bring me all of your dreams,

You dreamers,

Bring me all of your

Heart melodies

That I may wrap them

In a blue cloud-cloth

Away from the too-rough fingers

of the world."

—Langston Hughes, American poet and author of *The Dream Keeper*

we have some work to do. You may notice that most (if not all) science fiction movies about the future are bleak, scary, and dark. Do these images come from our dreams? We need to listen and work with our dreams. It could be that the state of Earth's health depends on people and their relationship to their dream life. When we work with our dreams, we become Dream Weavers because we are then using our dream life to help us make our choices. Dream Weavers don't ignore their dreams. Dream Weavers use their dreams to help improve their own lives and the lives of others. Debra, in the example on page 169, joined Al Anon because of her dreams. This is just one small example of a positive choice someone made due to a dream. Debra is a Dream Weaver.

There are a lot of people on the planet right now who don't think that dreams are important. Perhaps it is that attitude which contributes to the ill health of the planet as a whole. If so, it depends more and more on you, the Spiritual Warriors of your generation, to weave the dreams that can heal the planet.

"Then your I is no longer your mundane little self but the I of the Big Dreamer who is dreaming the whole universe."

—FRED ALAN WOLF, PHYSICIST

What you can do to help weave the planet into a healthier, better place:

- Start remembering, recording, and working with your dreams.
- Make yourself a dream pillow.
- Hold a Dream Circle.
- Find a dream partner and share your dreams regularly.
- Whenever you dream about a friend or relative, and it is comfortable for you, share the dream with them.
- Make a Dream Catcher.
- Ask your school psychology, sociology, drama, or writing class to have a class session on dreams.
- Write a play from your dreams and present it to the community.

Remember, dreams provide us with clues about who we want to be and how to get there; they connect us with our deepest longings, our greatest wisdoms, our spiritual selves, and the rest of the cosmos.

Books, Resources, and Wisdomkeepers Related to This Chapter

The Complete Book of Dreams, by Julia and Derek Parker (DK Publishing, 1998). Great companion to this chapter and for those who want to continue their dream work. Explains how you can interpret your dreams yourself.

Dreams Are Wiser Than Men, by Richard Russo (North Atlantic Books, 1987). A collection of several Dream Weavers' thoughts, experiences, and ways of working with dreams.

Dream Cards, by Stephen Kaplan Williams (Fireside Books, 1991). A set of 66 Dream Cards and 66 Wisdom Cards along with a book explaining how to interpret and learn from your dreams.

Laurel Ann Reinhardt, Ph.D., LP
Dream Weaver
e-mail: DreamWay@aol.com
A resource if you or your school want more information on dream circles or dream weaving.

The Penguin Dictionary of Symbols, by Jean Chevalier and Alain Gheerbrant (Penguin, 1996). A very useful dictionary to help you interpret your dreams.

Online Resources

The Association for the Study of Dreams
www.asdreams.org
Provides information on the science behind dreaming—the nature, function, and significance of dreaming. There is also a FAQ page, further reading suggestions, and journal and magazine research articles and excerpts.

DreamGate
www.dreamgate.com
This site is small but provides links to other sites and the opportunity to participate in online classes about the science of dreaming.

Dream Interpretation
www.dreammoods.com
This site includes a dream dictionary, dream forum (where you can share your dreams), and insights about dreams.

Dreamlover, Inc.
www.dreamloverinc.com
This site is devoted to the psychological and spiritual study of dreams, with a dream dictionary of more than 300 symbols, information on how to interpret dreams, and pages to help us understand what consciousness is, our sleep cycles, and dream research and theories.

Chapter Eight

Natural Highs and Altered States

Shiatsu to Drum Making to Reaching the Zone

"I don't need drugs. I *am* drugs."

—SALVADOR DALI, ARTIST

THE DESIRE TO GET HIGH is universal. Getting high, or experiencing altered or non-ordinary states, simply means to have an experience that is *outside* the bounds of "ordinary." In many rituals, reaching an altered state is a way to broaden one's experience. With this kind of altered state people receive insights, gifts from the spirit world, healings, and powers they can use to help themselves and their community. Prayer, meditation, Yoga, Shiatsu, chanting, drumming, dancing, and ritual are some ways to reach non-ordinary states and make contact with a Greater Power, the Greater Power within ourselves and everywhere around us.

"My favorite high is floating out on a lake in a canoe listening to an Alpha Blondy tape. I just listen and float. I feel as if I'm being pulled by another boat. . . ."

—TOM, AGE 17

"The best mind-altering drug is truth."

—LILY TOMLIN, COMEDIENNE

Creating altered states is a way to have a spiritual experience—to experience a spiritual connection to something bigger than ourselves. In ancient cultures altered states have traditionally been used to connect with the Divine. The purpose of reaching altered states is to be "empowered with energies" that we can use to improve our lives and the lives of our community.

Salvador Dali is right. The best high is *within* ourselves and therefore within our reach at all times. When he painted, he reached heights that no drug could furnish him. Drugs and alcohol provide small, frail experiences in comparison to the highs attained by many through painting, writing, meditating, drumming and dancing, racing, taking shamanic journeys, or going on vision quests. Giving in to such soulful and safe experiences teaches us that drugs and alcohol typically limit us.

"My experiences with altered states include both drug-induced and drug-free highs. The drug-free experiences are far superior, because of the 'after effects.' I come away with something that strengthens me when my 'trip' is a natural one. Drugs and alcohol had a way

of diminishing me. The real highs in life will lift us up and give us confidence in our self and our life, not bring us down."

—BRENT, AGE 23

Those of you who have tried drugs or abuse substances such as marijuana, alcohol, ecstasy, or cocaine may find that once you taste the highs of the *real* stuff, alcohol and drugs won't seem worth the money or time you give them. If you are using drugs or alcohol now, consider taking a vacation from them as you apply the wisdom found in this book. Many forms of getting high naturally are offered in this chapter, from an ancient Japanese form of releasing the natural energy in your body, called Shiatsu, to reaching to "the Zone" in athletics. Experiment and play with any or all of these ideas when you find yourself in the mood to get high.

Ancient wisdom teaches us that joy is our natural state. It is not something we have to win or constantly pursue. Ancient wisdom also teaches us that when we pursue happiness too much, it seems to escape us. Usually we "get high to feel happy." But we quickly discover that getting high in unnatural ways takes away our happiness. Enduring happiness is inherent; we simply need to use the ancient tools to bring forth this happiness. Lasting joy will not be found in another person (or relationship), object, or circumstance. **Getting high naturally is about bringing forth what is already within us.** This is what the Wisdom-keepers have taught for thousands of years—true joy is our natural state of being. So we needn't "do" anything unnatural to acquire it. Instead we need to realize that our desire to get high is our desire to feel happy. The ancients then offer us ways to remove the blocks to our innate happiness, such as through Shiatsu, meditation, chanting, drumming, dancing, and running. . . .

"When we get really silly and let ourselves just play we reach awesome states. Play is one of our natural highs. Especially when we let it take us where it wants, we arrive in a place that always offers us some surprise."

—ERIN, AGE 17

"I know that we all have a hunger for spiritual things and if it gets pushed under—then there is a hunger that always exists."

—MARIE SHERMAN, MEDITATION TEACHER

High on Shiatsu

"Find your center and you will be healed."

—Taoist proverb

"(The flower) says: 'Just be, Alice. Being is sufficient. Being is All. The cheerful, sunny self you are missing will return, as it always does, but only being will bring it back.'"

—Alice Walker, African American writer, author of *The Color Purple*

"The Tao's principle is spontaneity."

—Lao-tzu, ancient Taoist sage and author of *Tao-te-Ching*

Shiatsu is a form of Japanese *acupressure*. When certain areas of the body are pressed with the finger or thumb (thumb works best), the body responds to this pressure in a favorable way. Applying pressure to special places on the body releases certain physical, emotional, and psychological sensations. You can experience this natural "high" by placing pressure on certain "self-Shiatsu points" in your body. It's not only a natural high but benefits your mental, physical, and emotional well-being too. Shiatsu (Japanese) and acupressure (Chinese), have been around for at least 5,000 years. Humans in every culture have used acupressure instinctively and intuitively since the beginning of time. Have you ever found yourself holding your head when you have a headache, or pushing on other parts of your body to relieve yourself of pain? Have you noticed how we hold our chest when we are sad? When you instinctively put pressure on a point, such as a muscle that has gotten a cramp from running, you are encouraging the flow of energy to that area.

When we press the points described below, we are loosening energy in the body that may be stuck and congested. In Oriental medicine this energy in our body (and in every living thing) is called "Chi." Emotions are a form of Chi. Our energy levels (tired, intense, lazy, anxious) are all forms of our body's Chi, or energy. Like electricity, our energy is not something we can "see" but it is something we feel and experience. The health of our Chi affects our overall well-being. By placing pressure on certain areas on our body we can get our Chi moving, which will result in different body and emotional sensations ("highs"). Tibetans refer to this energy as *lung* (pronounced loong) and the Eastern Indians call it *prana*. Christians refer to it as "the breath of life." The Navajo refer to it as *nilchi'i;* the Japanese refer to it as *kami.* Every culture has a name for this energy that can be tapped in to through such practices as meditation, chanting, and Shiatsu.

Depending on what kind of "high" we want to achieve, we choose certain points on which to apply pressure. Activating these pressure points enhances our physical, emotional, mental, and spiritual well-being because it opens up the flow of energy throughout our entire body and mind. It also increases the oxygen and blood flow throughout the body and brain. Just as drugs and alcohol create certain physical and mental responses when we ingest them, Shiatsu achieves a high too.

One of the greatest advantages of Shiatsu is that you can do it yourself—it doesn't cost anything to experience its benefits.

Releasing Anxiety

Before you begin, there are two simple stretches that are excellent for relieving your body and mind of built-up pressure and anxiety. They are good for starting and finishing the day. If you consider yourself "uptight" or are worried about an upcoming event, they are good exercises for moving the Chi to all parts of the body. They also loosen you up for Shiatsu. You may feel soft tingling sensations and a sense of peace and well-being.

Remember to breathe!

Stand with your knees apart and bent slightly. Have your shoulders relaxed and down (not tight against your neck). Let your arms hang loose from your shoulders and swing them back and forth, back and forth, loosely and freely. Let your arms carry the motion. Move from your waist. Do this for a couple minutes. Notice the tension leaving your body. After finishing, stand still while breathing comfortably. Notice the different feelings and sensations in your body.

Rolling Off Tension

This loosens up your spine and whatever may be keeping your body tight and tense. (It is also helpful if you're constipated.) Make sure you do it on a mat or carpeted floor. And don't forget to breathe as you roll.

"The first step toward planetary healing is to walk toward the beauty in thee—to see the beauty in your own heart, to forgive those ideas and correct those thought forms that obscure the true wisdom fire in your mind."

—DHYANI YWAHOO, CHIEF OF NORTH AMERICAN YWAHOO LINEAGE

Hug your knees gently to your chest. Place your chin on top of your knees. Roll back and forth gently on your spine. Roll with your knees to your chest at least ten times. Notice how this loosens up your back. Notice anything else "loosening up" as you roll? Lie for a few minutes on your back with your knees up, breathing gently and noticing various body sensations.

Finding the Chi

When doing the following points on your body, you will know you have found the correct spot if it is *tender* to your touch. In Japanese this "tender spot" is called *Tsukai,* meaning "it hurts good." In order to achieve the natural high felt when your Chi starts to move, it is also important that you *focus your mind on what you are doing.*

Shiatsu instructor Mark Duhamel recommends that you wear loose, comfortable clothes when practicing the following routine. However, these "pressure points" can be used anytime you need them, regardless of what you are wearing. They are all easily accessible. **Breathing while you are working on a given pressure point, though, is essential to receive the benefits.** Each exercise has a particular effect on your emotional, mental, and physical state. The names of these pressure points, such as "Big Tomb," are Japanese names that date back thousands of years. As you will discover, the names represent the type of altered state and benefit you will experience when you do them.

The "Outer Barrier"

The "Outer Barrier" point (*Gaikan* in Japanese) is considered a central point that allows your Chi to reach all needed parts in the body and mind. It opens you up. It will increase your energy and in a sense "wake you up." Much like a large dam, this outer barrier opens up and lets out all the energy. You may want to do this exercise in the morning before an athletic competition or performance.

Finding the point: This point is on the back of your wrists, three fingers from the wrist crease, between the two bones of the forearm (2" behind the wrist). Place your fingers on the tender spot and press (not too hard) while you breathe and focus.

What to pay attention to: Notice how it feels to have the Chi begin to reach all parts of your body. What sensations do you feel as your body wakes up? Sometimes your mind feels more alert and you feel a soft buzz throughout your body.

The "Inner Barrier"

When the "Inner Barrier" *(Nai Kan)* is pressed, it protects the heart, while at the same time opening it up to receive Chi.

In Oriental medicine the heart is considered the *residence of the mind and spirit* (consciousness). Tibetans as well as Native Americans and others believe we *think* with our *heart*. So when we open up our heart, we are opening up our ability to think and create as well. To *protect* our heart means to not allow harm to come to us.

Finding the point: This point will be found on the palm side of your wrist, three fingers above the wrist, between the tendons. As in all points, apply pressure to the tender spot and breathe in and out as you push.

What to pay attention to: Focus on your heart as you press and breathe. Imagine your heart opening up. Let it open up to all the goodness that is trying to get in. At the same time notice a guardian at the front of your heart that won't allow any negativity or harm in. Notice your emotions.

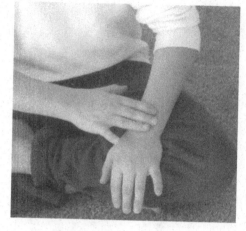

The "Outer Barrier" point

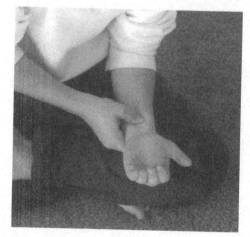

The "Inner Barrier" point

The "Big Tomb"

The "Big Tomb" point *(Dairyo)* "clears the heart and quiets the spirit." This spot is useful for centering and grounding yourself when you feel your

Thunder-energy rising up in you like a storm. This is a good "maintenance" point to apply pressure to on a regular basis. It will help you focus—while preparing for an exam or a performance or when you really need to listen.

Finding the point: This point is in the middle of the crease of the wrist.

What to pay attention to: Notice the "grounding" sensations as the intensity is transformed into a more even flow of energy. As you feel more calm in your body you may feel more connected to the earth, or more centered.

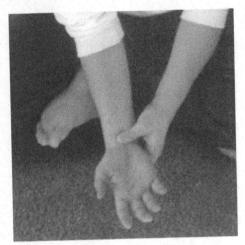

The "Big Tomb" point

The "Huge Void"

The "Huge Void" point (*Koket su*) stabilizes the spirit by freeing what is stuck inside of you. If you have bottled up feelings this will help release them. If you have bottled up your creativity, it will help release that too. It is also called the "alarm" of the heart and is considered a favored point. It is fairly easy to find because it is usually quite tender to the touch. You may notice a wave of feelings and thoughts when you push on this spot.

Finding the point: This point is in the center of your upper belly. It is not too far below your breast bone, about a quarter of the distance between the end of your breast bone and navel. It is quite sensitive when you push on it. It is very important that you breathe (don't hold your breath) as you push on this and all points.

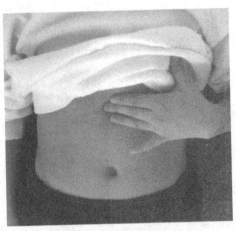

The "Huge Void" point

What to pay attention to: Focus on the different sensations that may rise up throughout your body when you do this point. Some experience tingling sensations, some experience a subtle rushing feeling.

The "Big Rush"

The "Big Rush" point *(Tai sho)* helps regulate and balance your Chi. Use this spot anytime to achieve a sense of balance. It is great for when you are angry, resentful, or frustrated as it will help you channel these emotions in a healthier, more beneficial way.

Finding the point: This point is between the first and second toe. Slide your finger between the toes toward your ankle and find the sensitive spot where the finger stops.

What to pay attention to: Notice what overall body sensations occur simply by breathing and pressing on this point.

"My head seemed to 'open up' and I felt light-headed in a good way."

—CRAIG, AGE 17

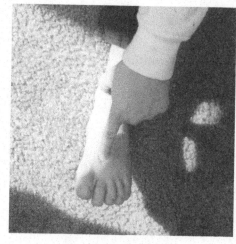

The "Big Rush" point

Group Chi

"I pray and I sing. And sometimes my prayer is my singing."

—BOBBY MCFERRIN, MUSICIAN AND SONGWRITER

When these Shiatsu practices are done in a group, the participants often discover that they get higher by creating a "group Chi" that builds upon everyone's participation and intensifies the experience. Try it in a big group or class sometime and notice the difference. Much like at a party, dance, or ritual, group energy can make for a more altered and pleasurable experience.

The body holds a thousand natural ways to get high. Stretching, breathing, exercising, practicing Yoga or Qigong (Taoist exercises for enhancing health and longevity), running, or doing Karate, are only a few other possibilities. If Shiatsu works for you, great. If not, venture out and find some of the many other alternative ways to use your body to reach a natural and healthy altered state.

Drum Medicine

*"I've been drumming and dancing since I was 8 years old.
I love drums and now I'm finally making my own."*
—JENNY, AGE 15

**"A village without
a drum is a
dead place."**

—AFRICAN PROVERB

Jere Truer guides groups through the use of stories and drumming, believing that everyone needs a drum. As a young man he struggled with his family's alcoholism and found that making music and writing songs kept him safe, strong, and connected! Here is what he discovered on his own journey as a Spiritual Warrior.

**"To the wind you
sing and the wind
whispers;**

**to the fire you cry
and the fire snaps;**

**to the ocean you
yell and the ocean
echoes;**

**to the earth you
drum and the earth
arrives."**

—WALKER
BLACKWELL, TEEN
POET, AGE 16

Drumming Your Thunder

by Jere Truer, poet, musician, storyteller

Drumming is an essential part of most cultures. A culture without a drum is considered endangered because it has lost touch with the heartbeat of the earth. It is the drummer who keeps time for the other musicians and dancers and who provides the pulse or beat that invigorates us. Even armies knew this when, for thousands of years, the drummers would rat-a-tat-tat while the troops marched for days. Without the drums, the soldiers tired more easily and fell out of step with one another. For all these reasons, cultures around the world have used drumming to keep their communities together.

In Africa, drums are considered to be gods because they are made of living material (wood), have skin, and when you touch them, they talk to you. In some African villages even today, drumming goes on constantly from early morning till nearly sundown. At sundown the drummers take a break for an hour or so to reflect, pray, or meditate, and then they drum for a few more hours. Mind you, not everyone is drumming all the time. Everyone drums, but they take turns at it as they complete their other tasks and play. It is also interesting that each person has a distinct rhythm that is unique to them, and the chief drummer helps them find that rhythm.

In Japan, before it became Westernized, every village had what was called the Community Drum—it belonged to the community. You knew whether you belonged to that village, not by city limits, but by whether you could hear the drum. So larger villages needed larger drums. Imagine the size of drum Tokyo would need!

I am of Scandinavian descent and the earliest people there were the Sami. They are still there and used to be called Laplanders. The drum was more important to them than anything else on earth. Like the Inuit or Eskimo peoples, the Sami lived above the Arctic Circle, so they had to know how to survive under extreme conditions. Their shamans (spiritual healers and teachers) consulted the drum by playing it and listening for spirits to tell them where a good hunt might be or to warn them of danger. The drum is a sacred instrument, a way to contact Mother Earth and Great Spirit, and to live in harmony with all of nature.

Why is the drum so important? And why is it more important than, say, a saxophone? Let's start with the importance of all art in general, then music specifically, and then the drum. Scholars have written extensively on this and I'm only going to give you the briefest explanation. First, until only about 450 years ago, *all* art—including visual art, music, dance, poetry, and theater—was done for sacred or religious purposes. Art was also used for healing people. Music has a very special way of affecting the cerebellum, or midbrain, where our deep emotional responses lie. So, if when praying or meditating or doing some other spiritual practice, you incorporate something such as drumming, which affects the inner cortex of the brain, you then have a possibly profound way of shifting your consciousness (taking you to an altered state). Chanting, toning, and breathwork also accomplish this shift. Sacred classical music and hymns have a similar effect, opening us more toward Spirit. Drumming and low chanting affect us on a more physical level

"Where I come from we say that rhythm is the soul of life, because the whole universe revolves around rhythm, and when we get out of rhythm, that's when we get into trouble. For this reason the drum, next to the human voice, is our most important instrument."

—BABATUNDE OLATUNJI, NIGERIAN DRUMMER

and stir deep emotions within us. Some religious leaders have been afraid of what stirring those emotions would mean, so drums have often been excluded from Western religious life.

Drumming heals the body. It works on a deeply emotional level, connecting us to the earth and to our community. Still, why not the saxophone? The truth is that playing the saxophone will do all those things, too. If you play the sax, play your heart out! However, I believe that because the drum is one of the first instruments ever used by humans, it connects us in some unexplainable way to our earliest ancestors. The drum was first created by clanking sticks and stones together. A little later, early humans discovered the "membranophone" or the sound made by something with a membrane over it. They tapped an animal skin stretched over a hollow log and out came a resonant "toom-toom." The other early instrument was a hollow reed, which, when blown through, makes a primitive flute that also has special power.

Are you ready yet to get in touch with that kind of energy? Yes? Before you go on to the next part of this chapter where we take you through the steps of making your own drum (it's easy!), let me tell you how as a young boy I began drumming and found out all this good stuff. When I was 11, I joined the school band and wanted to play the trumpet. But the director put me in the drum section. I wanted to quit but my father made me stay. After a while I got good and then very good! I never felt popular or cool, but when others heard me play the drums, it was as though I mattered all of a sudden.

My family was alcoholic and we lived in a small Midwestern city where either everyone knew everything about you or you kept real big secrets. Maybe everyone knew about the alcoholic problems —I am not sure. But I carried a huge secret and felt all alone because of it. I felt a lot of anger and loneliness, and I lost control sometimes. **What I found was that I could lose control on the drums and stay together at the same time.** I felt better about myself. And sometimes I lost control on the drums so well that I played excellently. I crawled inside the music to get healed and to be safe. Some of my friends crawled inside of drugs and alcohol, others inside of sex, and even some inside of violence. When I crawled inside the music, I didn't get hurt or hurt anyone else. I didn't know about the sacred aspect of music and drumming till much later. Still, some part of me . . . or perhaps the Spirit around me . . . led me to this good, pure, sweet source of joy and love. I would like to take you there. This chapter points the way, at least. Peace, love, and joy be yours!

Making Your Own Drum

You can be part of bringing the "heartbeat," the drum, back into your community.

Once you find yourself drumming (and maybe dancing too) you will easily and quickly get yourself to an altered state. Drums will bring forth in you excited states of body sensations, emotions, and images. It's good for the body to move and the voice to make noises; it's good for you to feel the many vibrations within your own body that will come alive as you and others drum. And as Jere pointed out, drumming is a great way to let out your anger and intensity in a good and creative way.

Don't have a drum? Well, here is an easy and inexpensive way to make your own.

> "When you lose the rhythm of the drumbeat of God, you are lost from the peace and rhythm of life."
>
> —CHEYENNE PROVERB

What you will need:

- a five-gallon oak barrel (usually used for wine, liquor, or pickles). (Found at beer- and wine-making shops, nurseries, and distributors of different containers. Also, check the Web for possible sources.)
- 2′ x 2′ piece of rawhide, enough to cover top of the oak barrel. (Found at any Tandy leather shop, or other leather shops, tanneries, or some shoe repair shops.)
- sledgehammer

Step 1

- regular hammer
- large flat-head screwdriver
- bastard file (a big heavy-duty file)
- coarse sandpaper
- ¹/₂ inch tacks (about 30)
- pliers
- good sharp scissors
- varnish or paint (a small amount)

When you buy the rawhide you will notice it is hard and stiff. To soften it up you will need to soak it for at least *twenty-four hours* before the making of the drums. You can soak the hide in a sink or a bucket of water.

Step 2

Drum making itself can be a ritual or part of a ritual. It takes between one and two hours to make a drum (and another twenty-four hours for it to dry). You can do this with a group of friends, or a class. One group led by Jere Truer did it over a weekend, with a drumming at the closing ceremony where everyone used their new drums.

Step One: Take the sledgehammer and hit out both ends of the barrel. If you want, you can shout and yell as you hit out the bottoms. At the same time keep your concentration on what you are doing. You don't want to hit the rim of the barrel.

Step Two: Take the metal hoops off both ends. This can be done by putting the sharp end of the screwdriver up against the edge of the rim and hitting the handle of the screwdriver with your hammer. Some simply hit the rims off with a hammer. The ease with which the rims come off varies from barrel to barrel.

Step Three: File down the edges of both ends of the barrel. You'll want the "top" of your drum to be smooth, since this is the end you will put the skin on and and will be hitting with your hand. So, the top will be filed down quite a bit more than the bottom, making it nice and smooth. *Either* end of the drum can be chosen as the top; it is up to you.

Step Four: Sand down the entire barrel with the coarse sandpaper, paying particular attention to the *top* part of the drum, where you will be putting the hide.

Step Five: This is when you cut the hide. Remove the hide from the sink or bucket. Cut it with a sharp scissors or knife, making sure you leave plenty of hide to cover the top of your drum. There should be *at least* 4 to 5 inches hanging over the rim all the way around.

Step 3

Step Six: There are two sides to the hide. Use the *smooth side facing up* on your drum. (If by chance you choose the rough side of the hide by accident, don't worry, this will not in any way ruin your drum.) Now, stretch the skin over the barrel. Hammer in the first tack about 1 to 1$^1\!/_2$ inches down from the top of the drum. Then, cross over to the other side of the rim and pull the skin *out* and then *down,* tightly. This creates a ripple in the hide. Place the *second* tack on this other side, across from the first tack. Put in the next two tacks so that the first four tacks make a "+," pulling the hide very tight, out and then down each time. This is when it is useful to have someone help stretch and hold the hide as you tack it down. After the first four tacks are in, the top should be free of ripples. If there is a small ripple, putting in the remainder of the tacks will take it out. Next, place another four tacks between

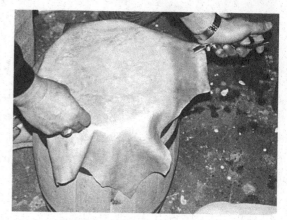

Step 6

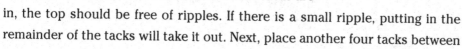

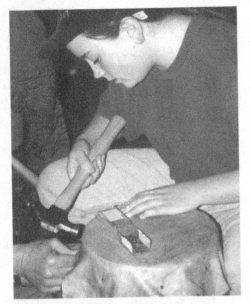

Step 6 continued

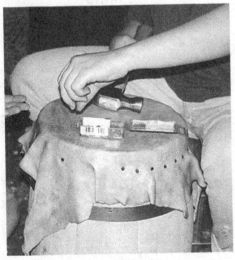

Step 7

the first four in the same manner. This will create a double cross on the skin.

Step Seven: Hammer in the remainder of the tacks all around the rim of the drum, spacing them about 1 inch apart. It takes 24 to 32 tacks to nail down the hide securely.

Step Eight: Cut the trim of the skin off. Most people choose to cut the trim close to the tacks. If you want you can cut yours in different lengths and shapes. Remember that the hide hardens and becomes very stiff, so you won't want any sharp edges. Once it hardens that will be its permanent shape.

Let the drum sit for at least twenty-four hours, until the hide is stiff. Once it is dry, you can begin to beat on your drum. You can decorate the sides of your drum with paint, or simply put lacquer or varnish over the wood. *Don't paint or varnish the hide* since that will affect the sound of your drum and the paint will later crack and peel.

Finding the Beat of Your Drum

Let the drum talk to you. You don't have to be a musician to enjoy a drum. Each drum is believed to have its own rhythm or "spirit." You find this beat by simply playing with it. Talk to the drum by hitting it and it will talk back to you with the sound it makes. In Jere Truer's Drum Medicine workshops, he suggests that you ask for the "voice" or beat of the drum to come to you in your dreams. Before going to sleep the night you've made your drum, ask to dream about the drum's rhythm. You don't have to remember the dream for it to work. Trust that a beat is coming to you and begin to play the drum freely. You have your own special beat and you will find it. (How do you think human beings came up with the first sounds? Pretend *your* drum is the first drum!) It's better to play around with your drum for a while before you get any lessons from a drum instructor. This allows you to hear the voice of your drum and to not get caught up with how it "should" sound.

> *"I'm a happy person. My friends notice this about me; they say I took a happy-pill at birth! I drum a lot. And, I don't drum because I'm happy; I'm happy because I drum."*
>
> —LANCE, AGE 20

Altered by Sound

> *"The sounds of the old Hebrew alphabet are quite powerful. My grandfather told me this. He said, just the sounds alone affect us in a very deep and meaningful way. My grandfather doesn't call it chanting but he'll speak to me in old Hebrew and I feel he's chanting to me."*
>
> —EBIN, AGE 22

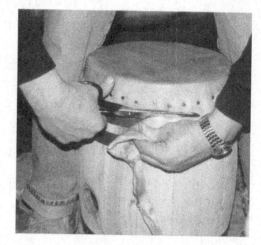

Step 8

Many of you have probably been to a pep rally where the group gets itself all excited by chanting cheers. Cheerleaders keep the crowds excited when the team isn't doing so well. The "noisemakers" or "containers of the energy" keep a ritual's energy up by drumming and shouting (See chapter 5, The Ceremonial Circle). Most of us sing or chant hymns at religious gatherings to arouse a spiritual connection to others and our Greater Power. Making sounds with our voices generates vibrations in our bodies and between us. Simply getting together in a group and making the same sound, or shouting and singing together, can cause us to experience intense physical sensations and emotions.

Find the beat of your drum

Tibetans and other Buddhists chant mantras. The very sounds of these mantras open the chanters up to the power within and create certain altered states, as well as call upon the blessings of various deities. Mantras are used to heal, inspire, and protect, as well as to bless the one chanting. Each mantra creates a certain condition outside and inside the body and mind. Chanting is used in many healing rituals of the Native American traditions, as well as in African and Australian Aboriginal rituals and by many sects of the Christian faith. Many popular recordings are now available on chanting.

Even though singing, cheering, and chanting are valued worldwide, we have too often been silenced and discouraged from making sounds with our own voices. Perhaps you have been told to shut up when singing along with a popular song. Some have been discouraged by being told to "lip" the words in choir and not actually sing. One teenager's mother told her daughter to pursue other careers after hearing her daughter sing. These are all ways our voices get quieted. Whether or not we have beautiful voices, *we can all sing.* We can all chant. We can all make impressive sounds with our voices.

Singing, shouting, and chanting are wonderful and natural ways to bring out our voices, to get high on the vibration of sound, and to experience feelings of exhilaration, peace, joy, connectedness to others, and excitement. Simply shouting out can open us up to feelings and experiences we hold inside of us.

A Holy Sound

There is a sound that is believed to be the first sound we make when we are born and the last sound we utter before we die. Many Buddhist, Hindu, and other traditions believe this to be a very sacred sound. The sound is believed to hold special powers through the vibration it produces in our bodies. Many use this sound to balance and heal themselves. This sound is the sound of a *sigh*—"AH." "AH" is actually a seed syllable mantra, meaning that it is a storehouse of power. It is believed that seed mantras such as "AH" and "OM" contain all the mysteries and wisdom of life. So, speaking or chanting these syllables invokes great powers in you.

> "History tells us that certain forms of non-ordinary states (ritual, drumming, and dancing) can be extremely productive, healing, and transformative, and are essential to our well-being."
>
> —CHRISTINA GROF, AUTHOR OF *THE THIRST FOR WHOLENESS: ATTACHMENT, ADDICTIONS, AND THE SPIRITUAL PATH*

Group Chant

You can intensify the power of this holy sound by chanting with a group. If you are with a small group of friends, simply sit in a circle facing each other. If you are part of a large group of people, twenty-five or more, you can all be facing the same direction. Have one designated leader to begin and end the chant. This person can be part of the circle or sitting in front facing the larger group. Together you all chant the sigh sound:

"AHHHHHHHHHHHHHHHHH . . ."

Take a nice deep breath in and on the out breath let out the "AAAAHHHHHH." Keep making the sound over and over. The room becomes one continual sound of "AHHHHHHH." Chant it strongly but don't force it. This sound has its own volume. Let it come out naturally. As you chant, pay attention to the feelings and sensations in your body. Notice where this sound "vibrates" inside of you. Notice how sitting in a room where many are making this sound together brings up certain emotions and experiences. Let yourself feel the high of this sound. Then, when you finish, sit in silence for a few moments noticing the sensations and experiences that arise in the silence.

> "Joy is not in things;
> it is in us."
>
> —CHARLES WAGNER,
> AUTHOR OF *SIMPLE*
> *LIFE (1904)*

Friendship Breath

Another way to experience the "AH" mantra is by sharing the sound and energy with a partner. This can be done in a small or large group, or with just one other person. Have everyone pair up. Each of you will take turns being the *breather*. The breather will lie comfortably on the floor next to his or her partner (the *sitter*). Have the one on the floor close his or her eyes and simply breathe naturally for a minute with eyes closed. The sitter then begins to breathe along with the breather. The sitter follows the breather's breath as he or she breathes in and out, until their breathing matches. The sitter concentrates on the breathing of the breather while the breather just relaxes and breathes. After about a minute, the *sitter* will start making the "AH" sound on each out breath. The sitter will continue to breathe *in* quietly with the breather and sigh an "AHHHH" on each *out* breath, for about three to five minutes.

You will need a way to time each breathing session. After one has breathed, change places so the breather becomes the sitter. After both have been the sitter and the breather, take a few minutes to share your experiences with each other or the group. It is a way to feel very close to someone without talking to them.

High on Sports

"You can and will reach altered states if you push beyond your limited view of yourself."

—SYDNEY, AGE 21

Human beings have always used physical activity as a way to achieve incredible altered states in natural and safe ways. You may have heard of the term *runner's high.* This is a common experience among runners and others who do an activity that pushes the body to perform physically. Athletes speak often of the high they get from their sport, called "the Zone." You reach the Zone when you get to a certain point in your physical activity where "you and the activity become one." You are the movement of running; you are "in the flow" of the exercise. Much like an artist gets in the "creative flow" and naturally creates a painting, athletes experience a lot of their achievements such as winning races or scoring points when they are in the Zone. When someone reaches the Zone during an athletic experience they report a change in perceptions, intense emotions, exceptional performances, intense sensations in the body, and a clear mind that sees beyond the ordinary. They also experience a sense of togetherness with others. Once a person experiences all this, it is hard *not* to return to this high again and again.

To achieve this high you need to be willing to commit yourself and to *concentrate fully on what you're doing.* The intent here is not winning or losing. In fact, you are not as likely to experience the Zone if your focus is only on winning or losing. Your focus needs to be on the *activity,* on your body, and on what you are attempting to accomplish. Reaching an altered state in athletic activities is too often overlooked in today's competitive sports.

"The beauty of the rite . . . is the beauty of one's essential nature. By participation in the rite, by uniting the mind with that beauty, by walking the way of the god, one becomes profoundly composed. . . .

The way of the god is the way to the seat of energy within the soul."

—JOSEPH CAMPBELL, PHILOSOPHER AND MASTER STORY-TELLER, FROM *THE POWER OF MYTH*

We can learn from ancient traditions around the world that value intense physical activity for its ability to create highs. Games and sports were an integral part of each Native American tribe's culture and religion. Most games were played to benefit the entire community—such as playing a game to call for rain. They were also intended to strengthen community relationships, to bring people together.

Foot races have been an important athletic activity for Native Americans since ancient times. The Apache included distance running in their warrior training for young men. Apache women run during their coming-of-age ceremony.

Running and other athletic activities prepare the body for adulthood, helping us to become strong inside and out. When athletic achievement is in a healthy context, it opens up feelings that motivate us to do more, to be more, and to hope for more. Whenever you push yourself beyond your normal limits you're opening up to what is possible for you. This is a great high in itself.

How to Get to "the Zone" in Sports

1. Use your imagination *actively* to see yourself doing better. Imagine yourself jumping higher, running faster. See it happening.

2. Focus on what you are doing. Take your focus *off* your "performance" for others. Let go of the worry of doing it for your parents, your grandparents, or for the fans (if there are any).

3. Let yourself get psyched up. Get excited and "into" what you are doing. It is no different from writing a book, painting, or singing —let yourself really get into it. Make the physical activity the focus of your meditation. Open up to what's possible. This possibility is *inside* of you.

4. Bring your love and dedication to the sport you choose. This commitment and love will bring you to an incredible high state no drug could even come close to matching.

5. Try not to force the Zone experience. It happens spontaneously, while you are focused (meditating) on what you are doing.

"Running is also a means of communicating with the forces of nature. Ritual foot races are conducted to induce rain and bountiful harvests in the Southwest, to locate buffalo on the Plains, and to accompany the spirits of the dead in the Arctic."

—FROM *THE NATIVE AMERICAN ALMANAC*

6. Have fun and enjoy yourself. If you are too uptight and take yourself too seriously you won't experience the high. Mindless competition is destructive. When you mindlessly compete you lose sight of the meaning of the sport, which is to do your best, not necessarily to "beat" the other guy. Compete with *respect* for those you are competing with. If you get too competitive and are only in it to win you will be upset every time you lose. You will also forget that your opponents are trying as hard as you are to do well. Lighten up and enjoy, and the high will come, and so will the hole in one, or the speed needed in the race.

"Life must be lived as play."

—PLATO, GREEK PHILOSOPHER

The athletes that don't experience the Zone typically have their focus on winning, or making a goal, and *not* on the activity of playing the game. They are lacking a deep connection to their activity, and thus come away feeling less fulfilled. They may have won the game, but they missed a chance to connect with something bigger and more lasting than winning. That leads to a tendency to seek other highs, such as through drugs, alcohol, violence, or sex. Perhaps this is why we hear of many popular athletes who abuse drugs, or are violent. Winning alone has never been known to offer lasting happiness.

"Let your nature be known and proclaimed."

—HURON PROVERB

Shinzen Young, a meditation teacher, offers an audio tape—*Meditation in the Zone*—that gives instruction on how to turn a workout into a high-quality meditation. He invites us to come into the Zone where our "physical excellence and spiritual growth join hands."

A Few Words of Caution

> **"Life is playfulness . . . We need to play so that we can rediscover the magic all around us."**
>
> —FLORA COLAO, SOCIAL WORKER SPECIALIZING IN CHILD ABUSE

In its best form, participation in a sport will bring joy, an experience of community, and good health. But it has a dark side too: it can become a distraction from other valuable experiences in life. A sport, just like dancing, meditation, or Shiatsu, is only a link in the diverse chain of life experiences. When we give too much time to one sport, or *watching* sports, there is a lot we will miss. If we let one activity completely dominate our life we may feel defeated and incomplete when that one sport or other activity doesn't bring us success or happiness. If we put all our energy into one sport but don't make the team, or get an injury that prevents us from playing, we can become depressed and troubled. At this time in your life, try to give your many talents and interests a chance— experience the many activities that make you feel good.

> *"During my first year out of high school I was completely lost. I went from being a high school jock to being just another guy in college. Now I play hockey and ball for fun. And I take myself a little less seriously. I have friends with other interests too, which expands my experiences. All of life is not about how well I play ball."*
>
> —JOEL, AGE 21

"Within your own house dwells the treasure of joy; so why do you go begging from door to door?"

—SUFI SAYING

Ending on a Smile

"We shall never know all the good that a simple smile can do"

—MOTHER TERESA, CATHOLIC SISTER AND PEACE ACTIVIST

The "smile meditation" is taught by many Buddhist teachers to show us the power of a smile, and that happiness does indeed dwell within us all.

"The sense of living is joy enough."

—EMILY DICKINSON, AMERICAN POET

Sit in a meditation posture (refer to chapter 6 on meditations) *and focus on your breathing for a few minutes. Simply watch the breath move in and move out of your body. Then, begin to bring a small smile to your face. Let your whole face feel this smile, as you sit there, eyes closed, breathing naturally. . . . Smile. Then feel the smile throughout your entire body. Sit in this "smile" for a few minutes. Notice the different thoughts and feelings that arise in your mind and body as you sit and smile.*

Then later in the day, for no particular reason, smile at someone else and notice the response. Notice how a smile lights up both of you.

Books, Resources, and Wisdomkeepers Related to This Chapter

Many books and tapes on Yoga, Tai Chi, and Qigong/Chi Kung are available in libraries and bookstores.

Acupressure Potent Points: A Guide to Self-Care for Common Ailments, by Michael Reed Each (Bantam Books, 1990). Easy to understand and follow for all ages. Recommended for those who want more instruction on self-acupressure.

Drumming at the Edge of Magic: A Journey into the Spirit of Percussion, by Mickey Hart with Jay Stevens (HarperCollins, 1990). You may also want to get Mickey Hart's companion disc to this book: *At the Edge* (RCD 10124/RACS).

Jere Truer
Drum Medicine
3009 Holmes Avenue South
Minneapolis, MN 55410
(612) 824-9745
For more help on drum making and drumming, or for information about Drum Medicine workshops.

Freedom Chants from the Roof of the World, by the Tibetan Gyuto monks (RCD/20113/RACS).

Meditation in the Zone, audio tape, by Shinzen Young
Sounds True Audio
(800) 333-9185
http://shinzen.org

Online Resources

American Running Association
www.americanrunning.org/index.htm
Lots of information on equipment and apparel, training, general health and fitness, and injuries associated with the sport of running.

Breathmastery
www.breathmastery.com
This site discusses many forms of breathwork and movement such as Qigong/Chi Kung, Prana Yoga, and ways to breathe away anger, which may lead to lasting improvements in physical, emotional, and spiritual health.

Seven Circles Foundation
P.O. Box 559
Lagunitas, CA 94938
(510) 236-3512
www.sevencircles.org
A nonprofit organization dedicated to Native American lifeways. Offers educational programs, sweats for people in recovery, and a newsletter. Check out their Web site for calendar of events.

Yoga Inside
210 Sixth Avenue
Venice, CA 90291
(888) 569-9642
www.yogainside.org
Yoga classes for teens that can be brought into your school. Also offers classes for youth who are

incarcerated or in detention facilities. An excellent resource for those of you interested in bringing yoga into your community.

Cedar Mountain Drums

www.cedarmtndrums.com

Resources and articles on drum making and drumming circles. Offers kits and materials for drum making from its Portland, Oregon store. Also building a national list of open drumming circles.

FoxDrums

foxdrums.s5.com

Makers of custom drums and community drums. Offers drum-making workshops.

Mike Flanagan's Shiatsu pages

www.shiatsu.8m.com

Mike's site gives a great description of what Shiatsu is and what it is good for, shows pictures of treatment poses, and provides links to local practitioners and other massage and bodywork sites.

RhythmWeb

www.rhythmweb.com

A fun site with separate pages for various percussion instruments, such as the djembe, doumbek, frame drum, handmade drums, and the drumset. It also includes pages of world cultures where drumming is an important aspect of life and society with audio clips of percussion performances.

White Horse Spirit Drums and Rattles

www.worlddrums.com

A site filled with Native American drum culture, how to make a drum, painting drums, and drumming stories.

Yoga

www.rivermaya.com

This site is divided into three parts: meditation (*sadhana*), exercises (*asanas*), and breathing (*pranayama*). The meditation part is a basic guide to beginning a meditation practice, the exercises show us many Yoga poses (including the Cobra, Lotus, Bow, and Wheel poses), and the breathing section tells us about the long, deep breathing that can help to relieve stress and eliminate toxins in the body.

One hot, summer day a lion and a boar arrived to drink at the same pool of water. They soon began to argue over who should drink first, and they ended up getting into a bloody fight. The fight became quite gruesome with each animal receiving dreadful bites and scratches from the other.

All tired out, they stopped to catch their breath. While resting, the lion and the boar saw some vultures flying above. The vultures' mouths were watering as they wondered which of the two would end up a corpse on the ground.

At this point the two fighters looked at each other and decided to stop their bloody battle.

"It would be better to be friends and share some water," they said to each other, "than to become tasty morsels for vultures."

—"THE LION AND THE BOAR," *AESOP'S FABLES*

Chapter Nine

The Thunderers

Acts of Outrageous Compassion

"The best possible work has not yet been done. If I were 21 today I would elect to join the communicating network of those young people, the world over, who recognize the urgency of life-supporting change, knowledge joined to action: knowledge about what man has been and is can protect the future."

—MARGARET MEAD, ANTHROPOLOGIST

"You gain strength, courage, and confidence by every experience in which you really stop to look fear in the face. . . . You must do the things you think you cannot do."

—ELEANOR ROOSEVELT, (1884–1962), FORMER FIRST LADY, ACTIVIST, AND HUMANITARIAN

"If you bring forth what is within you, what you bring forth will save you. If you do not bring forth what is within you, what you do not bring forth will destroy you."

—JESUS, GNOSTIC GOSPELS

WHAT DO YOU NEED to speak out about? What are your concerns in your personal life, in your community, in the world around you? What do you witness that upsets you? What do you sense would make the adults in your life uneasy if you *did* speak out about it? What needs to be talked about—and heard?

What are you passionate about? What moves your heart to com*passionate* action?

"Acting with compassion is not doing good because we think we ought to. It is being drawn to action by heart-felt passion. It is giving ourselves into what we are doing, being present in the moment—no matter how difficult, sad, or even boring it feels, no matter how much it demands. It is acting from our deepest understanding of what life is, listening intently for the skillful means in each situation, and not compromising the truth."

—RAM DASS, MEDITATION TEACHER AND SOCIAL ACTIVIST, FROM *COMPASSION IN ACTION*

The "truth" *is* the Thunder Wisdom you contain during your Thundering Years. This energy is a powerful force that can help those who are suffering and in need, including the planet itself. Compassionate action is "acting out" with purpose. It is using your Thunder-energy in a powerful, yet positive way—"Bring us your Thunder, so the RAINS will come."

Thunder Wisdom

We are not typically encouraged to listen to our anger. Instead, we are instructed to "control" it. While it is important not to harm anyone with our anger, this emotion is a valuable one. It's worth paying attention to and doing something with. Your intensity is an important part of who you are right now. And your anger, along with your need to "act out," is also part of this intensity. Getting your message *heard* can be a challenge. Speaking out about your feelings, protesting issues that concern you, expressing your anger creatively, and helping others speak out are central to the life of the Spiritual Warrior. Acting out with

"We are here

because there are things

that need our help.

Like the planet.

Like each other.

Like animals.

The world is like a garden,

and we are its protectors."

—B.B. KING, BLUES MUSICIAN

what Wisdomkeepers refer to as "skillful means"—rocking the boat without harming anyone—is part of the sacred journey into adulthood.

In many African tribes and in other indigenous cultures, it is accepted that the mental, spiritual, and physical health of the young people indicates the *overall health or disease of the community.* How the youth are doing says how the *community* is doing. Today there seems to be a lot of anger in teenagers. The world community needs to pay serious attention to you—your feelings, concerns, and desires. Your THUNDER. Your protests, your acting out, when done with purpose, are rites of passage. The thundering in the THUNDERing Years is the sound of your intensity, anger, and compassion.

> "Isn't it obvious what we would be angry about? . . . The condition of the planet, the constant need to be in competition with someone, the fear of what the future holds for us, parents ignoring us or forcing their lifestyles on us, teachers and schools being dishonest about the drug and alcohol abuse by students, fear of no career opportunities once we graduate, the system's way of educating us, adults 'teaching' one thing and doing another, the emphasis on athletes in high school and colleges, intolerance of differences, the gossip that goes on, and the way adults are putting younger and younger kids in prison. How could these NOT make a healthy, sane person angry?"
>
> —JACKIE, AGE 21

Anger can be an invitation to take a new road, or to *make* a new road, because *something* is not working with the old way. How do these and other problems call upon you to do something?

> "It isn't that they can't see the solution. It is that they can't see the problem."
>
> —G. K. CHESTERON, AUTHOR OF *SAINT FRANCIS OF ASSISI*

> "When I dare to be powerful—to use my strength
> in the service of my vision,
> Then it becomes less and less important whether I am afraid."
>
> —AUDRE LORDE, AFRICAN AMERICAN POET AND ACTIVIST

Start Where You Are

> "Small service is true service . . .
> The daisy, by the shadow that it casts,
> Protects the lingering dewdrop from the sun."
>
> —WILLIAM WORDSWORTH, ENGLISH POET

"If you think you are too small to be effective, you have never been in bed with a mosquito."

—BETTE REESE

". . . everything here

apparently needs us, this fleeting world,

which in some strange way

keeps calling to us. Us, the most

fleeting of all."

—RAINER MARIA RILKE, GERMAN POET

It's easy to get overwhelmed with the enormity and complexity of things you'd like to see done differently in the world. Before you get paralyzed into no action at all, stop . . . take a breath . . . and think of what you might do if you could change *one* thing. Keep it small. Keep it simple. It doesn't need to be big to make a big difference. None of us has to look very far to know we are needed.

Just look around—wherever there is pain, there is a need for help. Or, look inside yourself. Sometimes we choose to help others in the area that we have pain.

Chances are you will need to be a little outrageous to get your chosen message across. Just remember, you deserve to have your message heard. Even if life is very difficult right now, *you are not lost,* and your opinion is needed.

"I'm always getting in trouble for speaking up. Sure, it's frustrating, but what really upsets me is the high school teachers' reaction to my ideas. I can tell they don't really think much of what I think. I think we should have a school paper without any censorship. I think we should get gym credits for taking Yoga. But these ideas all get lost in the 'rules.' All the more reason I need to speak up, otherwise the school starts to assume we're all okay with the way things are."

—ANABEL, AGE 17

You may find your choice of clothes upsets some people or you've spoken up about an opinion that makes others uneasy. Your actions may result in you or others feeling *uncomfortable*. The intense life of those on the Spiritual Warrior's journey is often not very *comfortable* because it is always changing—important and challenging stuff is always going on.

"You (the young people) are one step ahead of us (adults) in redefining your reality. And we adults are trying to keep up with you. I know you have a prayer, a reaching, a spiritual desire—a calling that we need to listen to. *Everything you do is part of this prayer*—the clothes you wear, your songs, your music, your behaviors, the jewelry you wear and the drugs you may take. Everything. I understand these as your prayer and it's my responsibility to listen to you."

—Estaban, Principal of
Oneida Nations High School, Wisconsin

Sitting on the couch watching television takes less effort than trying to write a letter or put together a play. Choosing to "go along with the crowd" that is drinking and driving may be more comfortable than being the one who says, "No, I'm not coming if you're going to be drinking." *Have you ever gone along with something because it felt too uncomfortable to say no?* You are among the majority! If you choose to be on the path of the Spiritual Warrior, you may often feel part of a *minority*. Most people who have made great accomplishments—such as winning an Olympic medal, traveling to new places, winning a Nobel Peace Prize, taking risks to help others, or writing a book—are those who *don't* just follow the crowd. They are willing to take risks that separate them from others—risks that may make them feel uncomfortable for a while.

Radical Harmlessness: A Warrior's Creed

"Darkness cannot drive out darkness; only light can do that.
Hate cannot drive out hate; only love can do that."

—Dr. Martin Luther King Jr., minister and civil rights leader

To be a Spiritual Warrior is to fight against anything that keeps us down, anything that doesn't allow our essential and true nature (our "medicine") to come forth. On the other hand, an important part of compassionate action is understanding the effect our actions have on others.

"Everyday problems teach us to have a realistic attitude. They teach us that life is what life is: flawed, yet with tremendous potential for joy and fulfillment. Everything is workable."

—Lama Surya Das,
Buddhist lama,
author of
Awakening the Buddha Within

Buddhist Wisdomkeepers talk about acting *consciously*—being aware of the consequences of our speech and actions—because there is an understanding that all action results in a reaction. Everything we do has an effect. To become conscious of the effects of our actions is to take the more skillful path—a path that will have more rewards and benefits.

The code that guides all Spiritual Warriors—regardless of differences in religious beliefs, family experiences, or cultural and economic backgrounds—is to bring forth our power by being creative *and* intense, but without causing harm to ourself or to others. Our true nature is always good, although it can be disruptive. Our passion, our intensity about something, may *upset* people but this by itself does not mean we are causing them harm. The creed of *harmlessness* is inherent in most spiritual practices. You have likely heard this spiritual principle expressed in what is known as the Golden Rule: "Do unto others as you would have them do unto you." Living by this principle gives us permission to bring forth into a safe place that which is already within us. This means you can (and should be allowed to) express your intensity in your own way—doing many outrageous acts, experiencing altered states, and even being "destructive" as long as you do not cause harm.

The desire to express oneself through destructive acts is actually quite natural. In fact, *destruction is part of nature*. Nature is "destroying" itself all the time. Nature has a very dark side. It is part of nature's law: when something is being created, something else is being destroyed. This *balance* between destruction and creation is part of the natural evolution of all life on this planet. In teenagers, the child is being "destroyed" as the adult is being "created." Body cells, muscles, and organs are continually in this process of destruction and creation. *Destruction is part of the creative life process.* The pairing of destruction and creation gives an intensity to every creative act—be it making a simple sketch, running a race, or beating on a drum. Destruction is part of birth and creation is part of death. A bird is born, its shell is destroyed. *Yet, nothing is harmed.*

"All I was doing was kicking a rotten pumpkin down a hill. A cop stopped and questioned me. I told him, 'I'm kicking a rotten pumpkin

"What is the purpose of life? I believe that satisfaction, joy, and happiness are the ultimate purposes of life. And the basic sources of happiness are a good heart, compassion, and love. If we have these mental attitudes, even if we are surrounded by hostility, we will feel little disturbance."

—His Holiness the 14th Dalai Lama

down the street.' I don't do drugs. I 'do' games. I play games and I design games. If rolling a rotten pumpkin down a vacant street is 'delinquent behavior' then we are all in a lot of trouble. I stood my ground with this cop, who acted like he was going to take me in to the station. When he finally left, I kept kicking the pumpkin down the street. The whole experience gave me a great idea for a computer game about this tension between cops and teens."

MICHAEL, AGE 18

In nature there is a natural balance of destruction and creation. With us, however, there is too often a great *imbalance*.

"The way I see it, each of us is a small replica of Mother Earth. We have our positive and our negative, and the good works with the bad. It's just that there's an imbalance in a lot of people. They go too far either one way or another."

—JACKIE YELLOW TAIL, CROW WOMAN,
FROM *WALKING IN THE SACRED MANNER*

Even though the people before you, and some of the adults around you now, have caused themselves or others harm, *you can live your life differently.* You can live in more balance—creating with regard to what's being destroyed. This is the responsibility of the Warrior on the spiritual journey—to be aware of our surroundings, and to be more in tune to the consequences of our decisions and actions. (Even when those around us are not so brave!) If we want to make something good from our lives we have to commit to practices like that of the Spiritual Warriors of the ancient Tibetan culture who respected everyone and everything. According to Tibetan lama Chögyam Trungpa, "The essence of Warriorship, or the essence of human bravery, is refusing to give up on anyone or anything."

This great tradition of living in balance and harmlessness helps us to find greater meaning and more happiness in our own lives. The box of sacred wisdom quotes on the following two pages is just a sample of the many traditions that share this belief. It is a principle has worked for thousands of years; it will work for you too.

"Consciously or unconsciously, every one of us does render some service or other. If we cultivate the habit of doing this service deliberately, our desire for service will steadily grow stronger, and will make, not only for our own happiness, but that of the world at large."

—MAHATMA GANDHI,
INDIAN NATIONALIST
AND SPIRITUAL
LEADER

"Write the wrongs that are done to you in sand, but write the good things that happen to you on a piece of marble. Let go of all emotions such as resentment and retaliation, which diminish you, and hold on to the emotions, such as gratitude and joy, which increase you." —Arabic proverb

"God's way is gain that works no harm." —Taoism

"No one of you is a believer until he desires for his brother that which he desires for himself." —Sunni, Islam

"Therefore all that you wish men to do to you, even so do you also to them; for this is the law of the prophets." —Matthew 7:12, Christian

"All men shrink from suffering, and all love life; remember that you too are like them; make your own self the measure of the others, and so abstain from causing harm." —Buddhist Book of Proverbs

"Therefore I tell you: Be humble, be harmless." —Hinduism

"Regard your neighbor's gain as your own gain and your neighbor's loss as your own loss." —T'ai Shang Kan Ying P'ien, Taoism

"Thou shalt love the neighbor as thyself." —Leviticus 19:18, Judaism

"Take the time to develop a good heart and your life will be filled with happiness."—His Holiness the 14th Dalai Lama

"That nature alone is good which refrains from doing unto another whatsoever is not good for itself." —Dadistan-i-dinik 94:5, Zoroastrianism

"Ascribe not to any that which thou wouldest not have ascribed to thee, and say not that which thou doest not." —Baha'u'llah, Hidden Words, Arabic 29, Baha'i

"What you do to others, you do to yourself." —Unitarian Universalist

"Do what ye will, but harm none. What ye shall do unto others: be it for evil, it shall return sevenfold; be it for good, tenfold." —Traditional Wiccan creed

"We need to go toward Spirit now. We have to shift our attention back to the earth and stop causing harm to Mother Earth and its peoples." —Oneida elder

"The main thing is to be good to each other and cause no person or living thing harm. From such a place of harmony, the dream world is possible." —Australian Aboriginal elder

"A Spiritual Warrior's battle is for safety, sanity, and respect. This wisdom has been around since the beginning of time. Live fully and meaningfully and cause no harm." —Tibetan physician

"Be not estranged from another for in every heart pervades the Lord." —Sri Guru Granth Sahib, Sikkism

"In happiness and suffering, in joy and grief, regard all creatures as you would regard your own self." —Yoga-Sastra, Jainism

"Surely it is the maxim of loving-kindness: Do not unto others what you would not have them do unto you." —Analects 15:23, Confucianism

"This is the sum of duty: Do naught unto others which would cause you pain if done to you."—Mahabharata 5:1517, Brahmanism

"Do no wrong nor hate your neighbor; for it is not he that you wrong; you wrong yourself." —Shawnee chant

"Be wise as serpents and harmless as doves."—Matthew 10:16, Christian

The sacred words from these numerous traditions are showing us a way to true happiness and fufillment. Following them does not mean we won't make lots of mistakes. But after each mistake, we have something to come back to—wisdom that has guided millions of people over the years. This is why a spiritual tradition is often called a spiritual "practice," because we are all just practicing. And the more we practice, the happier we become. It takes bravery to go out into the world as a Spiritual Warrior holding on to such principles as radical *harmlessness*. But the rewards are worth the effort.

"You see things and say, 'why?' but I dream things that never were and say, 'why not.'"

—GEORGE BERNARD SHAW, PLAYWRIGHT

Fighting Back

"A little bird sat in a cage near a window. As night fell she started to sing her song. A bat flew by and heard her singing. He came up and asked why she never sang during the day, but only in the dark.

'I have my reasons,' replied the caged bird. 'You see, I was once singing during the day and was captured and put in this small cage! This is a lesson I will never forget!'

'It doesn't do you any good to be careful now,' said the bat. 'You should have learned this lesson *before* they caught you.'

—"THE CAGED BIRD," *AESOP'S FABLES*

"We must be the change we want in the world."

—MAHATMA GANDHI, INDIAN NATIONALIST AND SPIRITUAL LEADER

Not causing harm (or being "spiritual") does not mean you will never need to fight back against those who are causing *you* harm. To live by the principle of harmlessness does not mean to put yourself in any experience that is unsafe or disrespectful. You need not agree to anything that is against your beliefs. There will be times you will need to stand up and fight for something. As illustrated by the story that follows, it is okay to protect and defend yourself.

A young woman in India took it upon herself to practice meditation every day. She practiced hard, hoping she would someday be a teacher to others. Sitting in her room, she would fill her heart with loving-kindness, first for herself, then for all others in the world. When she left for school each day she would feel this love in her heart, until she met up with the neighbor down the street who would subject her to unwelcomed touches and comments about her body. She would send him loving-kindness and forgiveness every morning when she meditated and then feel awful when she encountered him at the store or on the street. One day she could stand no more from him and began to chase this older man down the street with her upraised umbrella. To her dismay she passed her meditation teacher standing on the side of the street observing her. Embarrassed and ashamed she went to her next meditation session expecting to be rebuked for her anger and lack of compassion.

"What you should do," her teacher kindly advised her, "is to fill your heart with loving-kindness, and with as much mindfulness as you can muster, hit this unruly guy over the head with your umbrella."

Today, you could send this man loving thoughts *and* charge him with sexual harassment. It is just and fair to file charges against someone who is harassing you since this is a natural consequence of his (or her) harmful behavior. At the same time, you can hope and pray he learns a better way. "Wishing him better" is an act of compassion and courage on your part.

Compassion in Action

"In our era, the road to holiness passes through the world of action."

—Dag Hammarskjold, Swedish peace activist
and former Secretary General of the United Nations

All social action—protesting, speaking out, demonstrating, caring for others, helping a stranger, being kind to others, and volunteering—is part of a spiritual path. Innovative thinkers such as Martin Luther King Jr., Mahatma Gandhi, Ram Dass, St. Francis of Assisi, Margaret Mead, Chögyam Trungpa, Black Elk, and Henry David Thoreau, to name a few, all say that *social action is an important part of the spiritual life*. The reason this is true is because social action comes from the part of you that sees clearly—that knows that something isn't right, or sees that someone needs help. It comes from your view of the world (from the mountaintop), which is *your* truth. It comes from the Thunder-energy that wants to change and improve things.

Here are just a few ideas for putting your passions into action. As you will see, many begin with yourself.

Write poetry, an essay, or play about your anger and give a performance to your community. Set up a play or show in your school, campus, or neighborhood to express your concerns. Take risks in what you write and say—make others feel uneasy. Make others think. Create or join a Poetry Slam. Go read some poetry or prose at an open mike on campus, or at a local coffeehouse. Publish a poem or article in a local paper. The written word is a very powerful way to get your message across.

Destroy a habit. Change a pattern today. Daily life is a series of habits—from the time we get up, to what we eat for dinner. Who we talk to, when we eat lunch, the classes we attend, where we sit, how we wear our hair, how we greet people, such things are mostly done out of habit. Science has documented that when we change even a small habitual movement, for example, brushing our teeth differently, a new neuropathway is created in the brain! Imagine the effect of changing a simple pattern such as eating lunch with a different group of people!

Begin by noticing what small, harmless habits you engage in on a daily basis. Then, choose to end one of those habits. You will be surprised to find how challenging this can be and how it will change the way you feel or see things.

Organize a group around an issue that needs changing. This can be done through certain classes (political science, for example), on your own, or with

"Resolve to create a good future. It's where you'll spend the rest of your life."

—CHARLES FRANKLIN KETTERING, INVENTOR OF THE ELECTRICAL IGNITION SYSTEM

"Listen carefully to what you hear. In the measure you give you shall receive."

—MARK 4:24, BIBLE

Teenage Sweet

I am teenage Sweet
I'm cigarettes and summer heat
seventy miles an hour
and smoking
And I don't care where the road leads

I am teenage High
I'm fireworks worth the sky
I'm still driving
and smoking
and I don't know where I am

I am teenage Love
I'm lust and I'm cheap drugs
Please see me—
find me
I want a *real* companion

I am teenage Joys
cheap thrills and childish toys
They don't let me grow up
I'm determined to grow up
But I will never be like *them*

I am teenage Angst
I'm bitter, pulling at the ranks
I can't seem to get out—
Don't know how to stay here

I am teenage Fire
They call it rebellion, call me a liar
Sometimes I forget that I'm better than *That*
But I'm better than *That*
Teenage Sweet.

LIA ELLESON, AGE **16**, POET AND ACTIVIST,
FROM *BUTTERFLIES IN THE MUD*

The Thunderers

the help of a mentor or an already active group. Keep your goal simple, so that you and the group can stay focused around it. One group of teen athletes painted posters protesting the lack of sports for the disabled in their school. They ended up helping with the Special Olympics that year and they got the attention they hoped for from the community. In California, Arizona, and other states bordering Mexico, many small groups of teenagers protested the law that attempted to prevent children of illegal immigrants from getting an education or health care. Group organizing is about having a "louder" voice for a message you feel is important enough to be heard. Also, you can contact your local paper, in hopes of getting an article published about your cause. Change takes time—getting your point noticed is the important first step.

Stay active. Physical activity is an important part of a spiritually healthy person. Exercise can quickly transform negative energy into positive energy.

- Breathe and walk in the fresh air.
- Turn on some music and dance.
- Sing or chant.
- Practice Yoga.
- Stretch.
- Beat on your drum.
- Go play.

Kill your television. Some of us decided to "kill our televisions." One family gave away their television to a shelter and two loaned theirs to friends for a few months. The one shared experience was an awareness of how much TV they watch. They all found they did more when they went without television.

You can try this too without actually "killing" your television. Let your life be free of television for at least a month and see what that's like for you. Anger can come as a result of BOREDOM! Did you know that? When we sit around too much and are not involved in something, we build up negative, intense emotions such as resentment, jealousy, boredom, and depression. You will likely find that you begin to DO more when the television is off. Then try to watch less

"Life's most urgent question is, what are you doing for others?"

—MARTIN LUTHER KING JR., MINISTER AND CIVIL RIGHTS LEADER

when you do go back to it. You may want to break a habit of always watching a certain show.

Volunteer your time and energy. There is an abundance of people and places that need help, where your time and effort can make a difference. It can be a local organization such as a home for the elderly or a national organization advocating for a healthier environment. Listed at the end of this chapter are just a few possibilities to explore. The opportunities to volunteer are endless. You will find that volunteer work will give you more purpose and direction in your life. And you will discover more about yourself and be able to make better choices of what you want to do as you move further into your adult life.

> "In my freshman year at high school I found myself getting depressed, confused, and withdrawn from my friends. I couldn't seem to find anything that helped. I was so insecure and scared. And I'm not sure why. Then my dad suggested I VOLUNTEER. it sounded like another bad idea, until I went to a local child care center that helped special needs kids. I started helping after school and then stayed to help in the summer. The children were wonderful and something shifted in me. My time there lifted me out of this major funk I was in. I ended up volunteering there for 4 years. I'm thinking of being a child advocate or lawyer for children."
>
> —CAYCE, AGE 20

"I don't know what your destiny will be, but one thing I know: the only ones among you who will be really happy are those who have sought and found how to serve."

—DR. ALBERT SCHWEITZER, ALSATIAN THEOLOGIAN, PHILOSOPHER, PHYSICIAN, AND MUSICIAN

When His Holiness the 14th Dalai Lama was asked what gave him the greatest pleasure, he responded, "Helping someone." Helping others is a way to make a strong statement about what is important to us. Volunteering also gives us the ability to "walk in another's shoes." This, in turn, gives us more compassion and understanding of others' experiences. It broadens our perspective—we begin to get a clearer picture of all that goes on outside of ourselves. When we start helping someone, something inside of us opens up. We start to find that we are less angry with everyone. Nothing cures an angry heart more than making a positive difference in someone *else's* life. Everyone we help, helps us become the person we are meant to be. The happiest people I've encountered, all have one thing in common—they give of their time and resources to help others.

Drop out of school. Many high school and college students redeem themselves by dropping out of the traditional school system. While some go back later, many go on to find alternative educational opportunities ranging from home schooling to various alternative schools. Those who use this time to *find themselves* succeed in ways they wouldn't have had they remained in the traditional mainstream of education. As far as education goes, "one size does not fit all," and going in search of alternatives can often save your real interest in being educated. The parents of one creative, intelligent young woman—who was barely sustaining herself in public school—had the insight to let her finish her education "at home," outside the walls of the local public school. She immediately began to design a life full of meaning and purpose. She volunteers at a local crisis center, writes poetry, and designs and sews her own clothes. She offers pageants of her dresses for the local girls who want unique prom dresses to wear. She couldn't receive school credit for any of these activities, but she was able to receive "life credits" that helped her get accepted into college.

Those who have dropped out suggest that you "drop out with a plan"—not just aimlessly end your formal education. There are many paths to an education, as there are many roads to happiness and success. Find the one that works for you.

Participate in a peaceful but powerful protest. You can use your Thunder-energy and vision to make a statement—to protest the wrongs you see around you, "to protect the future" as anthropologist Margaret Mead said (see page 209). There are times when making a statement through protest will be the most effective way of speaking out and getting your point across. The Spiritual Warrior is "at war" with such things as abuse, pollution, ignorance, and cruelty. To protest is to state a position—to assert your opinion enough so it is noticed by others. Protesting is about speaking out about something you feel strongly about. You can do a protest alone, organize a group, or join up with others protesting something.

You can protest at a peaceful rally, write and sign petitions, write letters to

"Volunteering is good for the soul."

—STEVE ALLEN, COMEDIAN

"Only a life lived for others is a life worthwhile."

—ALBERT EINSTEIN, PHYSICIST

224

those in political office, join a letter campaign (where many send letters on a topic to the general public), make protest signs, sit in, or walk out. A simple but powerful form of protest is to not agree to do something you feel is wrong.

Speak out. One way to act out with purpose is to speak up—to *say what's on your mind.* If you come from a family that does not encourage you to speak out, find people who will listen to what you have to say.

> *"The biggest problem is no one wants to be different but everyone wants to be unique, special. Know what I mean? We are afraid to speak out about unpopular things."*
>
> —JESSE, AGE 19

> *"We need to be willing first to be honest with each other. We are too sensitive to what other kids think of us and as a result won't speak up with a different or new opinion."*
>
> —ERIN, AGE 17

Be honest and outspoken with those who have authority in your life, even when you disagree with them. *It is not illegal to disagree with someone.*

> *"It's stupid just to teach abstinence from sex. We need to make sex nothing to be ashamed of. It's natural to have sexual feelings at our age! We should be recognized as having sexual feelings just like adults. Teenagers are embarrassed to go in a store and ask for condoms. Now that's a problem. Abstinence is a good choice, but we should still be seen and understood as having sexual feelings."*
>
> —TOM, AGE 17

If you are put down by an instructor for having a difference of opinion, consider reporting this to your school counselor, principal, or college adviser. *You have a right to express differences.*

End an abusive, dead-end, or painful relationship. Get out of a gang that promotes violence. Getting out of a destructive relationship will add peace to your life and to others. Ending a dead-end or abusive relationship, or ending

> **"A society grows great when old men plant trees in whose shade they do not expect to sit."**
>
> —GREEK PROVERB

> **"It is no use walking anywhere to preach unless our walking is our preaching."**
>
> —ST. FRANCIS OF ASSISI, FOUNDER OF THE FRANCISCAN ORDERS

your involvement in a hostile group, will open your life to new and better relationships. Relationships take up a lot of time, energy, and commitment on our parts. Is there a relationship in your life that needs to be "destroyed" through the harmless act of letting it go? This Sufi fable says so much . . .

> A blackbird found a large piece of food in the village and flew up into the big peaceful sky with the food in its beak. A flock of other blackbirds chased after him and aggressively attacked the food, pulling it from his beak. The blackbird finally let go of the last piece and the frenzied flock left him alone, flying off fighting over the food. The bird swooped through the big blue sky, diving up and then down and thought, "I have lost the food but I have regained the peaceful sky."

Declaring Independence

So much of our Thundering Years is about coming into our own—discovering who we are and then telling that to the world. Yet it is also a time of intense pressure to fit in—to a societal mold, to our parents' expectations, to our chosen group of friends.

Becoming part of a gang can be a powerful and exciting rite of passage. Feeling as if you belong—having an identity and a sense of clear purpose. But while gangs may seem to protect and nurture you, and define who you are, they can also strip away your independence—your ability and freedom to choose what is best for you.

The Wakeup Call

If you are part of a gang that promotes violence, chances are, you or someone you know will be dead, addicted to drugs, or seriously injured within the year. Even when the odds are strongly against you, you can reach outside your circumstances and design your own life. If your parents are angry, neglectful, unhappy people, to break this pattern will take a great amount of courage and energy on your part. If you look, you will find someone who can help you get beyond your circumstances and free yourself.

It may not be a named gang that is trying to recruit you; it may be a few young people who have "dropped out" and want you to join up with them. The violence that they advocate may be against yourself such as scarring, abusing drugs, or taking dangerous risks—encouraging you to act out in ways that harm your body, mind, and spirit.

The Escape Hatch

You will have to be brave and assertive if you want to get out of the gang or cycle of violence you are in. Several teens who were once part of gangs and are now out, invite those of you wanting to get out, or those of you wanting to help someone else out, to consider these suggestions:

First, decide that you want out and be prepared to be committed to changing your daily routine. You must have a conviction to live differently or you will easily be scared or seduced back into the gang or violent scene. You have to be willing to end these relationships and hang out at different places. Your commitment must be strong.

Second, find an adult who will help you out of the situation. Do your parents know of your involvement with these people? If both or one of your parents is involved in your well-being, tell them what you need to do and get their help. If your parents are unable to help you, then you may need to go outside of the family for help. Sometimes grandparents or other relatives are great resources. David B. said it was his grandfather who saved him. When he decided to end his connection to a violent group he moved in with his grandfather to get his High School GED and apply to colleges. You can attend Al Anon meetings, go to your school counselor or college adviser, or go to the youth director at your church or synagogue for help. The adults in your life are supposed to help make certain your environment is safe for you.

Third, get involved in activities that involve others such as sports at the local Y's, bands, local youth organizations, and activities that are *sponsored by adults and mentors.* Join up with other groups that are active in the community in other ways.

"The tree falls the way it leans."

—BULGARIAN PROVERB

Fourth, don't argue with the group or gang about your leaving. *You don't owe them an explanation.* Even if you have agreed to stay with them or have made some pact, it is still okay to leave. A pact is not binding unless you continue to agree to it. It's typical that such groups try to make you feel obligated to them—this is a way *they control you.* Don't let your life be controlled by anyone or any group.

Debra Goldentyer, in her book *Gangs,* says that the best way to leave is to "fade out." Fading out means you leave quietly but *slowly.* You show up less and less for activities, become less and less available. In some cases, however, it may work better to leave quietly and *quickly.* Most gangs do not want you to leave once you have joined up. They consider you their "property."

Fifth, change schools or move, if it is necessary and possible. Sometimes the only way to get out of a gang or violent situation is to get away, at least for a while. If you are being hassled on school grounds *it is the school's legal obligation to make it safe for you.* Safety at school is a right that is guaranteed to you by law. We understand that you are not likely to report these individuals to the school authorities (although it is an option).

Sixth, if you're abusing drugs (which includes alcohol), stop. Get help. There are twelve-step groups available across the country for all ages. If your connection with the gang is your dependency on drugs *then someone else owns you by this dependency.* That makes you weak and vulnerable, not strong and secure. You will never have control of your own life as long as you are dependent on someone else for your high.

Seventh, write your local senator or congressman, and/or the President of the United States. Tell them about the ongoing violence that you are in contact with. Send a copy of your letter to your local paper. The great majority of adults are ignorant about the very real violence that you may encounter on a daily basis. They need to be alerted and held more accountable for the increasing violence that you are up against. Tell the truth. We all need to hear it. Also, warn other kids younger than you of the dangers and pitfalls of gangs and violence.

Finally, never give up on yourself or your future. The future belongs to you (and to your children). Don't let someone else take that from you. Breaking free from a gang may be the hardest passage you move through during your Thundering Years. Remember that asking for help is not a sign of weakness but a sign of strength and courage—courage to take action in order to make a change in your life. You'll discover along this passage old and new friends, people who survived the journey before you, and Wisdomkeepers (such as those described in the next chapter) who can help guide you in the next phase of your journey in life.

Books, Resources, and Wisdomkeepers Related to This Chapter

In all the sacred texts, the meaning of compassion is expressed: the Bible, the Koran, the Dhammapada, the Bhagavad Gita, the Ramayana, the Tao-te-Ching, and the Popul Vuh. Consult any of these and they will instruct you toward compassionate action. Here are five other contemporary texts with ideas worth checking out:

Compassion in Action: Setting Out on the Path of Service, by Ram Dass and Mirabai Bush (Crown Publishers, 1992). Book includes Ram Dass's spiritual journey and how serving others lifts us up. Full of inspirational guidance and ideas. Includes an extensive resource list of volunteer organizations.

How to Make the World a Better Place: A Beginner's Guide to Doing Good, by John Hollender (William Morrow, 1990). A book filled with ideas for effecting positive social change. Includes lists of organizations and publications.

Learning Outside the Lines, by Jonathan Mooney and David Cole (Simon & Schuster, 2000). Two Ivy League students with learning disabilities and ADHD (attention deficit hyperactivity disorder) give you the tools for academic success and educational revolution. Great for those headed off to college or who feel lost in the school system.

The Teenagers' Guide to School Outside the Box, by Rebecca Greene (Free Spirit Publishing, 2000). A very useful and enticing guide to "alternative" learning. If you are having trouble in school—get this book.

The Teenage Liberation Handbook: How to Quit School and Get a Real Life and Education, by Grace Llewellyn (Element Books, 1997). An inspiring book for anyone who drops out of high school.

Teens with the Courage to Give: Young People Who Triumphed Over Tragedy and Volunteered to Make a Difference, by Jackie Waldman (Conari Press, 2000). Has useful contacts after each story, if you want to volunteer or find out more. "Although you wouldn't know it from today's headlines, America is full of young people like those in this book, who are doing remarkable things to make this a better world. After reading their stories, it's hard not to be optimistic about the future." —Scott Peterson, Executive Director, The Prudential Spirit of Community Awards.

Amnesty International
322 Eighth Avenue
New York, NY 10001
(212) 807-8400
A human rights organization that focuses on the release of prisoners of conscience. See online resources below for Web site information.

Break the Cycle
P.O. Box 1797
Santa Monica, CA 90406-1797
(888) 988-TEEN
e-mail: btc@pacificnet.net
Contact them if you or someone you know is in an abusive relationship.

Center for Global Education
Augsburg College
731 Twenty-first Avenue, South
Minneapolis, MN 55454
(612) 330-1159
Offers a five-college program in Peace and World Security Studies.

Children of War
85 South Oxford Street
Brooklyn, NY 11217
(718) 858-6882
An international youth leadership training program. Builds partnerships between young people from war zones and U.S. teenagers.

National Association for Mediation in Education (NAME)
425 Amity Street
Amherst, MA 01002
(413) 253-5096
A good source for information about conflict resolutions in schools; maintains a directory of active programs.

Teens Against Gang Violence
2 Moody Street
Dorchester, MA 02124
(617) 282-9659
http://tagv.org/geninfo.htm
Bring a message of peaceful warriorship to your school. You can start a chapter of Teens Against Gang Violence by contacting the address above.

Online Resources

Action Camps
www.yesworld.org
This site offers locations of action camps for young adults ages 15 to 25. The camps teach how to be an activist with such skill building as how to fund-raise, how to speak in public, and how to initiate social change. Scholarships are available; without one it costs about $400 a week.

Amnesty International
www.amnesty.org/
Includes the latest human rights news from around the world, present Amnesty International campaigns, suggestions of what we can do to help the organization, and links to other human rights sites.

Crime Prevention
http://crime-prevention.org/ncpc
For more information about activities or publications on crime prevention. You can also e-mail them at ncpc@web.net.

Global Youth Assembly
www.oneday.org/unya.htm
This site works toward "supporting the dreams and visions of young people for a better world" by including ways for the ideas of young people to be heard such as online petitions, links to youth and peace organizations, and resources available for young people to take action.

Volunteer Opportunities
www.volunteering.org
This site can get you linked to a variety of volunteer opportunities in your area and help you learn more about what's possible.

Youth Crime Watch of America
www.ycwa.org
A resource for peaceful conflict resolution.

Youth Venture
www.youthventure.org
A site that helps you and your community create groups and organizations that benefit others.

The bud
stands for all things,
even for those things that don't flower,
for everything flowers, from within, of self-blessing;
though sometimes it is necessary
to reteach a thing its loveliness,
to put a hand on the brow
of the flower,
and retell it in words and in touch,
it is lovely
until it flowers again from within, of self-blessing.

—GALWAY KINNELL, POET,
FROM *MORTAL ACTS, MORTAL WORDS*

Chapter Ten

Wisdom Seeking

"Other people can't make you see with their eyes. At best they can encourage you to use your own."

—ALDOUS HUXLEY,
AUTHOR OF *BRAVE NEW WORLD*

"It's the blood of the ancients that runs through our veins. And the forms pass, but the circle of life remains."

—ELLEN KLAVEN, AUTHOR OF
THE VEGETARIAN FACTFINDER

"When the student is ready the teacher will come."

—CHINESE PROVERB

EVERY ONE OF US NEEDS the blessings and wisdom of a spiritual teacher, mentor, or elder. The Thundering Years are the best time to seek the wisdom of those who have walked successfully down the creative and spiritual path. Living your dreams can be a struggle in this chaotic world, where too many adults have given up. It's difficult to take healthy risks, stay off drugs and alcohol, work hard in school, and be creative when so many around you are being destructive to themselves or others. To successfully walk the road of the Spiritual Warrior we all need guidance from others who have journeyed ahead of us. The Navajo are guided on their spiritual journey by a spiritual teacher they call a *haatati*, or chanter (what we often refer to as a "Medicine Man"). Tibetans seek guidance from lamas (master spiritual teachers) or *tulkus* (someone who is a recognized reincarnation of a deceased lama). Tibetan lamas and Navajo chanters begin preparing for their position in the community at birth.

Those who have made it through some similar rough times—or have some special insight into your circumstances, whatever they may be—would be good spiritual guides for you. A mentor or spiritual teacher can be someone who is recognized as a spiritual guide (such as a meditation teacher), or a lesser-known person who is a gold mine of love and wisdom for you. He or she can be someone within your family—a grandparent, uncle, aunt, or godparent—or someone outside your family such as a teacher, professor, church or synagogue member, neighbor, priest, rabbi, lama, or meditation instructor. *Anyone* has the potential to be a mentor. One teenager found his mentor while volunteering at a nearby retirement home. As it turned out, the mentor was an elder from his Finnish community and loved helping his young "student" through the telling of stories. The young man has been keeping a journal of these stories that may likely become a book someday.

"Why should young people suffer the ordeals of self-knowledge if there's no one waiting to welcome them home?"

—MICHAEL MEADE, CELTIC STORY-TELLER, AUTHOR OF *MEN AND THE WATER OF LIFE: INITIATION AND THE TEMPERING OF MEN*

"Find and learn more about your cultural background. This will help you get through many things. Knowing who you are, being connected to your history and your culture can help you overcome many difficulties. And, understanding of other people's beliefs, this is important too. This is all part of living the creative life. Find good people to help you answer your questions."

—SALAKWA, ONEIDA NATION, AGE 23

In Search of a Mentor

"Those who seek mentoring will rule the great expanse under heaven."

—SHU CHING, MARTIAL ARTS MASTER

"A mentor has walked the wisdom trail and is now able to open you up to this wisdom inside of you."

—MYRON ESHOWSKY, SHAMANIC HEALER

In those traditional cultures in touch with the value of mentoring—the Chinese, Tibetan, Native American, African American, and Celtic, for example—*the mentor will seek out the mentoree*. Since the mentor relationship is not fostered by our current Western culture, you may need to seek out a mentor for yourself. In your search for a mentor, here are some things to look for:

- Someone older (around 10 years or more), who has wisdom, integrity, and personal power.

- Someone who is not your counselor or one of your parents (although you may have a very good relationship with your parents).

- Someone who has found a way to live creatively and well in the adult world, without abusing drugs or alcohol.

- Someone who participates in play and work in ways that do not cause anyone (including themselves) any harm.

- Someone who has the ability to take healthy risks and learns from his or her mistakes.

- Someone who holds a unique understanding and fondness for you, but is not selfish with you.

- *Someone who does not want anything from you* (such as money, work, sex, or gifts) but is in your life to guide and teach *you*.

Myron Eshowsky, a shamanic healer who works with healing youth gangs, believes a mentor should be someone who "listens to you and understands the truth about you—has insight to what your purpose is. A mentor can see your

> **"If he is indeed wise, he does not bid you enter the house of his wisdom, but rather leads you to the threshold of your own mind."**
>
> —KHALIL GIBRAN, LEBANESE POET AND PHILOSOPHER, AUTHOR OF *THE PROPHET*

soul." A mentor is someone who is willing to give you the time and attention you need and share his or her knowledge and wisdom with you. Your mentor should be the same gender as yourself. And, he or she may have other things in common with you, such as sexual preference, religious or ethnic background, talents, and interests. The important thing is that your mentor is someone you can identify with. If you are gay or lesbian, you may want to seek a gay or lesbian mentor. If you are Hispanic, you may seek a Hispanic mentor to guide you. Or, your mentor may share spiritual ideals with you, or be into something you enjoy, such as hunting and fishing, or music. Steven found his mentor at the rodeo:

"I was heavy into weed. Most of the time I was stoned I was bored and lonely, even though I was hanging with a group of stoners like myself. Then I went to the rodeo and fell in love with horses. I met up with a group of other horse lovers and then met my mentor, Paul, who helped me learn to ride and do shows. Riding and caring for horses lifts me up, and Paul understands this."

—STEVEN, AGE 21

Your choice of a mentor needs to be someone who can commit to a relationship with you. Someone who actually has the time to guide you and be with you. A good mentor will encourage you to participate in activities that benefit you and help you to learn about all of your choices by getting exposed to different people and experiences.

On your journey through the Thundering Years you need the special help that only a mentor can give.

"Today, there are many products and services available for self-actualization, learning, and personal growth, usually in the form of self-help books, magazines, computers, and other audiovisual technology, seminars, retreats, and so on. Yet a very important component is missing from these methods of self-growth: that of individualized, tailored, one-to-one environments for giving and receiving the gift of wisdom—the time-honored process of mentoring."

—CHUNGLIANG AL HUANG AND JERRY LYNCH, AUTHORS OF
MENTORING: THE TAO OF GIVING AND RECEIVING WISDOM

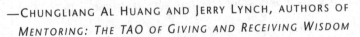

Your mentor's foremost responsibility is to help you know *all that is good about you,* while helping to guide you down a safe and good path.

Mentors are respected in their community because they have *earned* this respect through their own choices and behavior.

Mentors for Young Men

"There are men who wield power without pride, who are rich but simple in their ways, who are learned but have no arrogance. They are divine spirits in human form."

—Baba Muktananda, Indian elder

According to Robert Bly, a well-known elder and poet, a good choice in a mentor for young men would be a "strong man who deals with his anger in a healthy way. He also is a man who enjoys his work." Anger is a common emotion shared among young men today. This emotion is part of your Thunder-energy. Search out a mentor who doesn't escape into drugs and alcohol to cover up his anger or unhappiness, who expresses his anger in healthy and creative ways that help, rather than hinder, a situation.

"You can be big, without making someone else small."

—Terri Severson, teen mentor

A mentor isn't out to prove anything; he has become skillful and happy at just being who he is. Competition, winning, and proving oneself through physical strength are not a big deal to a man who feels his success from *within.* A truly strong man is part of a community of men who value each other for *who they are,* not just for what they do. A male mentor will demonstrate a successful life, without the intense competitiveness and hostility that is too often expected of the men in our culture.

Mentors for Young Women

"You have enough agendas placed upon you as a young woman. A mentor in your life should help you open up to the mystery and potential that is inside of you. This woman has succeeded at doing this for herself."

—Dr. Laurel Ann Reinhardt, psychologist and mentor

Young women need an *active* woman for a mentor. Too many girls and young women try to gain a sense of self-worth by seeking acceptance from others. Or they put all their hopes and dreams on a boyfriend (or relationship), losing touch with their own creativity and uniqueness. Although relationships are important and women are naturally gifted in building relationships, true and lasting self-esteem comes from within—not from others. Find a woman mentor who has discovered and demonstrates her own strengths and talents. Clarissa Pinkola Estes, a well-known Hispanic storyteller and mentor, speaks about the value of young women seeking the company of "wild" women. Wild women are those who have held on to and nourished their creative fire. Wild women are strong women who get their self-esteem from *within* themselves, rather than always having to be approved by others. A good female mentor would show signs that she values herself.

"Before you choose a counselor, watch him with his neighbor's children."

—SIOUX PROVERB

Male or female, a good mentor is someone who will:

- appreciate you and express this appreciation;
- teach you about things you are interested in;
- demonstrate such qualities as truthfulness, respect, curiosity, cooperation, and compassion for all things;
- ignite your creative spirit;
- motivate you to be all you can be;
- listen and learn from you;
- *not* impose his or her will upon you.

That Which You Are Searching for Is also Searching for You

Where to look? Where does one find a mentor? We all want to be in loving relationships with others. We all benefit from sharing our lives with those who share some common ground. A mentor *wants* to mentor, only he or she may not know that this kind of relationship is possible. We are not told that when we reach a

certain age we will begin to be mentored, or that we will mentor someone else. The tradition of mentoring has gotten lost, but many people are rediscovering the need and joy of such relationships and are offering ways to hook up young people with mentors.

Places to look for a mentor include your church or synagogue, or whatever spiritual or religious group you may belong to; twelve-step groups (AA/Alateen/ Overeaters Anonymous); Boys and Girls Clubs; your local YMCA/YWCA; community centers; meditation groups; Dharma centers; or ethnic organizations. A local nursing home can also be a good resource. You can also ask your school guidance counselor, college advisor, or teacher for ideas. At the end of the chapter is a list of groups you can contact.

"Seek and you shall find." Begin the search for your mentor, because he or she is also searching for you.

Come to the Council Fire

"All children of the earth will be welcome at our council fires."

—SENECA PROVERB

> **"The dream begins with a teacher who believes in you, who tugs and pushes and leads you to the next plateau, sometimes poking you with a sharp stick called 'truth.'"**
>
> —DAN RATHER, TV JOURNALIST

What follows is an account of wisdom collected in dozens of interviews and conversations with mentors, spiritual teachers, healers, and known elders from a diversity of cultures and experiences: African American, Irish, Guatemalan, various Native American, Australian Aboriginal, Tibetan, Asian, Caucasian, and Hispanic men and women.

Here is their collective message to you:

Imagine yourself in a council among elders from many cultures, including some from your own. You are sitting on one side of an open fire and many elders are sitting opposite you. Their faces are lit up by the orange flames and their shadows dance about, rising and falling with the flames. . . .

Wisdom Seeking

You have come to them for guidance and advice. Knowing they care for your well-being, you are prepared for what they have to tell you. You understand and respect that those present are wise and have the insight of those that have walked a truthful path. You are excited and grateful for this opportunity, and a little afraid of what they might expect from you.

They have no desire to control you in any way—they know it is useless to try to force you into anything. They know you will do what you want. They simply hope you will receive what they say as a gift. Those sitting around the fire know it is part of their responsibility as teachers or mentors to invest in you, the young Spiritual Warrior. They understand that the past was theirs and the future is yours. This council fire is a bridge between the past and the future.

You respect each other's place in the circle of time.

Now, sit back . . . open up . . . and listen to what they have to say.

Forgiveness . . . "We are sorry for any pain and suffering brought on you by your parents or other adults in your life. We regret any fear and hostility that has been part of your heritage. The truth is, our society has lost much of the respect and understanding of your time of life. Too many are afraid and are confused about what to say to you. Some are starting to bring back recognition and respect for you—but we need your help in this. Help us mend this broken alliance, help us heal from the mistakes of misunderstanding that have come between us.

"Accept this apology and our promise that we are here to help mend the sacred relationship between us.

"We understand that if you are in trouble, your trouble is an expression of the trouble in our communities—*you alone are not the problem* (no matter what you have done.)"

Now, some of the council members rise to place more wood upon the fire. The room is warming up. . . . Imagine the heat surrounding you and filling you . . . as they continue to share their wisdom.

Keeping Life Sacred . . . "One way to mend this sacred relationship, and our communities, is to hold rituals that celebrate and acknowledge the stages of life. Boys and girls need to be initiated into adulthood, to have rites of passage. Find adults who will offer you ceremonies as a way to celebrate and acknowledge this transition in your life. Spirit wants to talk to you. Ritual is a way to be acknowledged and to have a conversation with Spirit. It is a time to be recognized by your community as an adult."

A voice of an elder is heard from the back, his face is half lit up by the flames of the fire and although he speaks softly and low . . . everyone listens.

"Hold fast to the word of your ancestors."

—HOPI PROVERB

Once, Everything Was a Prayer . . . "Prayer was a part of everyday life. We would pray to receive blessings and power from the spirit world for everything we did. When the clothes were washed, we would sing and pray; when we hunted for our food, we would pray to the animal world; when we needed rain, we prayed . . . and if the spirits were happy, rain would come. There was a feeling of goodness and purpose about everything we did."

The flames seem to dance on the faces of all the teachers and elders. . . . You feel part of a circle of power.

The elder continues, "Hold a conversation with Spirit every day. Pray for help. Pray for guidance. Seek the help that is available to you. *You will be heard.* Be patient. Spirit wants you to have all you ask for . . . keep the conversation going. Spirit is listening. Then, find some time to sit quietly so when Spirit speaks to you, you will hear its voice."

Again, there is silence. . . . What wisdom do you seek? Are there questions stirring in you that you would bring to such a council of teachers? What

Wisdom Seeking

would you ask? . . . Now, imagine one of you getting up and adding wood to the fire.

You can hear the questions of your generation, and of your own soul . . .

> Why am I here?
>
> What is my purpose?
>
> Is Spirit real?
>
> Will things work out for me?
>
> How can I be happier?
>
> What is my destiny?
>
> Does it really matter what I believe?
>
> Where are the mentors in my life?

"Work hard, keep the Ceremonies, live peaceably, and unite your hearts."

—HOPI PROVERB

Then, someone begins to speak to you again, and the one voice sounds like many voices talking in unison.

"A special place was made for you the moment you were born. Your life matters. You were created for a reason. You are here for a reason . . . you are here for a reason . . . you are here for a reason. . . . Everything that is born into the world, whether it be plant or animal, a place is made for it. For you. Help honor your place in this great circle of life, by honoring yourself."

Now the council fire is burning down. . . . The shadows of the elders have grown smaller and they are whispering among themselves. They wonder about you. . . . Their thoughts and whispers turn into prayers, as you turn to leave and head home.

242

Books, Resources, and Wisdomkeepers Related to This Chapter

Mentoring: The TAO of Giving and Receiving Wisdom, by Chungliang Al Huang and Jerry Lynch (HarperSanFrancisco, 1995). A delightful book that describes Tao mentoring, written for those in a mentoring relationship.

Your local school and university are likely to have a mentoring program available. You may also want to do a search on the internet for mentoring programs.

ASPIRA Association, Inc.
1444 I Street, N.W.
Washington, D.C. 20005
(202) 835-3600　Fax: (202) 223-1253
Encourages and promotes leadership among Hispanic youth. Local offices offer youth leadership development and educational counseling. See online resources below for Web site information.

Big Brothers/Big Sisters of America
230 N. 13th Street
Philadelphia, PA 19108
(215) 567-7000　Fax: (215) 567-0394
e-mail: BBBSA@aol.com
Matches you up with an adult volunteer that serves as your mentor and role model. See online resources below for Web site information.

Myron Eshowsky
Foundation for Shamanic Studies
P.O. Box 1939
Mill Valley, CA 94942
www.shamanism.org
Works with youth gangs, communities, and shamanic healers on issues of nonviolence.

Indian Youth of America
609 Badgerow Building
P.O. Box 2786
Sioux City, IA 51106
(712) 252-3230　Fax: (712) 252-3712
A general referral source to local resources.

National Indian Youth Leadership　Development Project
P.O. Box 2140
Gallup, NM 87301
(505) 722-9176
Provides opportunities and contacts for Native American youth. Holds leadership training camps in 5 states.

National Network for Youth
1319 F Street, N.W., Suite 401
Washington, D.C. 20004
(202) 783-7949
e-mail: YOUTH-NET@aol.com
Promotes teen-adult partnerships, particularly with those who are considered "at risk." This means at risk of falling into a life of drug and alcohol abuse, crimes, or violence.

National Urban League Youth Development
500 E. 62nd Street
New York, NY 10021
(212) 310-9084
Promotes and develops leadership by offering opportunities for community service for young people up to the age of 18.

Online Resources

The Aboriginal Youth Network
www.ayn.ca
This site was made by Canadian youth to share ideas and information to keep cultural traditions alive. It is a fun site with a chat/rant space for us to voice our ideas, online games, news and current events relevant to Canadian youth, and answers to some of our health concerns.

ASPIRA Association, Inc.
www.aspira.org
This is a nonprofit organization "devoted to education and leadership development of Puerto Rican and other Latino youth" with leadership development, education, talent search, and youth and community development programs. The site contains links to other resources and to local offices of ASPIRA.

Big Brothers/Big Sisters of America
www.bbbsa.org
Big Brothers/Big Sisters of America is a youth mentoring organization. Their site includes ways for us to contribute and volunteer and has other mentoring and volunteering links.

A Message from His Holiness the 14th Dalai Lama

The 14th Dalai Lama is the spiritual and political leader of the Tibetan people. He has been in exile from his country since 1959, when the Chinese invaded Tibet. Millions of Tibetans were killed and millions now live in exile as refugees in countries around the world, including the United States. His Holiness knows what it is like to be without home and country. He knows suffering. He knows what it is like to have the future be a big question mark. Yet, in all of his difficulty he holds on to a strong and courageous belief in love and kindness. He speaks to us all when he encourages us to practice a "religion of kindness." He believes in the right for us all to be happy with our lives. In 1989 His Holiness won the Nobel Peace Prize.

His words are sent personally to you from his home in Dharamsala, India. His message is one of hope and commitment to the Spiritual Warrior's path.

"As human beings, whether we are rich or poor, educated or uneducated, whatever our nationality, color, or social status may be, each of us is just like everyone else. We all want to be happy and we do not want to be miserable.

"Because the very purpose of life is to be happy, it is important to discover what will actually give us the greatest satisfaction. Everything we experience, whether it is enjoyable or not, affects either our minds or our bodies. Generally, it is our minds that have the greatest influence over whether we are happy or not. As long as we are not ill and we have the food, shelter, and clothing we need, our bodies feel comfortable and we virtually ignore it. Our minds, however, register everything that happens to us, no matter how small.

"Our physical health is closely related to our state of mind. Scientific experiments have shown that if the mind is stable and calm, basic bodily functions such as digestion and sleep improve. On the other hand, when we are mentally distressed even the presence of friends,

comfort, and wealth will not make us happy. Therefore, it is worth-while finding out how to create a calm and joyful mind.

"As free human beings we can use our unique intelligence to try to understand ourselves and our world. But if we are unable to use our creative potential, we lose one of the basic characteristics of a human being. We say that somebody who is angry is 'mad' about something. It is true because when we are angry our intelligence becomes blind. Then we are more likely to become violent.

"Sometimes it seems that a problem can be solved quickly by using force or violence. But violence is unpredictable and because it is often destructive ultimately brings more harm than good. Similarly, you may feel that drugs make you feel happier, but when you cannot get them or the effect wears off, you feel worse than before. Like negative emotions, drugs muddle our intelligence and distort our natural awareness.

"There are many ways to create peace and happiness, some on your own and some with your friends. A good human being helps others as much as he or she can, but at least avoids doing harm. That means avoiding harming yourself as well as others. And that is why we need real alternatives to drugs and violence.

"In order to find mental stability and peace, the mind itself can be trained. Identifying negative states of mind such as anger, hatred, jealousy, and pride, we can work to eliminate them. At the same time we can cultivate positive attitudes such as compassion and love, tolerance and contentment. Training the mind in this way is both useful and realistic. Positive attitudes such as kindness, friendliness, and concern for others are not a luxury but a condition for health and happiness."

Bibliography of Quoted Wisdomkeepers

All Rivers Run to the Sea: Memoirs, by Elie Wiesel, Schocken Books, 1996.

American Indian Myths and Legends, selected and edited by Richard Erdoes and Alfonso Ortiz, Pantheon Books, 1985.

Animal-Speak: The Spiritual and Magical Powers of Creatures Great and Small, by Ted Andrews, Llewellyn Publications, 1993.

ANOQCOU: Ceremony Is Life Itself, by Gkisedtanamoogk and Frances Hancock, Astarte Shell Press, 1993.

Antonio Machado: Times Alone, translated by Robert Bly, Graywolf Press, 1983.

The Artist's Way: A Spiritual Path to Higher Creativity, by Julia Cameron, G. P. Putnam's Sons, 1992.

The Art of Dreaming, by Carlos Castaneda, HarperPerennial Library, 1994.

Awakening the Buddha Within: Tibetan Wisdom for the Western World, by Lama Surya Das, Broadway Books, 1997.

Black Elk Speaks, by John G. Neihardt, First Bison Book, 1988.

Boy into Man: A Fathers' Guide to Initiation of Teenage Sons, by Bernard Weiner, Transformational Press, 1992.

Brave New World and *Brave New World Revisited,* by Aldous Huxley, HarperCollins, 1973.

Buffalo Woman Comes Singing: The Spirit Song of a Rainbow Medicine Woman, by Brooke Medicine Eagle, Ballantine Books, 1991.

Butterflies in the Mud, by Lia Ellason, chapbook, 2000.

Circle Game, by Margaret Atwood, Anchor Books, 1998.

The Color Purple, by Alice Walker, Pocket Books, 1982.

Compassion in Action: Setting Out on the Path of Service, Ram Dass and Mirabai Bush, Bell Tower, 1992.

The Crack in the Cosmic Egg: Challenging Constructs of Mind and Reality, by Joseph Chilton Pearce, Crown Publishing Group, 1988.

In Defense of Hunting, by James A. Swan, HarperCollins, 1995.

The Dhammapada, translated by Ross Carter and Mahinda Palihawadana, Oxford University Press, 1987.

Dictionary of Native American Mythology, by Sam D. Gill and Irene F. Sullivan. Oxford University Press, 1992.

The Dreamer: A Voyage of Self-Discovery, by Ralph Thorpe, Element Books, 1997.

The Dream Keeper and Other Poems, by Langston Hughes, Knopf, 1996.

Dreams and Spiritual Growth, by Louis Savary, Paulist Press, 1984.

Dreams Are Wiser Than Men, edited by Richard A. Russon, North Atlantic Books, 1987.

The Elements of Celtic Tradition, by Caitlín Matthews, Element Books, 1997.

Explorations in Human Potentialities, by Herbert Otto, Charles C. Thomas Publishers, 1966.

A Fable for Critics, by James Russell Lowell, Ayer Company, 1977.

The Four-Fold Way: Walking the Paths of the Warrior, Teacher, Healer, and Visionary, by Angeles Arrien, Ph.D., HarperSanFrancisco, 1993.

Bibliography

The Gift: Poems by HAFIZ, translated by Daniel Ladisky, Penguin, 1999.

The Gnostic Gospels, by Elaine Pagels, Vintage Books, 1979.

A Gradual Awakening, by Stephen Levine, Anchor Books, 1989.

Grandmother of Time: A Woman's Book of Celebrations, Spells, and Sacred Objects for Every Month of the Year, by Zsuzanna E. Budapest, HarperSanFrancisco, 1989.

The Heart of the Goddess, edited by Hallie Iglehart Austen, Wingbow Press, 1990.

If You Want to Write, by Brenda Ueland, Graywolf Press, 1997.

I Know Why the Caged Bird Sings, by Maya Angelou, Bantam Books, 1983.

The Ink Dark Moon: Love Poems by Ono No Komachi and Izumi Shikibu, Women of the Ancient Court of Japan, translated by Jane Hirshfield with Mariko Aratani, Charles Scribner's Sons, 1988.

Iron John: A Book About Men, by Robert Bly, Addison Wesley, 1990.

Lakota Belief and Ritual, by James R. Walker, University of Nebraska Press, 1980.

The Lesson: A Fable for Our Times, by Carol S. Pearson, Gibbs Smith Publishing, 1998.

Life Is a Dream, by Pedro Calderón de la Barca, Consortium Publishing, 1999.

The Little Prince, by Antoine de Saint-Exupery, Harcourt Brace, 1968.

Loving-Kindness: The Revolutionary Art of Happiness, by Sharon Salzburg, Shambhala Publications, 1995.

The Meaning of Shakespeare, by Harold Goddard, University of Chicago Press, 1965.

Men and the Water of Life: Initiation and the Tempering of Men, by Michael Meade, HarperSanFrancisco, 1994.

Mentoring: The TAO of Giving and Receiving Wisdom, by Chungliang Al Huang and Jerry Lynch, HarperSanFrancisco, 1995.

Mortal Acts, Mortal Words, by Galway Kinnell, Houghton Mifflin, 1980.

The Nag Hammadi Library, edited by James M. Robinson, HarperSanFrancisco, 1990.

The Native American Almanac, by Arlene Hirschfelder and Martha Kreipe de Montano, Prentice-Hall, 1993.

Native American Stories, Told by Joseph Bruchac, from Keepers of the Earth, by Michael J. Caduto and Joseph Bruchac, Fulcrum Publishing, 1991.

News of the Universe: Poems of Twofold Consciousness, by Robert Bly, Sierra Club Books, 1980.

A Night Without Armor: Poems, by Jewel, HarperCollins, 2000.

An Open Life: Joseph Campbell in Conversation with Michael Toms, selected and edited by John M. Maher and Dennie Briggs, Harper & Row, 1989.

Passion, by Barbara De Angeles, Delacorte Press, 1998.

A Path with Heart: A Guide Through the Perils and Promises of Spiritual Life, by Jack Kornfield, Bantam Books, 1993.

Phenomenon of Man, by Pierre Teilhard de Chardin, HarperCollins, 1980.

The Philosophy of the I Ching, by Carol K. Anthony, Anthony Publishing, 1981.

The Power of Myth, by Joseph Campell, with Bill Moyers, Anchor Books, 1991.

The Power of Place: Sacred Ground in Natural and Human Environments, by James A. Swan, Theosophical Publishing, 1991.

The Prophet, by Kahlil Gibran, Alfred A. Knopf, 1951.

Rainbow Tribe: Ordinary People Journeying on the Red Road, by Ed McGaa, Eagle Man, HarperSanFrancisco, 1992.

Ritual: Power, Healing, and Community, by Malidoma Patrice Somé, Swan Raven and Company, 1993.

Saint Francis of Assisi, by G. K. Chesterton, Blackstone Audio Books, 1991.

A Sand County Almanac, by Aldo Leopold, Oxford University Press, 1996.

The Search for the Beloved, by Jean Houston, Jeremy P. Tarcher, 1997.

Seasons of Magic: A Girl's Journey, by Laurel Ann Reinhardt, Llewellyn, 2001.

Selections from Ralph Waldo Emerson, edited by Stephen E. Whicher, Houghton Mifflin Company Riverside Editions, 1957.

Shambhala: The Sacred Path of the Warrior, by Chögyam Trungpa, Shambhala Publications, 1984.

Shared Spirits: Wildlife and Native Americans, by Dennis L. Olson, NorthWord Press, 1995.

Shouting at the Sky, by Gary Ferguson, St. Martins Press, 1999.

Simple Life (1904), by Charles Wagner, Kessinger Publishing Company, 1942.

The Song of God: Bhagavad-Gita, translated by Prabhavananda and Christopher Isherwood, Barnes & Noble Books, 1995.

The Soul Would Have No Rainbows If the Eyes Had No Tears, and Other Native American Proverbs, by Guy A. Zona, Simon & Schuster, 1994.

Spinning Inward, by Maureen Murdock, Shambhala Publications, 1987.

The Spiral Dance: A Rebirth of the Ancient Religion of the Great Goddess, by Starhawk, HarperCollins, 1989.

The Spirit of Intimacy: Ancient Teachings in the Ways of Relationships, by Sobonfu E. Somé, Berkeley Hills Books, 1997.

Stone Soup for the World: Life Changing Stories of Kindness and Courageous Acts of Service, edited by Marianne Larned, MJF Books, 1998.

The Thirst for Wholeness: Attachment, Addiction, and the Spiritual Path, by Christina Grof, HarperSanFrancisco, 1994.

Traditional Celtic Stories, by Lyndsay Clarke, Thorsons Publishers, 2000.

The Vegetarian Factfinder, by Ellen Klaven, Little Bookroom, 1997.

Walden, by Henry David Thoreau, Knopf, 1992.

Walking in the Sacred Manner, by Mark St. Pierre and Tilda Long Soldier, Simon & Schuster, 1995.

Wherever You Go, There You Are: Mindfulness Meditation In Everyday Life, by Jon Kabat-Zinn, Hyperion Publishers, 1994.

The Wisdom of No Escape and the Path of Loving-Kindness, by Pema Chödrön, Shambhala Publications, 1991.

Your Mythic Journey: Finding Meaning in Your Life Through Writing and Story Telling, by Sam Keen and Anne Valley-Fox (contributor), Bantam Books, 1989.

Zen Mind, Beginner's Mind: Informal Talks on Zen Meditation and Practice, by Shunryu Suzuki, Weatherhill, 1991.

Zen Soup: Tasty Morsels of Wisdom from Great Minds East and West, by Laurence G. Boldt, Penguin, 1997.

"The creation of a thousand forests is in one acorn."

—RALPH WALDO EMERSON, AMERICAN ESSAYIST, POET, AND SPIRITUAL PHILOSOPHER

Index

Index to Wisdomkeepers

Index